T0207319

Lecture Notes of the Institute for Computer Sciences, Social Informatics and Telecommunications Engineering 507

The LNICST series publishes ICST's conferences, symposia and workshops.

LNICST reports state-of-the-art results in areas related to the scope of the Institute.

The type of material published includes

- Proceedings (published in time for the respective event)
- Other edited monographs (such as project reports or invited volumes)

LNICST topics span the following areas:

- General Computer Science
- E-Economy
- E-Medicine
- Knowledge Management
- Multimedia
- Operations, Management and Policy
- Social Informatics
- Systems

Ruidong Li · Min Jia · Tarik Taleb
Editors

Mobile Wireless Middleware, Operating Systems and Applications

11th EAI International Conference, MOBILWARE 2022
Virtual Event, December 28–29, 2022
Proceedings

 Springer

Editors
Ruidong Li 🆔
Kanazawa University
Kanazawa, Japan

Min Jia 🆔
Harbin Institute of Technology
Harbin, China

Tarik Taleb 🆔
University of Oulu
Oulu, Finland

ISSN 1867-8211 ISSN 1867-822X (electronic)
Lecture Notes of the Institute for Computer Sciences, Social Informatics
and Telecommunications Engineering
ISBN 978-3-031-34496-1 ISBN 978-3-031-34497-8 (eBook)
https://doi.org/10.1007/978-3-031-34497-8

This Springer imprint is published by the registered company Springer Nature Switzerland AG
The registered company address is: Gewerbestrasse 11, 6330 Cham, Switzerland

Preface

We are delighted to introduce the proceedings of the 11th International Conference on MOBILe Wireless MiddleWARE, Operating Systems, and Applications (MOBIL-Ware 2022). This conference brought together researchers, developers and practitioners around the world who are leveraging and developing middleware, operating systems and applications for mobile wireless networks.

The technical program of MOBILWare 2022 consisted of 23 full papers, in oral presentation sessions. The conference sessions were: Session 1 - Middleware, Wireless and Future Networks; Session 2 - Integrated Satellite-Terrestrial Information Network; Session 3 - Integrated Satellite-Terrestrial Intelligent Information Processing, Decision and Planning (1); and Session 4 - Integrated Satellite-Terrestrial Intelligent Information Processing, Decision and Planning (2). Aside from the high-quality technical paper presentations, the technical program also featured 1 keynote speech, and two invited talks. The keynote speech was given by Min Jia from Harbin Institute of Technology, China.

Coordination with the steering chair, Imrich Chlamtac, was essential for the success of the conference. We sincerely appreciate his constant support and guidance. It was also a great pleasure to work with such an excellent organizing committee team for their hard work in organizing and supporting the conference. In particular, the Technical Program Committee, led by our TPC Co-Chairs, Xin Liu, Dalian University of Technology, China, Abdelkader Lahmadi, University of Lorraine, France, and Yingde Li, Demon Group, China, completed the peer-review process of technical papers and made a high-quality technical program. We also thank the workshop chairs, Xiongwen He, Tsinghua University, China, Zhenhui Dong, Beijing Institute of Spacecraft System Engineering, China, Wei Wu, Beijing Institute of Spacecraft System Engineering, China, Zhaojing Cui, Beijing Institute of Spacecraft System Engineering, China, Dan Wang, Beijing Institute of Spacecraft System Engineering, China, Fan Bai, Beijing Institute of Spacecraft System Engineering, China, Sheng Yu, Beijing Institute of Spacecraft System Engineering, China, Jionghui Li, Beijing Institute of Spacecraft System Engineering, China, and Ling Tong, China Academy of Space Technology, China. We are also grateful to EAI staff, Martin Vojtek, Radka Vasileiadis, Viliam Farkas and Mikita Yelnitski for their great support and to all the authors who submitted their papers to the MOBILWare 2022 conference and workshops.

We strongly believe that the MOBILWare conference provides a good forum for all researchers, developers and practitioners to discuss all science and technology aspects that are relevant to middleware, operating systems and applications. We also expect that the future MOBILWare conferences will be as successful and stimulating, as indicated by the contributions presented in this volume.

Ruidong Li
Min Jia
Tarik Taleb

Organization

Steering Committee

Imrich Chlamtac   University of Trento, Italy

Organizing Committee

General Chair

Ruidong Li   Kanazawa University, Japan

General Co-chairs

Min Jia	Harbin Institute of Technology, China
Tarik Taleb	University of Oulu, Finland

TPC Chair and Co-chair

Xin Liu	Dalian University of Technology, China
Abdelkader Lahmadi	University of Lorraine, France
Yingde Li	Demon Group, China

Publicity and Social Media Chairs

Zhenyu Na	Dalian Maritime University, China
Yun Lin	Harbin Engineering University, China
Zhengxin Yu	Lancaster University, UK

Workshops Chairs

Xujie Li	Hohai University, China
Yong Wang	Chongqing University of Posts and Telecommunications, China

Sponsorship and Exhibit Chair

Xinyu Wang   Harbin Institute of Technology, China

Publications Chairs

Xiaojin Ding   Nanjing University of Posts and
                                    Telecommunications, China
Xiaoqiang Di   Changchun University of Science and
                                    Technology, China

Panels Chair

Lexi Xu   China Unicom, China

Tutorials Chair

Qiang Yang   Harbin Institute of Technology, China

Demos Chair

Liang Zhao   Shenyang Aerospace University, China
Dong Yan   Institute of Spacecraft System Engineering,
                                    CAST, China

Local Chair

Peiying Colleen   Ruan NVIDIA, Japan

Technical Program Committee

Xiaolong Yang   Brunel University London, UK
Kanglian Zhao   Nanjing University, China
Liang Ye   Harbin Institute of Technology, China
Rongfei Fan   Beijing Institute of Technology, China
Yong Wang   Chongqing University of Posts and
                                    Telecommunications, China
Hong Jiang   Southwest University of Science and Technology,
                                    China
Jian Jiao   Harbin Institute of Technology, China

Weizhi Zhong	Nanjing University of Aeronautics and Astronautics, China
Chenguang He	Harbin Institute of Technology, China
Shushi Gu	Harbin Institute of Technology, China
Qingjiang Shi	Tongji University, China
Peng Li	Dalian Polytechnic University, China
Xiaobo Zhou	Tianjin University, China
Jenq-Haur Wang	National Taipei University of Technology, Taiwan
Honglong Chen	China University of Petroleum, China
Bin Tang	Hohai University, China
Hamada Alshaer	University of Edinburgh, UK
Jéferson Campos Nobre	Federal University of Rio Grande do Sul, Brazil
Andreas Andreou	University of Nicosia, Cyprus

Contents

Integrated Satellite-Terrestrial Intelligent Information Processing, Decision and Planning (1)

Integrated Satellite-Terrestrial Intelligent Information Processing, Decision and Planning (2)

Contents

Middleware, Wireless and Future Networks

A Middleware-Based Approach
for Latency-Sensitive Service Provisioning
in IoT with End-Edge Cooperation

Canlong Sun[1](✉), Ting Li[1], Zihao Wu[1], and Cong Li[2]

[1] The 705 Research Institute of China State Shipbuilding Corporation Limited, Kunming,
Yunnan, China
362028257@qq.com

[2] Xi'an Institute of Optics and Precision Mechanics, CAS, Xian, Shanxi, China

Abstract. As modern mobile applications have become more and more complex,
mobile edge computing brings IT services and computing resources to the edge
of mobile networks to full fill various computing and application requirements.
Considering that mobile devices may not always have adequate hardware conditions, computation offloading, which can help devices take full advantage of extra
computing resources, has reached a broad audience in the edge environments.
However, due to the limited storage space of edge servers, it is very difficult to
manage services in middleware. Therefore, in the edge computing environment,
how to deal with a large amount of data from different edge nodes in the middleware is very important. In this paper, we regard an approach about improving
quality of sensitive data for middleware on edge environments. We have evaluated
our approaches on a real-world environment. The results demonstrate that our
approach can effectively reduce the response time.

Keywords: Edge Computing · Middleware · Latency-Sensitive Service · IoT

1 Introduction

With the popularity of the continuous development of the Internet of Things (IoT) technology, smart mobile devices (e.g., smart phones, tablet PCs, smart home appliances,
etc.) have played a increasing important role in people's life [1, 2]. Along with the rapid
development of the IoT, the concurrent huge network traffic also arises challenging issues
to deliver efficient IoT services with diverse Quality of Service (QoS). Especially, the
enormous network traffic load often causes severe network congestion, which eventually
impacts the service latency (e.g., response delay). In the field of IoT applications, as IoT
nodes usually need to frequently send/receive data to/from the core network server, it
greatly increases the load on the central network [3]. To solve the problem of limited
terminal resources, mobile edge computing [4, 5] technology offers a plausible solution
to empower cellular networks and deliver high bandwidth, low latency, and improved
QoS for diverse IoT applications, by placing part of cloud resources (e.g., computing,

R. Li et al. (Eds.): MOBILWARE 2022, LNICST 507, pp. 3–12, 2023.
https://doi.org/10.1007/978-3-031-34497-8_1

storage, and networking capacities) within the edge of radio access network (RAN). As edge computing servers are closer to mobile user terminals, compared with the remote cloud server, the computationally intensive and latency-sensitive applications can be supported by mobile edge computing. Besides, by migrating computing tasks from end device with limited resources to the edge of network, a large portion of mobile traffic will be diverted to edge servers. Thereby, the service-related data can be placed on edge servers to minimize the latency in users' data retrieval [6]. This is especially important for latency-sensitive applications, e.g., gaming, navigation, augmented reality, etc. Popular service often accounts for a large percentage of the mobile traffic data over the internet. Thus, caching popular service as data on edge servers can significantly reduce the traffic load on the internet backbone. According to [7], it is expected to reduce mobile traffic data by about 35% in IoT via the mobile edge computing paradigm.

In this paper, we propose a novel mobile edge computing-based middleware (MDS) approach in IoT to improve the QoS for sensitive data in edge environments. Specifically, we design a novel collaborative service mitigation framework for IoT in the edge environment with MDS. Then, we theoretically formulated the service latency model under MDS in end-edge computing environment, where part of task data is offloaded to an appropriate edge node via the MDS and the other remain to be processed locally. Additionally, we devise an algorithm to effectively sort the processing order of the data arriving in the middleware. Finally, we carry out extensive real-world environments to evaluate the feasibility and effectiveness of the proposed approach in terms of service delay, in comparison with conventional approaches.

The rest of this paper includes the following sections. Section 2 reviews the related work. Section 3 describes system model. Section 3 introduces our proposed MDS approach of replaceable services. Section 4 presents our experimental environment and gives the analysis of experimental results, followed by Sect. 5 that concludes our work and gives the future work.

2   Related Works

The author in [8] propose a novel framework called SpeCH and introduce a new paradigm for partitioning a set of data-items into geo-distributed clouds. In [14], the authors propose a data-centric programming model called Fog Function is proposed, which uses the underlying orchestration mechanism. The authors in [9] propose an approach which is based on a QoS-aware meta orchestration modelling of a given pipeline and an orchestration builder generating deployable Edge-specific orchestrations. The authors in [15] propose an algorithm that divides tasks into four types in real time and then offloads them cooperatively. In [16], the authors propose a Data-intensive Service Edge deployment scheme based on Genetic Algorithm (DSEGA). The authors in [10] propose an edge-enabled federated learning framework for smart grid to deliver intelligent power services for individuals. The authors in [12] develop a novel blockchain system for private data audit in IoT with edge-cloud cooperation. These viewpoints are all based on edge computing or fog computing. They only consider edge nodes and do not consider middleware well. Moreover, data intensive services often transfer large amounts of data over a wide Area network (WAN) because of their scalable fault tolerant protocols

[13]. The authors in the [9] characterize the network stability region and design the first throughput-optimal control policy that coordinates processing and routing decisions for both live and static data streams. The work in [11] proposes an MA-based approach to solving the problem of distributed DWSC in an effective and efficient manner. In particular, the authors in [11] develop an MA approach that combines e-commerce and local search technology with service distance. However, most of these views start from the hardware performance of each node, without considering the thread problem.

3 System Model

3.1 Execution Time of Data Services Under Local Computing

Let $\mathbb{I} = \{1, \ldots, i, \ldots, I\}$ be the set of IoT devices. For the computation task Φ, its execution time of data processing at the local IoT device $i \in \mathbb{I}$ can be computed as:

$$et_{local} = \frac{\alpha_i D_i}{f_i}, \tag{1}$$

where $N_i = \alpha_i D_i$ denotes the number of required CPU cycles to complete the computation task Φ. Here, $\alpha_i(\alpha_i > 0)$ is a parameter related to the computation complexity of the computation task Φ. D_i is the size of the computation task Φ. f_i is the CPU frequency of the IoT device i, which also indicates the local computing resource available for task Φ. Moreover, the corresponding energy consumption in executing task Φ can be computed as:

$$E_{local} = \chi_i(f_i)^3 et_{local} = \chi_i \alpha_i D_i (f_i)^2, \tag{2}$$

where χ_i is the CPU capacitance-related parameter of IoT device i.

3.2 Execution Time of Data Services Under Edge Computing

Let $\mathbb{J} = \{1, \ldots, j, \ldots, J\}$ be the set of edge nodes in the IoT. Under edge computing environment, considering the existence of MDS, the execution time consists of the data transmission latency to the MDS and the edge nodes, the data processing time on edge servers, and the synchronization latency between the MDS and the edge servers. According to [18], the time of downloading services data at edge node $j \in \mathbb{J}$ can be computed as:

$$dt_{edge} = \frac{d_v}{Tx_v} + \frac{wl_c}{c_c} + Q_c + \frac{d_o}{Tx_o}, \tag{3}$$

where Tx_v and Tx_o are the data transmission rate (in Kbps) at the location where the middleware starts to transmitting to each other data about the service c to/from an edge node j, respectively. To calculate Tx_i and Tx_o, We first need to find the location of the middleware through the trajectory model of the middleware, and then use the signal strength of its location to determine its transmission speed. wl_c is the middleware workload, d_v and d_o mean the granularity of the data. Let $\rho \in (0, 1)$ be the output/input ratio of the task Φ. We have

$$\rho = \frac{d_v}{d_o}. \tag{4}$$

c_c is the CPU capacity (in MIPS) for the middleware. Q_c is the waiting time that edge service c stays in a queue to be executed in the middleware. Moreover, the execution time of data processing at the edge node $j \in \mathbb{J}$ can be calculated as:

$$et_{edge} = \frac{\alpha_i D_i}{f_j}, \tag{5}$$

where f_i is the CPU frequency of the edge node j, which indicates its available computing resource to process the task Φ. Then, the overall service latency can be computed as the sum of the data downloading delay and data processing delay, i.e.,

$$t_{edge} = dt_{edge} + et_{edge} = \frac{d_{i,j}}{Tx_{i,j}} + \frac{wl_c}{c_c} + Q_c + \frac{d_{j,i}}{Tx_{j,i}} + \frac{\alpha_i D_i}{f_j}. \tag{6}$$

The energy consumption in data transmission from the IoT device to the edge node is $E_{trans} = \frac{d_v}{Tx_v} P_i$. Here, P_i is the transmit power of IoT device i. Typically, compared with the original input size of the task, the output size of task (i.e., the task processing result) can be usually negligible. Thereby, the energy consumption of transmisitting the processed task data is neglected. As such, the overall energy consumption in executing task Φ can be computed as:

$$E_{edge} = \frac{d_v}{Tx_v} P_i + \chi_j (f_j)^3 et_{edge} = \frac{d_v}{Tx_v} P_i + \chi_j \alpha_i D_i (f_j)^2, \tag{7}$$

where χ_j is the CPU capacitance-related parameter of edge node j.

4 The Proposed Service Provisioning Approach with MDS

4.1 Execution Time of Data Services Under End-Edge Computing with MDS

In practical IoT applications, part of the task can be processed locally while the other part of the data can be effectively offloaded to nearby edge nodes for processing, thereby improving the QoS of latency-sensitive IoT services. Under the end-edge computing paradigm, the time of downloading service (i.e., dt_{mc}) data under MDS approach is calculated by

$$dt_{mc} = E_{mc} + \frac{wl_{mc}}{c_{mc}} + Q_{mc}, \tag{8}$$

where wl_{mc} is the MDS approach's workload, c_{mc} is the CPU capacity (in MIPS) for the middleware. Q_{mc} is the waiting time in a queue to be executed in the middleware. E_{mc} is the time spent processing data.

Let $\kappa \in [0, 1]$ denote the ratio of locally procedded data, then the overall service delay can be computed as:

$$t_{end-edge} = \max\{\kappa \times et_{local}, dt'_{edge} + (1 - \kappa) \times et_{edge}\}, \qquad (9)$$

where dt'_{edge} is the newly time of downloading services data at edge node $j \in \mathbb{J}$, i.e.,

$$dt'_{edge} = \kappa \frac{d_v}{Tx_v} + \frac{wl_c}{c_c} + Q_c + \frac{d'_o}{Tx_o}, \qquad (10)$$

where d'_o means the output data size of the partially offloaded task size. Then, the explicit form of the overall service delay can be expressed as:

$$t_{end-edge} = \max\left\{\kappa \frac{\alpha_i D_i}{f_i}, \kappa \frac{d_v}{Tx_v} + \frac{wl_c}{c_c} + Q_c + \frac{d'_o}{Tx_o} + (1 - \kappa) \frac{\alpha_i D_i}{f_j}\right\}. \qquad (11)$$

The energy consumption under the proposed scheme can be computed according to Eqs. (2) and (7).

4.2 Framework of the Proposed MDS Approach

Figure 1 illustrates the detailed workflow of the proposed service provisioning approach with MDS. As shown in Fig. 1, the edge node sends the data generated by the service to the middleware, which is sorted in real time by the MDS component of the middleware, and finally the middleware processes the data in this order.

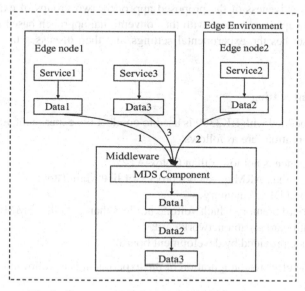

Fig. 1. Framework of the proposed MDS approach.

4.3 Algorithm of the Proposed MDS Approach

The following Algorithm1 is used in the MDS component, which can effectively sort the processing order of the data arriving in the middleware.

Algorithm1
___

```
int counter = 0;
int winner = randint (0, totaltickets);
job_t *current_job = head;
While (current_job != null)
{
    counter = counter + current_job->ticket;
    if (counter > winner)
        break;
        current_job = current_job -> next;
}
current_job.do ()
```

---

5 Performance Evaluation

To verify the effectiveness of the proposed approach, two groups of experiments are designed in this paper to compare with the conventional approach based on QT5. This section first describes the experimental settings and then discusses the experimental results.

5.1 Experiment Setting

A hardware embedded with RK3399 is used to conduct the experiment, and its relevant hardware configurations are as follows:

1) CPU performance is not lower than Cotex-AT2;
2) GPU is no less than ARM quad core processor like Mali-T860;
3) Support 2G and DDR3 memory;
4) Support onboard memory which volume not less than 64G like EMMC;
5) Development board gigabit network card;
6) GPIO interface provided by development board.

The detailed software configuration of the experiment is as follows:

project	Software name	Version
Operating system	Debian	Debian9
Library files or supporting software	QT	5.7.0
	GCC	6.3+
	FFmpeg	3.2.9+
programing language	C	C99
	C++	C++ 11
Communication environment	TCP/IP Protocol	SOCKET2.0+
	CAN	CAN2.0B

5.2 Experiment Results

In the first experiment, we verify whether the proposed MDS approach can optimize the processing time when the data generated by multiple services in multiple edge nodes is sent to the middleware. In Experiment Setting 1, the number of edge node services is regarded as a variable, and five edge nodes are built. A total number of 10, 20, and 100 services are distributed on the five edge nodes (average distribution). To ensure that other variables are the same, the same services are used in Experiment Setting 1. Each group of experiments has verified 50 times and taken its average value. The experimental results are shown in Fig. 2.

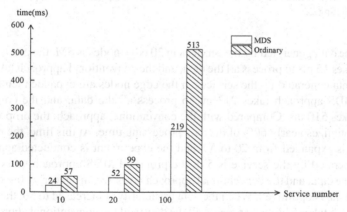

Fig. 2. Evaluation results of the proposed MDS scheme in terms of response time under Experiment Setting 1.

When the number of services is 10, the response time of the conventional approach is 57 ms, and the response time of the MDS approach is 24 ms. If the number of services is increased to 20, the response time of the conventional approach is 99 ms, and the response time of the MDS approach is 52 ms. If the number of services is increased to 100, the response time of the conventional approach is 513 ms, and the response time of the MDS approach is 219 ms. As seen in Fig. 2, with the increase of the number of services, the proposed MDS approach can always shorten the response time by about 50% compared with the conventional approach.

In the next experiment, four groups of comparative experiments are conducted. In the Experiment Setting 2, 20 edge nodes and 50 edge nodes are adopted to transmit 5M granular data and 50M granular data generated by node services to the middleware respectively. In this way, it is verified whether the MDS approach is still Y when the number of edge nodes and the granularity of data generated by services change. The experimental results are shown in Fig. 3.

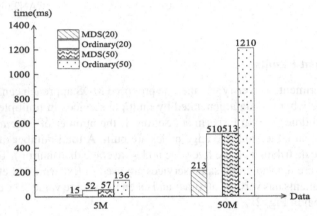

Fig. 3. Evaluation results of the proposed MDS scheme in terms of response time under Experiment Setting 2.

When the data generated by the services in 20 edge nodes is 5M, the proposed MDS approach takes 15 ms to process all the data, and the conventional approach takes 52 ms. When the data generated by the services in the edge nodes are expanded ten times, the proposed MDS approach takes 213 ms to process all the data, and the conventional approach takes 510 ms. Compared with the conventional approach, the proposed MDS approach optimizes nearly 60% of the data processing time. At this time, the number of edge nodes is expanded from 20 to 50, and the experiment is conducted again. When the data generated by the service is 5M, the proposed MDS approach takes 57 ms to process all the data, and the conventional approach takes 136 ms. Nearly 50% of the data processing time is optimized. When the data granularity is increased to 50, the proposed MDS approach takes 513 ms to process all the data, and the conventional approach takes 1210 ms. It can be seen that the proposed scheme can obtain nearly 55% reduction of the data processing time.

6 Conclusion

In this paper, we regard the discovery and scheduling problem of replaceable services replacement as the discovery and scheduling component based on the cache, and develop an optimal approach based on similar replaceable service form the app vendor's perspective for solving the none cached replaceable services environment. Such approach allows adapting of computation from clients, reducing response latency, backbone bandwidth, and the client's computational requirements. We also develop an optimal approach based on similar replaceable service form the app vendor's perspective for solving the none cached replaceable services environment. We have evaluated our approaches on a real-world environment. The results demonstrate that our method can effectively reduce the recovery time after s system failure as the mirror increases.

References

1. Cisco, T., Internet, A.: Cisco: 2020 CISO benchmark report. Comput. Fraud Secur. **2020**(3), 4 (2020)
2. Wang, Y., et al.: A survey on metaverse: fundamentals, security, and privacy. IEEE Commun. Surv. Tutor. (2022). https://doi.org/10.1109/COMST.2022.3202047
3. Lai, P., He, Q., Abdelrazek, M., Chen, F., Hosking, J., Grundy, J., Yang, Y.: Optimal edge user allocation in edge computing with variable sized vector bin packing. In: Pahl, C., Vukovic, M., Yin, J., Yu, Qi. (eds.) ICSOC 2018. LNCS, vol. 11236, pp. 230–245. Springer, Cham (2018). https://doi.org/10.1007/978-3-030-03596-9_15
4. Mao, Y., You, C., Zhang, J., Huang, K., Letaief, K.B.: A survey on mobile edge computing: the communication perspective. IEEE Commun. Surv. Tutor. **19**(4), 2322–2358 (2017)
5. Wang, Y., et al.: Task offloading for post-disaster rescue in unmanned aerial vehicles networks. IEEE/ACM Trans. Netw. **30**(4), 1525–1539 (2022)
6. Wang, Y., Su, Z., Luan, H.T., Li, R., Zhang, K.: Federated learning with fair incentives and robust aggregation for UAV-aided crowdsensing. IEEE Trans. Netw. Sci. Eng. **9**(5), 3179–3196 (2022)
7. Patel, M., et al.: Mobile edge computing – introductory technical white paper. ETSI White Pap. **11**, 1–36 (2014)
8. Atrey, A., Van Seghbroeck, G., Mora, H., De Turck, F., Volckaert, B.: SpeCH: a scalable framework for data placement of data-intensive services in geo-distributed clouds. J. Netw. Comput. Appl. **142**, 1–14 (2019)
9. Cai, Y., Llorca, J., Tulino, A.M., Molisch, A.F.: Dynamic control of data-intensive services over edge computing networks. arXiv preprint arXiv:2205.14735 (2022)
10. Su, Z., et al.: Secure and efficient federated learning for smart grid with edge-cloud collaboration. IEEE Trans. Industr. Inf. **18**(2), 1333–1344 (2022)
11. Sadeghiram, S., Ma, H., Chen, G.: Composing distributed data-intensive Web services using a flexible memetic algorithm. In: 2019 IEEE Congress on Evolutionary Computation (CEC), Wellington, New Zealand, pp. 2832–2839 (2019)
12. Wang, Y., et al.: SPDS: a secure and auditable private data sharing scheme for smart grid based on blockchain. IEEE Trans. Industr. Inf. **17**(11), 7688–7699 (2021)
13. Anantha, D.N., Ramamurthy, B., Bockelman, B., Swanson, D.: Differentiated network services for data-intensive science using application-aware SDN. In: 2017 IEEE International Conference on Advanced Networks and Telecommunications Systems (ANTS), Chengdu, China, pp. 1–6 (2017)

14. Cheng, B., Fuerst, J., Solmaz, G., Sanada, T.: Fog function: serverless fog computing for data intensive IoT services. In: 2019 IEEE International Conference on Services Computing (SCC), San Diego, USA, pp. 28–35 (2019)
15. Anisetti, M., Berto, F., Banzi, M.: Orchestration of data-intensive pipeline in 5G-enabled edge continuum. In: 2022 IEEE World Congress on Services (SERVICES), Barcelona, Spain, pp. 2–10. IEEE (2022)
16. Liu, C., Liu, K., Xu, X., Ren, H., Jin, F., Guo, S.: Real-time task offloading for data and computation intensive services in vehicular fog computing environments. In: 2020 16th International Conference on Mobility, Sensing and Networking (MSN), Tokyo, Japan, pp. 360–366 (2020)
17. Chen, Y., Deng, S., Ma, H., Yin, J.: Deploying data-intensive applications with multiple services components on edge. Mob. Netw. Appl. 25(2), 426–441 (2020)
18. Castro-Orgaz, O., Hager, W.H.: Shallow Water Hydraulics. Springer, Cham (2019). https://doi.org/10.1007/978-3-030-13073-2

Deep Reinforcement Learning Based Congestion Control Mechanism for SDN and NDN in Satellite Networks

Ziyang Xing[1], Hui Qi[1], Xiaoqiang Di[1,2(✉)], Jinyao Liu[1], and Ligang Cong[1]

[1] School of Computer Science and Technology, Changchun University of Science and Technology, Changchun, China
dixiaoqiang@cust.edu.cn
[2] Information Center, Changchun University of Science and Technology, Changchun, China

Abstract. In a satellite network, the content-centric information center network can reduce redundant data and decouple the location of network entities from the content, which is especially suitable for sending massive data from satellites to the ground. Influenced by outages, the information center network congestion control is inefficient and adaptive, the congestion policy cannot be changed from a global perspective, and the paths saved in the FIB and PIT are prone to failure. This paper proposes a congestion control algorithm based on deep reinforcement learning: RL-ICN-CC, which uses a software-defined network controller to obtain the state information of the whole network, deep reinforcement learning realizes an adaptive congestion control mechanism, and consumers adjust the interest packets according to the global state of the network CWND of the sending rate to avoid congestion. In this paper, FIB and PIT are redesigned. When the saved path easily fails, consumers can still calculate other cache locations to obtain content. Compared with other algorithms in multiple scenarios, the throughput of the proposed scheme is improved by 11%, and congestion adaptability is achieved.

Keywords: satellite network · congestion control · deep reinforcement learning · ICN

1 Introduction

Low-orbit satellite networks (LEOs) have the advantages of wide coverage and low cost and have become a future network development trend. In the highly dynamic network environment of LEO, the network architecture has difficulty meeting the needs of massive data transmission, and it is difficult to distribute satellite data to the ground [1]. Therefore, content-based network architecture (ICN), which is designed to solve the problem of large-scale content distribution [2], separating content from location, retrieving data throughout the network through content identification [3], supporting multiple access, etc., was developed. The traditional end-to-end transmission mode can realize multiterminal asynchronous data transmission, which greatly improves the transmission efficiency. The ICN congestion control directly affects the success of content retrieval, but the ICN routers (with routing and caching functions) are distributed. However, it is very difficult to collect global information of the entire network, and the congestion control mechanism cannot be implemented globally. Congestion control is inefficient [4], and it is easy for consumers to fail to obtain content. To solve this challenge, software-defined network (SDN) technology was introduced. The SDN controller is used to centrally control the entire network, open and configurable, etc., to obtain the status information of all links and realize online learning of artificial intelligence reinforcement learning from a global perspective [5]. The controller generates punishment and reward values in real time according to the status information. Through the process of "exploration-learning-application-summary-upgrading and testing", the system determines the optimal strategy, realizes adaptive congestion control [6], and has the characteristics of high efficiency and intelligence.

In addition, the satellite network topology has the characteristics of periodic connection and disconnection. In the TCP/IP network, the server will retransmit to solve the problem of data loss. However, in the information center network, the content of the producer is stored in the cache. When a link is disconnected (there are multiple satellite links and other links are connected), the path information in the FIB and PIT will be invalid. Therefore, this paper modifies FIB and PIT and proposes FIB and PIT based on geographic location (longitude and latitude). When a satellite link fails, the predictability of satellite topology is used to find other available cache content from FIB and PIT to improve consumption. The success rate of the user hitting the cache.

The main contributions of this paper are as follows:

(1) The FIB and PIT based on geographic location in the satellite network are proposed, and fields such as latitude and longitude are newly added. When a certain path fails, other cache paths can be found.
(2) Under the software-defined information center network, the adaptive congestion control algorithm of artificial intelligence reinforcement learning online learning is proposed, and congestion control is realized according to the state information of the entire network.
(3) To verify the modified FIB and PIT and the reinforcement learning congestion control algorithm, the Iridium constellation is designed in STK to simulate different network states, and it has been proven by a large number of experiments that congestion control can be achieved.

The rest of this paper is organized as follows: Sect. 2 introduces the related work of this paper, Sect. 3 details the adaptive congestion control algorithm for artificial intelligence reinforcement learning online learning under the software-defined information center network, Sect. 4 evaluates the performance of the proposed scheme, and finally, the conclusion and the prospect of future work.

2 Related Work

Network congestion means that the transmission volume exceeds the maximum load capacity of the link, and it is also an important indicator that affects the transmission performance. One of the goals of studying congestion control is to adjust the congestion window according to the real-time bandwidth to minimize the communication delay and avoid the impact of link interruption data transmission. Since the information center network congestion is different from the traditional TCP/IP congestion control mechanism, it is necessary to implement congestion control according to the characteristics of the information center. In recent years, scholars at home and abroad have mainly studied NDN network congestion control from the following aspects:

Congestion control for each hop, that is, to control the queue length for each hop. Lan D et al. [7] designed a hop-by-hop congestion control method to detect the queue length of interest packets in the queue of intermediate nodes. When the queue occupancy rate is low, the router port is allowed to forward the Interest packets; otherwise, the Interest packets are directly discarded. When the delay in LEO is too large, it will affect the monitoring rate of the data packets in the monitoring queue of the router. This solution cannot be applied on a large scale in LEO.

Receiver-driven congestion control. In the literature [8], this type of congestion control mechanism is similar to TCP/IP by confirming congestion through RTT delay and then avoiding congestion by adjusting the data transmission rate of Interests by the receiver to adapt to the transmission performance of the link (also known as "Interest Shaping"). Interest packets stored by nodes in the ICN correspond to different data. When there is a data request, the data packets corresponding to the Interest packets may be returned from different nodes [9]. The different positions of the nodes have a greater impact on the calculation of the returned data RTT [10]. Furthermore, LEO The RTT caused by the simultaneous connection and disconnection of the medium link is inaccurate, and it is also impossible to accurately determine the congestion.

In addition, many scholars have applied artificial intelligence to congestion control. Xu et al. [11] designed a framework DRL-TE based on the reinforcement learning deep deterministic policy gradient (DDPG). Using the link bandwidth, the experiment shows that the utilization of the link is improved and the end-to-end delay is reduced, but the dynamic network is not compared in the experiment.

In summary, although there have been many research results on the optimization method of information center network congestion control, due to factors such as the periodic connection and disconnection of satellites and the limited processing capacity of satellites, congestion control is still unable to adapt itself. There are few schemes for congestion control under dynamic networks. Based on this, this paper uses SDN to collect overall network status information and uses punishment and reward to achieve self-adaptation under dynamic network congestion.

3   System Architecture

According to the iridium constellation structure, the entire system architecture is designed as shown in Fig. 1. There are producers, switches with NDN functions, consumers (multiple), controllers, ground station nodes, etc., to form a software-defined information center network, simulating the realization of iridium constellation sends data to terrestrial consumers.

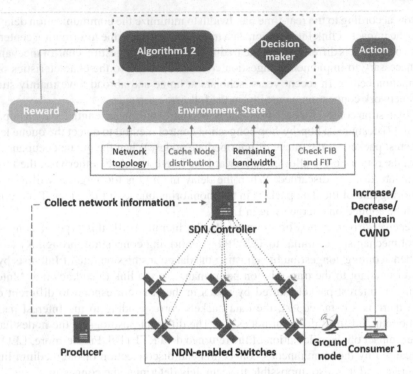

Fig. 1. System Architecture.

Producer: publishes content.

Consumer 1: Get some content.

Switches with NDN functions: There are 66 switches in the SDN network (see Sect. 4.1 for details), with NDN functions, such as caching and routing, and communicate with the controller through the openFlow protocol. The modified FIB and PIT are installed (see Sect. 3.2 for details).

Controller: The core of the entire network, which collects link network status, issues and installs flow tables. The controller is equipped with an artificial intelligence module, which can realize artificial intelligence online learning to achieve adaptive congestion control (see Sect. 3.3 for details).

The whole architecture realizes the content released by the producer, the storage path of FIB and PIT, the content cached, and the content obtained by the consumer. The controller collects the status information of each link, realizes the congestion control of artificial intelligence online learning, and adjusts the sending rate CWND of the consumer to achieve the purpose of increasing throughput.

3.1 Collect Network Status

The purpose of collecting the network status of each link is for the basis of artificial intelligence decision-making, and the status of each link is collected through the controller LLDP (Link Layer Discovery Protocol) protocol [12], mainly including the following:

Network topology: including the connection and disconnection of each link.

Cache distribution: Obtaining the cache distribution on switches with the NDN function is beneficial for consumers to obtain content.

Remaining bandwidth: This is an important parameter of congestion control, and congestion control is adjusted according to the remaining bandwidth.

Update FIB and PIT: Update cache path information, geographic location information, time, etc., in the table.

The above state information is collected to realize the parameters of artificial intelligence online learning decision-making and update them in the cycle. The artificial intelligence online learning algorithm will execute a certain action based on this to implement CWND that adjusts the consumer's sending rate.

3.2 Geo-Based FIB and PIT

The periodic on-off of the satellite network belongs to a dynamic network. Affected by the periodic interruption and connection of the satellite topology, the path saved in the FIB and PIT will fail, resulting in failure of consumers to obtain content. This article modifies the FIB and PIT according to the characteristics of the satellite network. Added information such as path generation time, longitude and latitude is shown in Table 1 and 2. When the consumer fails to obtain the content, the controller can retrieve all available content by looking up the FIB and FIT tables to deal with the periodic interruption and connection of the satellite, as in Algorithm 1.

Table 1. Modified FIB.

key	content	cache time	position	set
...				
130	C40	1663451240	(38,4)	[W4, W6,...]
140	C471	1663469240	(18,18)	[W1]
...				

Algorithm 1. Obtain the cache path algorithm.

input	Content unique Key
output	FIB unique Key or FIT unique Key
01	if FIB Content unique key ! = NULL and find with Longitude and latitude
02	return Content unique Key
03	else if FIT unique key != NULL and find with Longitude and latitude
04	return Content unique Key
05	else if wait for next period
06	return Content unique Key in next period
07	else
08	producer pull content again and update FIB/FIT

Table 2. Modified PIT.

key	content	cache time	position	set
...				
13	C436	1663451240	(38,4)	[W4, W6,...]
14	C472	1663469240	(18,18)	[W1]
...				

key: unique key.
content: content unique Key.
cache time: cache created timestamp.
position: longitude and latitude.
set: caching node set.

Lines 05–06: the consumer waits for the next cycle to obtain data again; Line 08: none of the other solutions are successful, and the producer pushes the content to the cache and updates the FIT, FIB and other information. According to Algorithm 1, due to the FIB With path invalidation in PIT, look for available cache content in the 3 selected tracks (see Fig. 2).

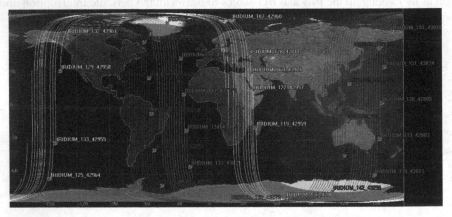

Fig. 2. 2D image with 3 tracks (yellow, red, blue) selected. (Color figure online)

3.3 Online Learning of Congestion Control

Congestion control online learning is the core of the entire architecture. As shown in Fig. 3, congestion control online learning applies deep reinforcement learning to generate real-time optimal solutions according to the network state information collected in the network state collection module. First, the agent extracts features through the convolution layer of the neural network according to the previously obtained state and then maps it into the probability of a certain action by the fully connected layer. To reuse

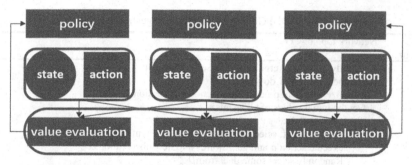

Fig. 3. MADDPG Congestion Control Online Learning.

the previous important experience, the experience playback mechanism is introduced, which can avoid related sequences. The samples affect the training and finally adjust the consumption sending rate CWND according to Algorithm 2.

The multiagent algorithm implements a DDPG algorithm for each agent, and all agents share a centralized critic network.

State: Define state S as composed of the following components: available link bandwidth, $S = (remainingbandwidth)$, obtained by the SDN controller.

Action: Define action A to adjust the consumer's sending rate. There are the following actions (see Table 3).

Table 3. Action execution types

Way of changes	Extent of Change (CWND)
Increase	+LAV, * LAV, * 2 * 1 LAV
Decrease	− LAV, * 0.75 * LAV, * 0.1* LAV
Maintain	0

LAV (last average value) = last time average value

They are the average value of CWND in the previous stage of the algorithm. When the action is "Increase", it is the average value of CWND in the previous stage, multiplied by the average value of CWND in the previous stage, and multiplied by 2 times the previous stage. Average value of CWND.

Reward: The reward function is to reward those that are beneficial to alleviating congestion and punish the other way around. as follows:

$$R = \alpha \times \log(throughput(t)) - \beta \times \log(RTT(t)) \qquad (1)$$

α and β are parameters between [0, 1], throughput(t) is the throughput at time t, and RTT(t) is the throughput at time t.

Algorithm 2. MADDPG Online Learning Congestion Algorithm.

input	Network topology G
output	null
01	Randomly initialize **Actor** and **Critic** of each agent
02	for period $e = 1 - E$ do
03	Initialize a random process N for action exploration
04	Get the initial values of all agents$x$
05	for $t = 1 \rightarrow T$ do:
06	for each agent i, select an action with the current policy$a = N + \mu(o)$
07	execute action a and get rewards and new observationsx'
08	Randomly select some data from$D$
09	for each agent, the centralized training **Critic** network
10	for each agent, the centralized training **Actor** network
11	for each agent, update target **Actor** network and target **Critic** network
12	end for
13	end for

The gradient of a deterministic policy is:

$$\nabla_\theta J \approx \frac{1}{N} \sum_{i=1}^{N} \nabla_\theta u_\theta(s_i) \nabla_a Q_\omega(s_i, a)|_{a=\mu_\theta a(s_i)} \tag{2}$$

Each agent is a separate DDPG algorithm that then integrates the results of each agent and finally outputs the conclusion after comprehensive processing.

4   Simulation Test and Performance Evaluation

This section compares the comprehensive performance of the proposed scheme, such as throughput, by simulating the satellite network environment.

Computer: Intel(R) Core(TM) i5 12400F CPU @2.50 GHz × 6 processor, 32 G memory. Operating System: Ubuntu 22.10.

Controller: Ryu [13], deployed in Geostationary Earth Orbit (GEO), the operation period is equal to the rotation period of the earth, and it is stationary relative to the ground station and can obtain satellite status information in LEO.

Analysis tool: Wiresharkv3.6.3 version, used for network protocol analysis, routing analysis, packet analysis, etc. [14].

Network traffic simulation tool: Manimahi is used to simulate network parameters in simulation experiments and can record and playback operations [15].

The ground station is located in Jiamusi, China, in the Northern Hemisphere.

4.1 Simulation Test

$$X' = \begin{bmatrix} 1 & X_{(1,2)} & X_{(1,3)} & \dots & X_{(1,k)} \\ X_{(2,1)} & 1 & X_{(2,3)} & \dots & X_{(2,k)} \\ X_{(3,1)} & X_{(3,2)} & 1 & \dots & X_{(3,k)} \\ \dots & \dots & \dots & 1 & \dots \\ X_{(k,1)} & X_{(k,2)} & X_{(k,3)} & \dots & 1 \end{bmatrix} \tag{3}$$

The position information of each satellite derived from STK is shown in formula (6), which represents the position matrix of each satellite in the iridium constellation. $X_{(j,k)}$. Since the iridium constellation switches every 60 s, it runs in sequence. When a satellite is connected to multiple satellites, this article ignores the link situation that is too far from the satellite, only discusses the one-to-one corresponding satellite link, and organizes the satellite distance matrix X' into the visibility matrix X, as follows.

$$X = \begin{bmatrix} 0 & X_{(1,2)} & X_{(1,3)} & \dots & X_{(1,k)} \\ X_{(2,1)} & 0 & X_{(2,3)} & \dots & X_{(2,k)} \\ X_{(3,1)} & X_{(3,2)} & 0 & \dots & X_{(3,k)} \\ \dots & \dots & \dots & 0 & \dots \\ X_{(k,1)} & X_{(k,2)} & X_{(k,3)} & \dots & 0 \end{bmatrix} \tag{4}$$

X is the satellite visibility matrix composed of 0 and 1 after being sorted by X'. In the X matrix, except for the value with too long a distance, when there is a link between satellites, it is recorded as 1; otherwise, it is recorded as 0, as shown in formula (7). The periodicity between satellites in the iridium constellation will follow the relationship of (7). See Algorithm 3 for the pseudo code of connection and disconnection, dynamic switching link.

Algorithm 3. Iridium Constellation Dynamic Network Algorithm.

input	matrix $X(X, X^2, \dots, X^N)$, $N = 66$
	$\Delta t = 60$
01	for each $X^n\ != null$ and $X^n \in X$ do
02	if $X^n = X^{\Delta t + n}$
03	do nothing
04	else
05	if $X^n_{(j,k)}\ != X^{\Delta t+n}_{(j,k)}$ and $X^{\Delta t+n}_{(j,k)} = 1$
06	put link $X^n_{(j,k)}\ X^{\Delta t+n}_{(j,k)}$ up
07	else if $X^n_{(j,k)}\ != X^{\Delta t+n}_{(j,k)}$ and $X^{\Delta t+n}_{(j,k)} = 0$
08	put link $X^n_{(j,k)}\ X^{\Delta t+n}_{(j,k)}$ down
09	end if
10	end for

In Algorithm 3, lines 02–03 indicate that one cycle has been run and its state remains unchanged. $X_{(j,k)}^n$ represents the value of the j row and k column element in the n visible matrix, the 05–06th row, when its value and the value of the element in the next cycle are 1, the chain The link is connected; in lines 07–08, when the value of $X_{(j,k)}^{\Delta t+n}$ is 0, the link is disconnected, and Δt is the satellite switching time interval, and the whole process simulates the satellite Periodic on and off.

4.2 Performance Evaluation

The experiments in this paper are implemented on the Mini-NDN open source software [16]. This software is a network simulation platform based on Mininet, which can realize all the functions of NDN and build a software-defined information center network together with the controller and switches with NDN functions. Consumers obtain the cached content through the software-defined information center network. According to Algorithm 3 and a switch with 66 NDN functions, the periodic disconnection and connection of satellites are simulated. The comprehensive performance of the algorithm in this paper will be compared through the following experiments. To eliminate the influence of other factors on the experimental results, the average of 20 experiments will be taken into the statistical results.

(1) Can it hit the cache

Due to the dynamic characteristics of low-orbit satellite networks (periodic connection and disconnection of intersatellite links), the path information cached in the FIB and PIT tables will become invalid; that is, consumers cannot obtain CS through the paths in the FIB and PIT content above. As shown in Fig. 4.

In Fig. 4(a), the consumer has been unable to obtain the content in the FIB and PIT tables and finally failed to obtain the content.

In Fig. 4(b), the consumer fails to obtain the content from the CS through the path in the FIB and PIT, but through the recalculation of the geographic location of the scheme in this paper, the routing data have been obtained from other caches, and the content is finally obtained successfully.

In Fig. 4(c), the consumer fails to obtain the content through the FIB and PIT. Through the recalculation of the geographical location in this paper, the producer provides the content again. Finally, the consumer succeeds in obtaining the content and updates the FIB and PIT.

In Fig. 4(d), the consumer fails to obtain the content through the FIB and PIT. According to the predictability of the satellite topology, the consumer waits again for the next cycle and reacquires the content according to the path in the FIB and PIT table; finally, the consumer obtains the content. Content succeeded.

(a)　The network link is interrupted, and the consumer fails to obtain the content

(b)　Recalculate the available cache, and the consumer obtains the content successfully

Fig. 4. Several situations in which consumers acquire content.

(c) The available cache is recalculated, and the consumer obtains the content successfully

(d) The consumer waits for the next cycle and obtains the content successfully

Fig. 4. (*continued*)

4.3 Throughput CDF

Figure 5 Comparison of CDF between the algorithm in this paper [17] and the DPCCP algorithm the literature proposes a no artificial network utility maximization (network utility maximization) model DPCCP (delay-based path-specified congestion control protocol) to solve congestion control. In this paper, this algorithm is applied to the network of simulation 5.1 and the algorithm in this paper. About throughput The CDF is shown in Figure x. The DPCCP algorithm selects the transmission path by calculating the performance of each path, but the characteristics of periodic connection and disconnection of satellites result in a maximum throughput of 16 Mb/s, which is lower than that of RL-ICN-CC in this paper. In addition, the algorithm cannot be self-adapted to congestion control, so the CDF of the DPCCP algorithm fluctuates greatly, while the throughput

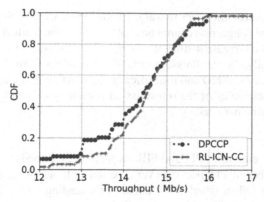

Fig. 5. CDF comparison between this algorithm and DPCCP algorithm.

of the algorithm in this paper is stable and does not fluctuate greatly. Reinforcement learning online learning can adapt to consumers in real time according to the network environment. Rate CWND to avoid congestion and thus improve throughput. The maximum throughput and average throughput of the RL-ICN-CC algorithm in this paper are higher than those of the DPCCP algorithm.

(2) **Buffer occupancy rate**

In this paper, the RL-ICN-CC algorithm adjusts the CWND according to the consumer's sending rate, so the occupancy of the buffer is extremely important; that is, the queue length is controlled to achieve stability. According to the algorithm (active queue management) and the experimental method in the literature [19], the number of data packets in the NDN flow is counted to analyze the buffer occupancy, as shown in Fig. 6.

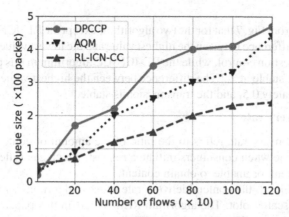

Fig. 6. Average queue length under different NDN flows for each algorithm.

With the increase in NDN flow, the average queue length in each algorithm increases, and the increase in DPCCP and AQM is significantly larger than that of RL-ICN-CC in this paper. This is because the other two algorithms have a weaker ability of consumers to adjust CWND. The congestion cannot be adapted well, which affects the transmission performance. With the increase in time, it is very easy for the buffer to be full and the data to overflow, and finally, the transmission fails. The RL-ICN-CC algorithm in this paper can adjust the real-time CWND and the buffer queue length without fluctuation and can cope with the characteristics of the transmission instability caused by the intermittent topology in the satellite network.

(3) Size of PITs

Since this paper remodifies PIT and FIB, its performance needs to be evaluated. The test counts the number of PIT packets over a period of time, and the difference in the number of PITs can reflect whether the consumer's sending rate is stable, that is, the pros and cons of congestion control.

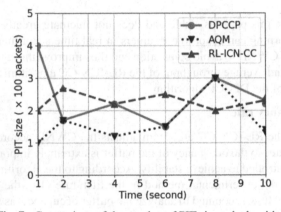

Fig. 7. Comparison of the number of PITs in each algorithm.

It can be seen from Fig. 7 that for the two algorithms except the RL-ICN-CC algorithm in this paper, the difference between the highest value and the lowest value is large, which reflects poor congestion control, while the RL-ICN-CC algorithm in this paper has small fluctuations and is stable at 2.2 The difference between the highest value and the lowest value is approximately 0.5, and the transmission is stable.

(4) Content delivery rate

The content delivery rate refers to the ratio of the amount of content obtained per unit time to the time when consumers initiate a request, which can reflect the speed of obtaining the content. or unable to obtain content.

As shown in Fig. 8, the content delivery rate of each algorithm within 32 s is displayed through a scatter plot. The algorithm RL-ICN-CC in this paper has remodified PIT and FIB. In the satellite network, the efficiency of content acquisition is significantly improved, and it can obtain content in a short time. DPCCP cannot cope with the drawbacks of periodic connection and disconnection of satellite network topology. All the time required is long, and sometimes the content cannot be obtained due to link interruption.

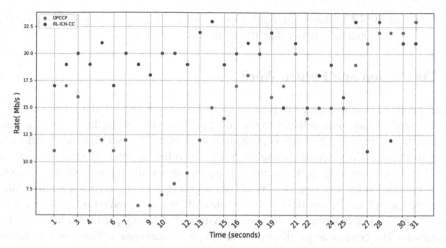

Fig. 8. Content Delivery Rate Comparison.

Furthermore, the average rate of the algorithm RL-ICN-CC is significantly higher than that of DPCCP at 11 Mb/s at 19 Mb/s, and the algorithm RL-ICN-CC is relatively stable and has less fluctuation, which can continuously transmit data and is suitable for the batch distribution of large files.

(5) End-to-end delay

The end-to-end delay is an important indicator of whether the entire link is congested or not and the performance of the link. The same link and content were selected in the experiment to compare the advantages and disadvantages of the algorithm in this paper and other algorithm.

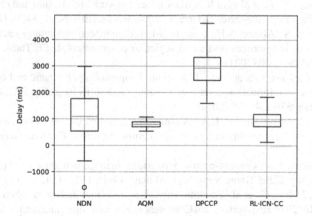

Fig. 9. Delay box diagram of each algorithm

As shown in Fig. 9, when the reinforcement learning NDN is not used, the delay is large, and the difference between the maximum value and the minimum value is also large. The RL-ICN-CC algorithm in this paper realizes adaptive congestion control, and the overall performance is better than that of the other algorithms.

5   Conclusion and Future Work

In this paper, a content-centric information center network is proposed to solve the problem of satellite mass data delivery to the ground. However, due to the dynamic nature of satellite topology, the network is prone to congestion, and user and cache paths are prone to failure. It is proposed to use the SDN controller to obtain the status information of the entire network. Reinforcement learning solves the optimal control strategy, avoids congestion by adjusting the CWND of the consumer interest packet sending rate, redesigns the PIT and FIB including the latitude and longitude, and refinds the content of other cache servers according to the characteristics of topology predictability, avoiding consumers. The content acquisition fails due to path interruption. Through simulation experiments, it is known that the proposed scheme has strong adaptability and generalization ability in the satellite network and improves the throughput. In future work, other deep reinforcement learning algorithms will be further studied to solve the problem of avoiding congestion in information-centric networks.

Acknowledgments. This research was funded by the National Natural Science Foundation of China under grant No. U21A20451, the Science and Technology Planning Project of Jilin Province under grant No. 20200401105GX and 20220101143JC, and the China University Industry-Academia-Research Innovation Fund under grant No. 2021FNA01003.

References

1. Li, J., Xue, K., Liu, J., et al.: An ICN/SDN-based network architecture and efficient content retrieval for future satellite-terrestrial integrated networks. IEEE Netw. **34**(1), 188–195 (2019)
2. Gupta, D., Rani, S., Ahmed, S.H., et al.: ICN-based enhanced cooperative caching for multimedia streaming in resource constrained vehicular environment. IEEE Trans. Intell. Transp. Syst. **22**(7), 4588–4600 (2021)
3. Leal, G.M., Zacarias, I., Stocchero, J.M., et al.: Empowering command and control through a combination of information-centric networking and software defined networking. IEEE Commun. Mag. **57**(8), 48–55 (2019)
4. Benedetti, P., Piro, G., Grieco, L.A.: A softwarized and mec-enabled protocol architecture supporting consumer mobility in information-centric networks. Comput. Netw. **188**, 107867 (2021)
5. Jmal, R., Fourati, L.C.: Content-centric networking management based on software defined networks: survey. IEEE Trans. Netw. Serv. Manag. **14**(4), 1128–1142 (2017)
6. Liu, Z., Zhu, J., Pan, C., et al.: Satellite network architecture design based on SDN and ICN technology. In: 2018 8th International Conference on Electronics Information and Emergency Communication (ICEIEC), pp. 124–131. IEEE (2018)
7. Lan, D., Tan, X., Lv, J., et al.: A deep reinforcement learning based congestion control mechanism for NDN. In: ICC 2019–2019 IEEE International Conference on Communications (ICC), pp. 1–7. IEEE (2019)

8. Carofiglio, G., Gallo, M., Muscariello, L.: ICP: design and evaluation of an interest control protocol for content-centric networking. In: 2012 Proceedings IEEE INFOCOM Workshops, pp. 304–309. IEEE (2012)

9. Ryu, S., Joe, I., Kim, W.T.: Intelligent forwarding strategy for congestion control using Q-learning and LSTM in named data networking. Mob. Inf. Syst. **2021** (2021)

10. Li, L., Xu, K., Li, T., et al.: A measurement study on multipath TCP with multiple cellular carriers on high speed rails. In: Proceedings of the 2018 Conference of the ACM Special Interest Group on Data Communication, pp. 161–175 (2018)

11. Xu, Z., Tang, J., Meng, J., et al.: Experience-driven networking: a deep reinforcement learning based approach. In: IEEE INFOCOM 2018-IEEE Conference on Computer Communications, pp. 1871–1879. IEEE (2018)

12. https://learningnetwork.cisco.com/s/article/link-layer-discovery-protocol-lldp-x

13. https://ryu-sdn.org/

14. https://www.wireshark.org

15. http://mahimahi.mit.edu/

16. https://minindn.memphis.edu/

17. Ye, Y., et al.: Delay-based network utility maximization modeling for congestion control in named data networking. IEEE/ACM Trans. Netw. **29**(5), 2184–2197 (2021)

18. Xu, Y., Ni, H., Zhu, X.: An effective transmission scheme based on early congestion detection for information-centric network. Electronics **10**(18), 2205 (2021). https://doi.org/10.3390/electronics10182205

19. Li, W., et al.: Charging on the route: an online pricing gateway congestion control for ICNs. IEEE Trans. Netw. Serv. Manag. **17**(1), 239–250 (2019)

Intelligent Automated Penetration Testing Using Reinforcement Learning to Improve the Efficiency and Effectiveness of Penetration Testing

Mohammed Y. A. Aqra[✉] and Xiaoqiang Di

Changchun University of Science and Technology, Changchun, China
mohammed.abokhadeje@gmail.com, dixiaoqiang@cust.edu.cn

Abstract. A penetration test is a process that involves planning, generating, and evaluating attacks that are designed to find and exploit vulnerabilities in digital assets. It can be used in large networks to evaluate the security of their infrastructure. Despite the use of automated tools, it can still be very time consuming and repetitive. The goal of this paper is to develop an intelligent automated penetration testing framework that uses reinforcement learning to improve the efficiency and effectiveness of penetration testing. It utilizes a model-based approach to automate the sequential decision-making process. The framework's main component is a partial observed Markov decision process that is solved using an external algorithm.

One of the biggest challenges in performing penetration tests on large networks is finding and evaluating clusters of vulnerabilities. This paper presents a method that combines a hierarchical network model with a cluster-based approach. It allows for faster and more accurate testing compared to previous methods. The results of the study show that the IAPTF method outperforms other approaches in terms of time, accuracy, and human performance. One of the main advantages of IAPTF is its ability to perform repetitive tests, which is typically not possible with traditional methods. This method could potentially replace manual pen testing.

Keywords: Machin learning · Deep Reinforcement Learning · IAPTS · HRL-GIP

1 Introduction

The rapid emergence and evolution of new wireless communication systems has caused a change in the way they work. The 5G and 6G technologies have already been deployed in various countries. With the increasing number of people using smartphones, the need for more effective and efficient wireless communication has also become more prevalent [1]. The 6G wireless networks are designed to provide high-speed and reliable connectivity. They need advanced network devices and techniques to meet their various requirements. In recent years, the literature has suggested that the main ideas for 6G are the use of

© ICST Institute for Computer Sciences, Social Informatics and Telecommunications Engineering 2023
Published by Springer Nature Switzerland AG 2023. All Rights Reserved
R. Li et al. (Eds.): MOBILWARE 2022, LNICST 507, pp. 30–42, 2023.
https://doi.org/10.1007/978-3-031-34497-8_3

terahertz communication, intelligent reflecting surfaces, and reconfigurable intelligent surfaces [2].

The IRS is a new type of wireless communication technology that is expected to be used in the 6G era. It is a thin metasurface that can reflect electromagnetic waves in an organized manner. This technology can be used to mitigate multi-path problems and is ideal for terahertz and millimeter wave communication [3]. The increasing popularity of IRS devices has led to the development of new technologies that allow them to provide high-speed wireless communication. Some of these include the ability to perform multiple tasks at the same time, such as power transfer and mobile edge computing. In addition, the use of mmWave technology has allowed for the development of unmanned aerial vehicles (UAVs) and smart cities [4].

The increasing popularity of IRS devices has led to the development of new technologies that allow them to provide high-speed wireless communication. Some of these include the ability to perform multiple tasks at the same time, such as power transfer and mobile edge computing [5]. In addition, the use of mmWave technology has allowed for the development of unmanned aerial vehicles (UAVs) and smart cities. Several studies have been conducted on the use of IRS in the design of wireless communication systems that are designed for different performance matrices. These studies are categorized into four main areas: cascade channel estimation, multiuser communication, phase shift optimization, and beamforming optimization [6].

Machine learning techniques are a revolutionary technology that can be used in the development of artificial intelligence (AI) systems. They are capable of learning from vast amounts of data and making predictions for the future [7]. Due to their capabilities, various ML techniques have been widely adopted in the design of wireless communication systems. The various types of deep learning techniques that are commonly used in IRS are labeled as deep learning, reinforcement learning, unsupervised learning, and federated learning. According to the studies conducted on the use of IRS, the advantages of using ML techniques are compared with the conventional methods [8].

The ability to use deep learning techniques in the design of wireless communication systems has been greatly improved by the use of ML. This technology can help improve the accuracy of the channel estimation process by extracting the relationship between the input and output signals. In particular, the use of DL-based IRS in the design of Massive MIMO and OFDM systems has been shown to be more reliable. In [9] study, the authors proposed a DL-based channel estimation method that can be used in the design of an IRS-based system. However, this method could cause issues due to the error propagation when estimating the direct channel. In another study, the authors proposed a method that can be used to estimate the cascaded channel using a convolutional neural network. The literature also covered the various techniques and technologies that are used in the design of IRS-based systems. In [10] study, the authors analyzed the performance of a multi-antenna assisted IRS system. They then conducted a performance analysis of the various techniques involved in the design of the system.

ML techniques are widely used in the design of wireless communication systems due to their capabilities. They can help solve various problems related to the design of wireless communication systems. A study conducted on the use of IRS-assisted technology in a wireless communication system revealed the state-of-the-art survey of the technology. The authors used microstrip patch antennas and a variety of antennas to study the operation principle of an IRS-based system. They also covered the properties of metasurfaces and their reflections [11].

The literature additionally covered the various techniques and technologies that are used in the design of IRS-based systems. In addition, the authors conducted a survey to learn more about the various aspects of the technology. They also discussed the multiple concepts and features of the channel model. The study additionally conducted a survey to learn more about the implementation structure of the IRS. The literature also covered the various techniques and technologies that are used in the design of IRS-based systems. One of the most important factors that can be considered when it comes to the development of an IRS-based system is the integration of multiple technologies.

1.1 Problem Statement

One of the most challenging issues in the development of machine learning systems is selecting the best method to automate the Agent Pen process. In Pozdniakov, et al., 2020, they present a method that avoids the use of pre-defined models by making the learning algorithm completely model-free. This approach significantly improves the performance of the system while still addressing the quality of attack sequences. Despite the increasing number of attackers and the complexity of the threat landscape, more automation is needed to effectively pentest systems. One of the most challenging factors that can be addressed is the accuracy of the results. To achieve this, they perform a variety of attacks against different targets, including Linux and Windows systems.

One of the most important factors that can be considered when it comes to developing an approximator is the number of features that will represent the state-action space of a given attack. This is because, while building an approximator, it is important to choose the most appropriate features for the specific attack. Another important factor that can be considered is the size of the feature set that will represent the state-action space. To achieve this, they use a recurrent neural network (RNN) that is designed to perform a variety of tasks, such as identifying and validating vulnerabilities. Unfortunately, too many features can negatively affect the performance of the learning algorithm and lead to time-consuming attacks. To address this issue, they have created an autoencoder that can reduce the number of features in the learning algorithm.

1.2 Aim of the Study

This study aims to focus on the use of machine learning (ML) in the field of PT practice to make it more intelligent and efficient. It can be extended to include the use of web and application testing. The study aims to introduce the importance of machine learning in the field of PT practice. It reviews various studies and surveys related to the subject. The last section of the study will introduce the proposed RL model and its various components. The proposed system is called IAPTS and it is mainly used for testing the effectiveness of various techniques related to physical exertion testing. This study also describes the various steps involved in the testing and the results obtained.

2 Literature Review

2.1 Overview of Deep Reinforcement Learning

The goal of the policy is to define the agent's plan of action and how it relates to the environment. The reward values that the environment gives to the agent are the numerical representations of the state's intrinsic desirability. The value function is a long-term function that calculates a discounted return from a specific state after a policy has been followed. The environment model is a representation of the behavior that helps boost the performance of the algorithm [12].

In a supervised manner, DeepMind Alpha Go applied Monte Carlo tree search techniques to a dataset. However, instead of imitating human strategies, it did not see data from human games. Instead, it played a variety of games against itself to learn how to win a game that was not known to humans. An agent is a type of entity that is involved in reinforcement learning. The goal of a reinforcement learning algorithm is to enable an agent to learn quickly and accurately the optimal policy. This process can be done through the representation of the symbol p, which indicates that the goal is to achieve the highest reward value. The goal of a given action is to make the agent closer to its target. The reward RT 2- R determines the reward if the agent is closer or if it is farther away [11, 13].

Deep reinforcement learning is a subfield of machine learning that uses the concepts of deep learning to provide an optimal solution for an agent's experience. This process is carried out through iterations and evaluation of a reward function to determine the ideal behavior for an agent. There are three main approaches to deep reinforcement learning: the value-based approach, the policy-based approach, and the model-based approach.

The goal of value-based reinforcement learning is to enable an agent to find the optimal policy by calculating its value function in the long run. In contrast, policy-based reinforcement learning is focused on finding the optimal policy by implementing the rules that are related to the objective function [14]. The former approach refers to the same action regardless of the state. The latter, on the other hand, involves the use of probabilistic evaluation methods to evaluate the actions taken in a given state. For model-based reinforcement learning, the agent is required to provide a model of the environment that describes the tasks that it can perform in that environment.

It is very challenging to directly compare the performance of model-based and non-model-based reinforcement learning algorithms. In their book, Mackworth and Poole stated that model-based learners are more efficient than their counterparts. They also claimed that fewer experiences are required to learn well with model-free methods. On its own, an agent might face errors and inaccuracies when learning the environment model. This can affect its performance and prevent it from achieving the required tasks. There are various approaches that are designed to integrate the model-free methods with the model-based ones. These include the Monte Carlo method, the value-based method, the policy based method, and the temporal difference method [15].

Although the different approaches are implemented in different ways, they share some of the same characteristics. The control that a reinforcement learning algorithm provides is a closed-loop approach. The reward is represented by the system's feedback, and this is delayed by the algorithm. The algorithms used in deep learning are designed to make decisions based on the sequence of actions taken. They also have long-term rewards that are dependent on the actions' duration. A concept known as credit assignment problem states that the system's dependence on time is due to the various actions that it performs [16, 17].

DRL is a framework that helps in the development of UAV control systems by providing a variety of tools that allow them to work with model-free algorithms. These include the ability to learn online how to perform the target without being trained, and to work in environments that are not familiar to the UAV. With the development of deep learning algorithms, there are now many new tasks that can be performed in the control area. For instance, controlling a swarm of UAVs with minimal resources can be performed safely [18].

2.2 IRS Hardware Architecture and Its Working Principle

The IRS hardware is based on the meta-surface, which is a two-dimensional meta-material. It can be used in the subwavelength frequency range with a large number of atomic layers. This is done through the use of a large number of meta-atoms. The signal response of an IRS Meta surface atom element can be changed by designing it according to the specific requirements of the wireless communication system. For instance, the size, shape, and orientation of the element can be changed to accommodate the dynamic wireless channels generated by the user's mobility [19]. The three main approaches to controlling IRS mechanical reflection are presented in the literature. These include the use of functional materials, electronic devices, and mechanical translation. Examples of electronic devices that are commonly used for this process include field-effect transistor (FETs), PIN diodes, and micro-electromechanical systems (MEMS) [19].

Due to their low energy cost and fast response time, electronic devices are widely used in today's society. In addition, they are also very advantageous for reducing the cost of designing and implementing IRS elements. To achieve the best possible performance, the IRS elements should be linked to a network to acquire knowledge about the environment [20].

This layer is composed of a copper plate, which is used to prevent the signal energy leakage during the IRS's reflection. A control circuit board then excites the element, which then changes the reflection amplitude and phase shift. The IRS smart controller then activates the reflection adaption. The IRS architecture allows the controllers to communicate with each other and with the various network parameters of a network, such as access points and base stations. Through a field-programmable gate array, the controllers can also control the flow of information between the multiple devices [21].

An example of this process is the reduction of the incident energy of a signal by the variation in the resistance of the IRS elements. This allows a scaling of the reflection amplitude to an effective level. This is similar to the work of a radio frequency identification tag, which can regulate the power strength of a signal by changing its load impedance. One of the most important factors that the IRS should consider when it comes to optimizing its reflection design is the availability of independent control over the phase and amplitude of the element. This can be done by implementing a more intelligent hardware design [22].

2.3 IRS Reflection

The channel model for wireless communication based on the IRS is composed of three components. These are the channel link between the IRS elements and the BS, the reflection of the IRS elements, and the channel between the two entities. In this type of channel, the characteristics of the signal are different from those of a traditional direct channel. The IRS utilizes a BS-based approach to receive and distribute superposed multi-path signals. Each element of the device receives and distributes the associated signal with an amplitude and phase that are ideal for a specific channel model [21].

2.4 IAPTS Memory, Expertise Management and Pre-Processing

The goal of this research is to develop a framework that will allow a large and medium-sized LAN to be equipped with a reliable and secure RL learning system. This will require dealing with a huge amount of intimations, which is very complex and can be difficult to solve given the limited computing power and time available. One of the most challenging aspects of this project is the modeling and simulation of the PT as a POMDP environment [1].

Resource management is a must in order to ensure that the resources are used efficiently. The system memory is used to store the data that the system processes. These include the environment attributes, which are used to define the policies and actions that an agent can perform within the environment, and the agent's memory, which is used to acquire knowledge and experiences. The first part of this study will focus on searching a policy as an agent acts in a certain environment [3]. The reward value will then be determined by a human expert. This method will allow researchers to conduct a research facilitation. This will allow IAPTS to adapt and adjust the tests that it deploys after a successful exploitation. It will also allow it to perform post-exploitation tasks such as privilege escalation and pivot [6].

This module will also allow researchers to develop a deeper understanding of the system's operations and procedures in order to provide it with the necessary "expert knowledge." In practical terms, this will allow IAPTS to perform various tasks such as extracting PGs and executing the testing plan. It will additionally allow it to keep track of the results of the tests and update its status in real time [7].A parallel knowledge-based system will also be implemented as part of the framework. This system will capture the details of the actions performed by the human expert. It will additionally extract knowledge from the data that the security system collects. This method will allow the system to perform post-exploitation tasks such as privilege escalation and pivot [1].

Despite the potential of artificial intelligence, it is still not able to model the intuition of humans. This issue will be solved by allowing the human expert to interact with the system. A mechanism that will allow security analysts to provide feedback will also be implemented to solve this issue[2].The feedback collected during the test will be stored in the system memory, which will then be used for future use. This method will allow the system to perform post-exploitation tasks such as privilege escalation and pivot. In addition to the human expertise, the memory will also feature a variety of features and workflows, such as the implementation of direct learning [5].

One of the most effective ways to improve the learning performance of the RL algorithms is by implementing a prioritized experience replay method. This method was initially implemented to enhance the learning capabilities of the system. However, in order to accommodate the technical requirements of the system, we modified the method. In addition to choosing the most relevant and plausible policies, we also injected other transition sequences that were validated by a human expert. These sequences allow the system to retrieve value function information from the previous tests and improve its efficiency. The resulting sequences can be replayed to reduce the number of POMDP observations and transitions, which improves the algorithm's efficiency [6].

In addition to the human expertise, the system will also feature a variety of features and workflows, such as the implementation of direct learning. One of the most important factors that will be introduced in this project is the GIP LP Solve algorithm, which was designed to improve the performance of IAPTS. This method will allow the system to capture the necessary expertise in form of a decision policy. Another effective way to demonstrate the importance of learning is by implementing a test scenario that is inspired by the real-world experience of re-testing a network after some upgrades or updates. This scenario will allow the system to perform multiple tasks such as extracting PGs. After the tests are performed, the system will use the previous generation of PGs as an initial belief in the output [7].

3   Testing the Model

The decision to embed RL within the practice of PT was based on its relevance and suitability. Its implementation also took into account the various decision-making problems that are involved in the process. The second challenge was to choose between two models: one that is model-free and another that is model-based. The concept of PT practice is that it involves choosing a decision-making task that is related to the relevant decision policy. This strategy helps minimize the number of iterations that the user has to perform in order to achieve the best possible outcome. In addition, the quality of the solution is related to the relevance of the decision policy. The first step in the process of solving is to identify the appropriate approach. In this paper, the researchers discussed the various advantages of using a model-free RL and the two options that are available for implementing this strategy: policy search and value iteration.

The next step was to choose between the two models. The decision to use policy search was made after considering the various advantages of the strategy. This strategy is supported by the initial goal of optimizing the process and fully automating the decision-making tasks within the PT practice. We then build a decision tree from the POMDP solution's output. After the selection of the appropriate model and the corresponding technique, the next step was to choose the appropriate solution modes. This process is carried out to enhance the efficiency and accuracy of the decision-making process. The goal of this work is to provide an intelligent automation of the tasks within the PT practice.

The paper also discussed the various advantages of using a comprehensive framework for developing and testing both the model-free and the model-based solutions. This approach allows the developers to start with the approximate mode and test both the proposed and the actual solution. After selecting the best solution, PERSEUS was the first algorithm to be implemented during the early stages of the project. Due to the importance of accuracy and efficiency, many exact solving algorithms were considered for inclusion in IAPTF. However, after assessing the various advantages of GIP, it was concluded that it was the most efficient candidate. To ensure that the solution is flexible and can handle different input types, multiple modifications were made to the GIP and PERSEUS versions.

The researchers tested and implemented the exact and approximate methods of solving the POMDP problem. The former method involves optimizing the value function of the model over all possible belief's states, while the latter method is more computational. For most applications, exact solutions are very challenging to perform due to their complexity. The exact solution that is used for calculating the value function of POMDPs is very cost-effective as it allows the user to perform the optimal action on any belief state. However, the computational power required to implement this algorithm is very high due to the exponential growth of the belief space. The approximate method is more inexact because it relies on a single choice of belief states. In this paper, the researchers will use the method known as Point-Based Value Iteration to perform a comparison and guidance exercise. It takes into account the initial belief and then picks the belief points according to a forward simulation.

The exact solution provided by the PBVI algorithm is an approximate representation of the value of the model that takes into account the various belief points in the model. It then ensures that the value function increases with every iteration. In practice, this method is very useful for solving large problems that involve multiple belief points. The PBVI algorithm also maintains a single value per point, which helps it to successfully solve large problems. In IAPTS, we implemented the PERSEUS algorithm, which performs a randomized point-based value optimization process on each of the POMDPs. It ensures that the value of the points in the belief set is improved in each backup stage. The Perseus algorithm also performs backup stages depending on the convergence criteria and the number of policy changes.

The exact solution provided by the PBVI algorithm is an approximate representation of the value of the model that takes into account the various belief points in the model. It then ensures that the value function increases with every subsequent belief. However, the computational power required to implement this algorithm is very high due to the complexity of the problem. To minimize the time required to implement this algorithm, the researchers decided to use a variety of algorithms that use a combination of linear programs and a prune-dominated vector.

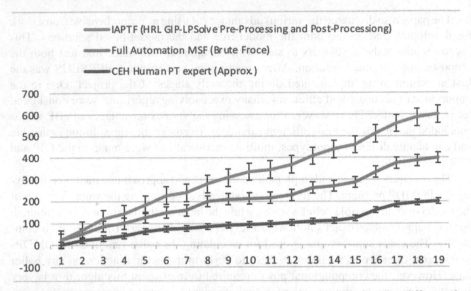

Fig. 1. Using different algorithm and belief handling techniques, this can solve different size POMDP problems.

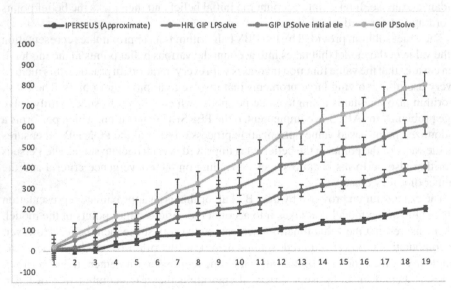

Fig. 2. Re-test the same network. After introducing a significant number of changes to the network configurations

4   Results and Discussion

The HRL approach requires around two days to perform compared with the regular RL-GIP. Going beyond the 100-machine size, HRL is more efficient and can reach 200 machine size. It performed almost as well as the PERSEUS algorithm. In addition, HRL-GIP can also be significantly faster than the previous generation. The HRL-GIP effect is widely used in large networks to perform effective value optimization. It can reach a good rate in 100-machine networks with over 20 clusters.

Security clustering often results in a large number of security clusters. This means that many small POMDPs are placed on top of these security clusters. This can result in IAPTF having to perform a lot of data manipulation and optimization to solve the problem. Using a model-free RL method is very advantageous for reducing the time required to implement the algorithm.

The goal of evaluating IAPTS is to provide a comprehensive analysis of the various aspects of the process, starting with validating the approach and examining the results in real-world situations. After that, the evaluation process continues with analyzing the accuracy and relevance of the results. The output of the program is then converted into a more understandable format by implementing policies graphs.

In addition to the time, it takes to solve the POMDP problem, other factors such as the number of tasks that need to be performed by the Metasploit MSF will also be taken into account to arrive at the overall time that IAPTS will spend testing on the test-bed networks. The results of the study presented in Fig. 1 and Fig. 2 show that IAPTS outperforms both the manual and automated versions of PT when it comes to solving algorithms on different LANs. The authors' experience as a consultant for PT also contributed to the findings. It is additionally clear that IAPTS is more cost-effective than both manual and automated versions of PT. In addition, the various discount rates that were considered during the development of IAPTS were aimed at preserving the realistic nature of the system.

Following the multiple simulations and testing, the discount rate for "0.5" was selected. We then decided to introduce some changes in the algorithm to improve its performance. One of these is the use of a more short-term approach to improve the performance of IAPTS. The researchers also decided to prioritize the observations and transitions through the use of the associated probabilities.

The results of the evaluation process were very good, with the new GIP-LP Solve achieving better performance than the previous generation. In addition, the improved performance of this variant was also evidenced by the significant time savings that it made in both the PG accuracy and time consumed. To further improve the performance of the program, we additionally re-tested the same network with or without changing the machine configurations.

The results of the tests were very impressive, especially when re-testing the same network that was shown in Fig. 2 The quality of the decisions that were produced by IAPTS was also beyond human expertise. In particular, when using the GIP LP Solve initial belief algorithm, the program was able to produce decisions that were more accurate than those that were produced by a human expert.

4.1 Simulation

Each performance was repeated five times with random seeds to ensure that the results were reproducible. The shading regions on the graph represent the variability in the runs. After training the agents, we are looking at two indicators: the number of steps that the agents have to take to reach their target and the maximum score that they can achieve. The HA-DRL algorithm can give an agent around 20 points depending on the scenario. It can also reduce the score by a small amount due to invalid actions it takes to reach the assets. We have tested the algorithm on various scenarios with different action space configurations.

The complexity of a scenario can increase the number of hosts and the number of actions in the action space. However, with only 2 additional agents to train, the number of actions in the action space can only increase from 49 to 4646. In all the tested scenarios, the HA-DRL convergence was superior to the IAPTS agent. In these scenarios, the complexity of the algorithm was significant enough to show its superiority, while the cost of training was not too high. Compared to the previous generation, the HA-DRL algorithm performed better in learning the optimal policy.

The performance of the IRS algorithm on different scenarios was unstable, especially when it was training with 20 and 30 hosts. It only managed to learn the optimal policy in one out of four runs. In the 50 hosts' scenario, the HA-DRL performed well, as it was able to train the agents successfully in one out of four runs. However, it was not able to get the most out of the training experience, as it took around 2,000 episodes to get the agents up to speed. The RIS algorithm was able to achieve the optimal number of actions in each scenario. This is the first demonstration of how deep learning can be used in an automatic testing system to handle large action pools.

5 Conclusions

This paper presents an approach to embedding RL techniques into the cyber security domain. We use a hierarchical RL representation to address the complexity of the PT domain. This method overcomes the scaling-up challenges that were encountered in addressing large POMDPs on networks with many nodes. The proposed approach involves segregating the network into small clusters and then processing the network's various attacking vectors in a way that is more effective than that of certified ethical hackers. This method can be used to deal with different types of networks and their complexity. The proposed IAPTF framework is a versatile and comprehensive approach that enables human experts to perform more complex tasks without requiring them to spend a lot of time. It can also reveal unexpected combinations that are typically ignored in manual testing.

References

1. Nomikos, N., Zoupanos, S., Charalambous, T., Krikidis, I.: A survey on reinforcement learning-aided caching in heterogeneous mobile edge networks. IEEE Access **10**, 4380–4413 (2022). https://doi.org/10.1109/ACCESS.2022.3140719

2. Rasheed, F., Yau, K.L.A., Noor, R.M., Wu, C., Low, Y.C.: Deep reinforcement learning for traffic signal control: a review. IEEE Access **8**, 208016–208044 (2020). https://doi.org/10.1109/ACCESS.2020.3034141

3. Park, D.Y., Lee, K.H.: Practical algorithmic trading using state representation learning and imitative reinforcement learning. IEEE Access **9**, 152310–152321 (2021). https://doi.org/10.1109/ACCESS.2021.3127209

4. Liu, D., Wang, Z., Lu, B., Cong, M., Yu, H., Zou, Q.: A reinforcement learning-based framework for robot manipulation skill acquisition. IEEE Access **8**, 108429–108437 (2020). https://doi.org/10.1109/ACCESS.2020.3001130

5. Liu, C.L., Chang, C.C., Tseng, C.J.: Actor-critic deep reinforcement learning for solving job shop scheduling problems. IEEE Access **8**, 71752–71762 (2020). https://doi.org/10.1109/ACCESS.2020.2987820

6. Li, M.L., Chen, S., Chen, J.: Adaptive learning: a new decentralized reinforcement learning approach for cooperative multiagent systems. IEEE Access **8**, 99404–99421 (2020). https://doi.org/10.1109/ACCESS.2020.2997899

7. Rothmann, M., Porrmann, M.: A survey of domain-specific architectures for reinforcement learning. IEEE Access **10**, 13753–13767 (2022). https://doi.org/10.1109/ACCESS.2022.3146518

8. Gasperov, B., Kostanjcar, Z.: Market making with signals through deep reinforcement learning. IEEE Access **9**, 61611–61622 (2021). https://doi.org/10.1109/ACCESS.2021.3074782

9. Lee, H., Cha, S.W.: Reinforcement learning based on equivalent consumption minimization strategy for optimal control of hybrid electric vehicles. IEEE Access **9**, 860–871 (2021). https://doi.org/10.1109/ACCESS.2020.3047497

10. Zhang, Q., Lin, J., Sha, Q., He, B., Li, G.: Deep interactive reinforcement learning for path following of autonomous underwater vehicle. IEEE Access **8**, 24258–24268 (2020). https://doi.org/10.1109/ACCESS.2020.2970433

11. Lee, H., Song, C., Kim, N., Cha, S.W.: Comparative analysis of energy management strategies for HEV: dynamic programming and reinforcement learning. IEEE Access **8**, 67112–67123 (2020). https://doi.org/10.1109/ACCESS.2020.2986373

12. Alharin, A., Doan, T.N., Sartipi, M.: Reinforcement learning interpretation methods: a survey. IEEE Access **8**, 171058–171077 (2020). https://doi.org/10.1109/ACCESS.2020.3023394

13. Hu, Y., Hua, Y., Liu, W., Zhu, J.: Reward shaping based federated reinforcement learning. IEEE Access **9**, 67259–67267 (2021). https://doi.org/10.1109/ACCESS.2021.3074221

14. Kubalik, J., Derner, E., Zegklitz, J., Babuska, R.: Symbolic regression methods for reinforcement learning. IEEE Access **9**, 139697–139711 (2021). https://doi.org/10.1109/ACCESS.2021.3119000

15. Chen, S.Y.C., Yang, C.H.H., Qi, J., Chen, P.Y., Ma, X., Goan, H.S.: Variational quantum circuits for deep reinforcement learning. IEEE Access **8**, 141007–141024 (2020). https://doi.org/10.1109/ACCESS.2020.3010470

16. Elavarasan, D., Durairaj Vincent, P.M.: Crop yield prediction using deep reinforcement learning model for sustainable agrarian applications. IEEE Access **8**, 86886–86901 (2020). https://doi.org/10.1109/ACCESS.2020.2992480

17. Mohammed, M.Q., Chung, K.L., Chyi, C.S.: Review of deep reinforcement learning-based object grasping: techniques, open challenges, and recommendations. IEEE Access **8**, 178450–178481 (2020). https://doi.org/10.1109/ACCESS.2020.3027923

18. Jin, M., Lavaei, J.: Stability-certified reinforcement learning: a control-theoretic perspective. IEEE Access **8**, 229086–229100 (2020). https://doi.org/10.1109/ACCESS.2020.3045114

19. Green, S.A., et al.: Mapping mental health service access: achieving equity through quality improvement. J. Public Health **35**(2), 286–292 (2013)

20. Thomson, L.J., Camic, P.M., Chaterjee, H.J.: Social Prescribing: A Review of Community Referral Schemes. University College London, London (2015)
21. Shepherd, M., Butler, L.: The underuse of couple therapy for depression in improving access to psychological therapies services (IAPTS): a service evaluation exploring its effectiveness and discussion of systemic barriers to its implementation. J. Family Therapy **43**(4), 493–515 (2021). https://doi.org/10.1111/1467-6427.12323
22. Ghanem, M.C., Chen, T.M.: Reinforcement learning for efficient network penetration testing. Information **11**(1), 6 (2020). https://doi.org/10.3390/info11010006

Time Slot Correlation-Based Caching Strategy for Information-Centric Satellite Networks

Rui Xu[1,2,3] , Xiaoqiang Di[1,3,4(✉)] , Jing Chen[1,3], Jinhui Cao[1,3], Hao Luo[1], Haowei Wang[1,3], Hui Qi[1,3], Xiongwen He[5], and Wenping Lei[6]

[1] School of Computer Science and Technology, Changchun University of Science and Technology, Changchun 130022, China
dixiaoqiang@cust.edu.cn
[2] School of Information Engineering, Henan Institute of Science and Technology, Xinxiang 453003, China
[3] Jilin Province Key Laboratory of Network and Information Security, Changchun University of Science and Technology, Changchun 130022, China
[4] Information Center, Changchun University of Science and Technology 130022, Changchun, China
[5] Beijing Institute of Spacecraft System Engineering, Beijing 100094, China
[6] Beijing Institute of Space Mechanic and Electricity, Beijing 100094, China

Abstract. With the successful manufacture of highly stable and high-performance satellite processors, caching on satellites has become possible. Information Centric Networking (ICN) is introduced to satellite networks to address the growing need for diverse data services. However, existing caching policies in ICN still suffer from the shortage of rational planning of cache locations and redundancy of cache contents. Consequently, the time slot correlation-based caching strategy for satellite networks (TSCCS) is proposed. Firstly, the index of time slot correlation is designed to quantify the neighboring time slots' coupling relationship, and then the DSAM network model with time slot correlation is established. Secondly, the significance of satellite nodes is evaluated from the local and global perspectives respectively based on the eigenvector centrality algorithm to filter out the dynamic set of cache nodes. Finally, probabilistic caching is performed at the set of caching nodes with the goal of reducing cached content redundancy, considering content popularity and access delay. The simulated outcomes indicate that the TSCCS caching policy is superior to the comparison method in the areas of cache hit rate, request latency, and server load.

Keywords: ICN · Satellite Networks · Network Model · Cache Nodes · Caching Strategy

1 Introduction

The sixth generation mobile communication network (6G) further integrates satellite networks with terrestrial networks to extend the communication scenario to land, sea, air, and underwater areas to achieve seamless global coverage. To fulfill the requirements for

R. Li et al. (Eds.): MOBILWARE 2022, LNICST 507, pp. 43–56, 2023.
https://doi.org/10.1007/978-3-031-34497-8_4

worldwide network accessibility for users in the 6G era, satellite networks have become one of the indispensable tools for providing wide area coverage [1]. Unlike ground-based telecommunication networks, satellite communication networks have the advantage of large communication range, independent of geography and climate, and high mobility, which are widely applied in many aspects such as weather forecasting, resource detection, navigation and positioning, environmental monitoring, and mobile communication. Although terrestrial communication networks are developing rapidly, they cannot provide good communication services in special environments such as oceans, deserts, and polar regions. Moreover, satellite networks provide continuous and effective communication connections in the above regions, as well as reliable connections in unexpected situations such as earthquakes, floods, and tsunamis when terrestrial communication facilities are destroyed. However, the periodic high-speed motion of satellite nodes, inter-satellite link interruptions and reconnections, and dynamic changes in network topology leave satellite networks in a non-stationary state, which leads to problems such as large propagation delays, intermittent connections, and inconsistent round-trip links during data transmission [2].

To solve the above serious problems, ICN architecture is introduced to satellite networks. ICN is a new information-centric network architecture that differs from traditional IP networks. By directly separating content from location, ICN employs content naming as a unique identifier for data transmission and provides a publish/subscribe model to retrieve content. In-network caching technology in ICN is proven to be a highly productive approach to enhancing content distribution capabilities in the areas of throughput, latency, and energy consumption [3]. With in-network caching technology, the proximity response of user requests reduces content acquisition delay for users and improves the quality of user experience. Moreover, distributed in-network caching reduces energy consumption for link transmission, conserves bandwidth resources, and reduces server load. Meanwhile, the cache nodes continuously work to provide content for users when the content providers are offline, which enhances the stability of satellite networks. However, existing ICN caching strategies are mostly designed for terrestrial networks, which cannot adapt to the characteristics of periodic dynamic changes in satellite networks, and there are problems such as a lack of reasonable planning of cache locations and redundancy of cached contents. Therefore, designing an effective caching policy is a meaningful attempt to boost the performance of satellite networks which is also one of the research focuses of ICN. The time slot correlation-based caching strategy for satellite networks is suggested. The main contributions are shown below.

- By defining the index of time slot correlation to quantify the adjacent time slots' coupling relationship, the satellite network is simplified into the DSAM network model by integrating inter-satellite link status in the current time slot and the evolution law between adjacent time slots.
- The cache node selection algorithm based on eigenvector centrality is suggested to assess the significance of satellite nodes from a local and global point of view, thus filtering out the nodes with high significance to form the dynamic set of cache nodes. By considering the content popularity and content access delay, the probabilistic caching scheme is devised to improve the caching probability of popular content on caching nodes.

- In the simulated scenario of the Iridium constellation, the caching performance of TSCCS is evaluated by varying the content request hotness and node caching capacity and observing the change in caching performance of each strategy. The results demonstrate that TSCCS applies to satellite networks and surpasses the comparison approach in the areas of cache hit rate, request delay, and server load.

The rest parts of this paper are structured as follows. Section 2 delineates the application of caching techniques in ICN for terrestrial and satellite networks. The description of the scenarios in this paper is given in Sect. 3. The implementation steps of the TSCCS are summarized in Sect. 4. Section 5 implements and evaluates TSCCS in a simulation environment. Section 6 summarizes this work in full.

2 Related Work

Caching strategies are one of the popular research topics in ICN, aiming to enhance cache utilization and decrease bandwidth consumption by rationalizing the use of cache resources in the network. Caching policies are categorized as on-path and off-path policies depending on where the cached content is stored on the backhaul route of the data. The data packets are backhauled and cached along the transmission route in on-path policies, ignoring other nodes outside the transmission route. The classic on-path policies in ICN include LCE [4], LCD [5], MCD [5], and Prob [6], etc. The on-path policies are easy to implement and are widely adopted in practical deployments. However, network nodes in the on-path strategy lack information of global network topology and cache state, and can only collaborate with nodes on the same path, which limits the caching performance. Meanwhile, all nodes with the same caching strategy allow duplicate placement of cached content on caching nodes, resulting in excessive redundancy of cached content [7]. The off-path caching strategies are not restricted by the transmission path between the user and the server and allow the content to be placed on any node in the network. Chai et al. present a policy (Betw) that is based on the BC measure and places data on nodes with large betweenness values for fast response to user requests [8]. Caching strategies such as BEP [9] and HCache [10] optimize the placement of cached content from the perspective of network topology and region division, respectively. The off-path strategies optimize the placement of cache contents and rationalize the utilization of cache resources by collecting state information of the network, such as node capacity, request distribution, and network bandwidth. However, when collecting network information, the off-path strategy invariably requires a large amount of additional overhead, resulting in a drain on network resources [11].

In-network caching technique in terrestrial networks has proven to be advantageous in improving network performance and enhancing network throughput. To enhance the capability of data transmission in satellite networks, scholars conduct meaningful research on caching schemes applied to satellite networks. To address the serious shortage of end-to-end routes in IST networks, Yang et al. suggest a network caching mechanism (TCSC) with time-evolving coverage sets for the effective distribution of files [12]. To address the management and efficiency problems arising from traditional network architectures, Li et al. suggest a novel satellite network architecture by merging the advantages of ICN and SDN, along with a cooperative caching scheme and an encoding caching scheme to improve the performance of content extraction [13]. Zhu et al. investigate a coordinated multi-layer edge caching policy in IST networks, where base stations, satellites, and gateways collaborate to serve content to terrestrial requesters, which in turn reduces the communication delay in the satellite-terrestrial link [14]. Ngo et al. propose a full-duplex transmission model supporting two layers of caching, deploying content caches to satellites and ground stations separately, thus reducing content transmission delay [15]. Existing caching strategies for satellite networks optimize caching performance in terms of cache content placement, edge caching, multi-layer caching, and collaborative caching to enhance content distribution efficiency and improve user service experience [16].

The existing caching strategies in topologically time-varying satellite networks face some unresolved problems. The selection of cache nodes lacks the consideration of node dynamics, which is not applicable to dynamically changing satellite networks and reduces the utilization of cache space. In addition, existing studies employ a single processing method for cache contents, resulting in redundant cache contents. Hence, the TSCCS caching policy is presented in this paper, in which the nodes with high importance are selected to form a dynamic set of cache nodes by estimating the significance of satellite nodes in a single time slot and from a global perspective, to achieve reasonable planning of cache content placement locations. On this basis, the probabilistic caching solution that is dependent on the content prevalence and access latency is designed to enrich the variety of cached content, while improving the caching probability of popular content on caching nodes and reducing the redundancy of cached content.

3 Scene Description

The satellite network model consists of the server, the satellite network, and subscriber terminals, as shown in Fig. 1. The inter-satellite link is the cornerstone for interconnection between satellite nodes, which in turn constitute the satellite network. The satellite network has a wide coverage area and provides data transmission services to terrestrial subscribers throughout the covered area. The satellite nodes in the ICN-based satellite network architecture all have content memories, and the content is stored and forwarded according to the caching strategy. The service process of the satellite network model is as follows. Firstly, the request from the terrestrial subscriber is delivered to the receiving satellite and the satellite's cache memory is searched to see if the requested content is stored. If it exists, the access satellite forwards the content to the terrestrial subscriber in the form of a data packet. Otherwise, the subscriber request is forwarded to additional satellites. Then, the cache space of other satellites in the satellite network is searched. If it exists, the requested content is routed via the inter-satellite link back to the terrestrial subscriber according to the original route. Otherwise, the subscriber request is transferred to the terrestrial server via the satellite-ground link. Finally, when the satellite network cannot satisfy the user's request, the ground-based server reacts to the subscriber's request and returns the data packet according to the original route.

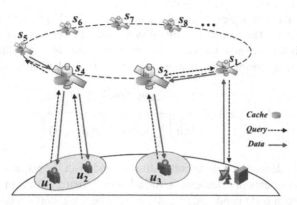

Fig. 1. System model illustration.

4 TSCCS Caching Strategy

Since caching resources are scarce in the information-centric satellite network, applying the default policy in ICN results in duplicate caching of the same content. Hence, this paper is devoted to improving the traditional caching strategy and suggests a caching policy that is predicated on time slot correlation. In this section, the DSAM network model is first detailed. The process of selecting the cache node corresponding to each time slot with the eigenvector centrality algorithm is then shown. Finally, the probabilistic caching scheme is introduced.

4.1 DSAM Network Model

The snapshot-based modeling approach in dynamic networks is a common treatment in many literatures, where a series of snapshots (time slices) are exploited to reflect the time-changing features of dynamic networks [17]. The snapshots are normally set as topology diagrams of the same duration, denoted as $S_1, S_2, ..., S_n$. By analyzing the connection of the links between satellite nodes, it is found that the inter-star links are connected and disconnected with regularity. There is no inter-star link outage while the satellite network is in a steady state that lasts for 1 or more snapshots. Therefore, adjacent snapshots with the same topology are merged under the condition that the satellite network topology is stable. Thus, the time slot sequence is captured, denoted as $P_1, P_2, ..., P_T$, and the duration of each time slot is noted as TS_i. Within the observed time (OT), a collection of time slots of different lengths captures the evolutionary features of the operating course of the satellite, and the inconsistency of time slots is shown by the difference in the weights. Furthermore, the weight matrix that corresponds to the time slot sequence is represented as the following equation.

$$W = [w_1, w_2, w_3, \cdots] = \left[\frac{TS_1}{OT}, \frac{TS_2}{OT}, \frac{TS_3}{OT}, \cdots \right] \tag{1}$$

Local correlation is one of the important indicators to gauge the adjacent time slots' coupling relations in dynamical networks, which mainly includes the following two measurements. The first approach reflects the local correlation of nodes from the perspective of their own neighbors in adjacent time slots, including CN [18] as well as CN-derived normalized indicators. The second is to quantify the local correlation of nodes by counting the shared neighbors of nodes in various time slots. Taking into account both research perspectives, the node correlations in adjacent time slots are derived as shown below.

$$C_j(t, t+1) = \frac{\sum_i a_{ij}(t)a_{ij}(t+1)}{\min\left[\sum_i a_{ij}(t), \sum_i a_{ij}(t+1)\right]} \tag{2}$$

where $C_j(t, t+1)$ denotes the node correlation of node j in the adjacent time slots P_t and P_{t+1}. $A_{ij}(t)$ represents the elements in the adjacency matrix of P_t. In time slot P_t, if a link exists between node i and node j, $a_{ij}(t) = 1$. Otherwise, $a_{ij}(t) = 0$. In both P_t and P_{t+1}, $a_{ij}(t) = 1$ and $a_{ij}(t+1) = 1$ if there are links between both node i and node j. In this case, $a_{ij}(t)a_{ij}(t+1) = 1$. Otherwise, $a_{ij}(t)a_{ij}(t+1) = 0$.

The variation of the adjacency relationship between nodes can be obtained by analyzing the node correlation of each node in the neighboring time slots. When the node correlation is large, it means that the majority of the satellite nodes are working online continually for a considerable period of time as well as there are stable inter-satellite links in the network. When the node correlation is small, it indicates that the proportion of satellite nodes and inter-star links that exist stably in the adjacent time slots is low, reflecting the high level of changes in network topology. On the basis of node correlation in adjacent time slots, the diagonal matrix is structured to indicate the time slot correlation, as shown in the following equation.

$$C^{(t,t+1)} = \begin{bmatrix} C_1(t, t+1) & 0 & \cdots & 0 & 0 \\ 0 & C_2(t, t+1) & \cdots & 0 & 0 \\ \vdots & \vdots & \ddots & \vdots & \vdots \\ 0 & 0 & \cdots & C_{N-1}(t, t+1) & 0 \\ 0 & 0 & \cdots & 0 & C_N(t, t+1) \end{bmatrix} \tag{3}$$

where $C^{(t,t+1)}$ denotes the time slot correlation of time slots P_t and P_{t+1}. $C_j(t, t+1)$ expresses the node correlation of node j in P_t and P_{t+1}. All elements outside the main diagonal are 0. N indicates the number of satellite nodes.

To completely portray the structure evolvement of the dynamic network and its dynamics process, the dynamic supra-adjacency matrix (DSAM) is introduced. Given that the layer-to-layer connectivity of different nodes should be different, the layer-to-layer connectivity between nodes is expressed with the node correlation in adjacent time slots, which ensures the difference between nodes. A dynamic network is picked as an instance of the DSAM network model as shown in Fig. 2. The connectivity among nodes inside a time slot is represented by a solid line in each time slot, and the connectivity of nodes in neighboring time slots is represented by a dashed line between time slots.

The DSAM network model accounts for the inter-layer and intra-layer relations of nodes and represents the impact of the network topology at the previous moment on the later moment with the ratio of time slot durations. In addition, the DSAM network

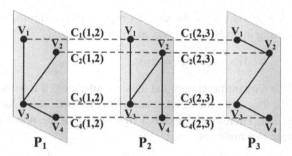

Fig. 2. Example of the DSAM network model.

model is specifically expressed as follows.

$$
A = \begin{bmatrix}
A^{(1)} & \frac{TS_1}{TS_2}C^{(1,2)} & 0 & \cdots \\
\frac{TS_1}{TS_2}C^{(1,2)} & A^{(2)} & \frac{TS_2}{TS_3}C^{(2,3)} & \cdots \\
0 & \frac{TS_2}{TS_3}C^{(2,3)} & A^{(3)} & \cdots \\
\vdots & \vdots & \vdots & \ddots
\end{bmatrix}
\tag{4}
$$

where A denotes the super-adjacency matrix based on DSAM. $A^{(1)}$, $A^{(2)}$,..., $A^{(n)}$ is represented by the corresponding adjacency matrix of each time slot. $C^{(i-1,i)}$ is indicated by a diagonal matrix composed of node correlations. TS_i shows the duration of the time slot i. The remainder of the elements in matrix A are indicated by 0.

4.2 Cache Node Selection Algorithm Based on Eigenvector Centrality

Due to the scarcity of on-board storage resources, selecting appropriate cache nodes becomes an important task to improve the cache performance and transmission performance in the network. So the cache node selection algorithm based on eigenvector centrality is suggested. In complex network theory, centrality algorithms usually evaluate the significance of nodes in a network, including DC, BC, CC, and EC. Among them, eigenvector centrality (EC) is a very effective evaluation indicator to quantify the significance of the test node by counting the significance of the neighborhood nodes that are directly linked to the test one.

$$
EC(i) = \lambda^{-1} \sum_{j=1}^{N} a_{ij} e_j
\tag{5}
$$

where λ is the main eigenvalue of the neighboring matrix, and the feature vector is $e = [e_1, e_2, \cdots, e_n]^T$. A_{ij} denotes the connectivity between node i and node j. If a link exists between node i and j, then $a_{ij} = 1$, otherwise $a_{ij} = 0$.

The EC is exploited to find the principal eigenvector in the constructed super-neighborhood matrix A, noted as $v = \{v_1, v_2, v_3, \cdots, v_{NT}\}^T$. The EC value of each node in the time slot i is recorded as $\{v_{(i-1)\times N+1}, v_{(i-1)\times N+2}, v_{(i-1)\times N+3}, \cdots, v_{iN}\}^T$. The vector length of each time slot is N, and there exist a total of T different time slots.

Therefore, the term $N \times (t-1) + i$ in the vector v represents the significance of node i in the time slot t, resulting in an $N \times T$ matrix as follows.

$$Ws = \left\{ ws_{it} | ws_{it} = v_{N \times (t-1)+i} \right\}_{N \times T} \tag{6}$$

The matrix Ws is a quantification of the local significance of the nodes. Depending on the duration of the time slots, the weight matrix W of the time slots has been computed in the previous section. Therefore, the global significance of the node, noted as We, is calculated with these two matrices.

$$We = \left\{ we_i | we_i = \sum_{j=1}^{T} Ws(i,j) \times W(j) \right\} \tag{7}$$

In the information-centric satellite network, a restricted amount of cache nodes are chosen to hold content copies, which helps to boost the efficiency of the caching system and reduce user acquisition latency [8]. The selection of appropriate cache nodes requires a balance between important nodes with local characteristics and important nodes with global characteristics. In the time slot P_i, the nodes are ranked by the EC value from highest to lowest, and the top K important nodes with local characteristics are selected as cache nodes. At the same time, the significance values of nodes from the global viewpoint are sorted in descending order, and the top K important nodes with global characteristics are also selected as cache nodes. Finally, $2 \times K$ nodes are acquired above to combine into a set of cache nodes.

4.3 Probabilistic Caching Scheme

Since the storage capacity of on-board routers is finite, the storage capacity of satellite nodes is bound to become saturated as the number of user requests increases and as time passes, which leads to the replacement of cache nodes. To lower the frequency of cache replacement, the content that has been requested by users a lot in the previous period and predicts the same popularity in the future period is screened in the network and placed on the router node. Therefore, the caching probability of content block c at satellite node p is obtained from the following equation.

$$\eta(c, p) = \frac{\rho(c)}{\max(\rho(i))} \times \frac{D_{p-S}}{D_{U-S} + 1} \tag{8}$$

where $\eta(c, p)$ means the caching probability of content block c at satellite node p. $\rho(c)$ indicates the content prevalence of content block c in the current time slot, and $\max(\rho(i))$ means the maximum value of the content popularity of all content in the network. D_{U-S} means the number of hops between the user and server, and D_{p-S} means the number of hops between satellite nodes to the server. The equation takes into account content popularity and access delay to improve the caching probability of content that has a high prevalence at cache nodes while reducing the redundancy of cached content.

Content distribution is achieved through data packet and interest packet processing and forwarding in an ICN-based satellite network. The router takes on the task of forwarding both interest packets and data packets to maintain the three modules essential for network communication, which are content store (CS), pending interest table (PIT), and forwarding information base (FIB). CS stores the content copies and is the table that the user requests to view first. PIT logs the uplink request information, including the path and interface information of the interest packet route. FIB records the content name and the receiving port to provide routing information for subsequent requests.

There are two parts in this paper to completely describe the process of implementing the TSCCS caching policy.

1. In the time slot with stable topology, the interest packet is transported over the inter-satellite link and forwarded at the satellite node, where the number of hops forwarded is recorded in the new field (hop) of the interest packet. When the interest packet is accepted by the on-star router node, it searches in its CS for content that has the same name as the content. If a successful match is made, the data packet is passed back sequentially up the access port. Otherwise, the lookup continues in the PIT. If the interest packet and the PIT match successfully, the access port is added and the interest packet is discarded. Otherwise, add a new entry in the PIT and forward the interest packet to the next-hop satellite node as documented in the FIB.
2. The interest packets containing the requested information are forwarded across the satellite network. When the user request is matched with the cached content in the server or satellite node, the content asked is passed back the original way following the forwarding route of the packet of interest. The satellite nodes all have a forwarding function, while the satellite nodes in the set of caching nodes have not only a forwarding function but also caching function. Therefore, when a satellite node accepts a data packet, it initially determines if the node has caching capabilities. If the satellite node is the selected caching node and has remaining capacity in its storage space, it stores the contents contained in the data packet in the present node and forwards it to the following hop satellite. If the node is a cache node but has no extra capacity in the cache space, it replaces the stale content based on the LRU (last recently used) [7] replacement policy and forwards the data packet to the following hop satellite. If the node is not a cache node, the data packet is transmitted to the following hop satellite. The process is terminated by the reception of the requested content by the terrestrial subscriber.

5 Simulation and Evaluation

5.1 Simulation Setup

ndnSIM is an NDN emulation module equipped on NS-3, which enables various network functions under ICN architecture [12]. The performance of the TSCCS caching strategy is verified by comparing it with the caching strategies of LCE [10], LCD [11], Prob(0.5) [12], and Betw [17]. The LRU cache replacement strategy is adopted for all caching strategies to ensure the objectivity of the simulation experiments. The average cache hit rate, average request delay, and average server load are selected as the main performance indicators in this paper, and the variation of cache capacity is monitored by altering the Zipf parameter and node cache capacity. The simulated setting is built by following the information of the Iridium constellation, comprising six orbits with an altitude of 780 km and an inclination of 86.4°, totaling 66 satellites [19]. The whole experiment lasts 40 s, in which the first 10 s are treated as the pre-warming time, and the experimental data of the last 30 s are extracted for the subsequent experimental analysis. The simulation environment and experimental parameters are listed in Table 1.

Table 1. Simulation parameters.

Parameters	Default	Range of variation
Number of server nodes	1	-
Number of ground stations	22	-
Number of contents	1000	-
Data packet size/KB	1024	-
Request rate/(req/s)	200	-
Zipf distribution parameter α	1.0	0.7~1.3
Node cache capacity	30	15~45

5.2 Evaluation Indicators

The following evaluation indicators are selected to comprehensively estimate the caching capability of the TSCCS policy.

1. Average cache hit ratio (ACHR)

ACHR is the percentage of subscriber requests that hit the cache compared to the sum of subscriber requests, which is one of the major evaluation indicators of the effectiveness of a caching policy. If ACHR is higher, the greater the utility of the caching scheme.

2. Average request delay (ARD)

ARD is the mean duration of the process from the outgoing of interest packets to the receipt of data packets, which is one of the metrics to assess the user's satisfaction with the caching scheme. If ARD is smaller, the caching scheme is more efficient.

3. Average server load (ASL)

ASL is the average of the number of interest packets processed by the server per unit time in each time slot, which is a measure of the stress on the server. When ASL is too high, it causes insufficient server processing capacity and affects the stable operation of the network.

5.3 Simulation Results

5.3.1 Impact of Zipf Parameter

Figure 3 evaluates the effect of user request popularity on cache capability in three aspects of ACHR, ARD, and ASL, respectively.

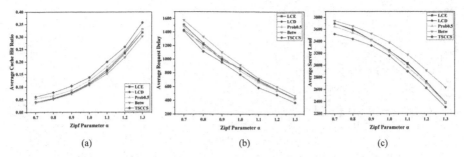

Fig. 3. Impact of Zipf parameter. (a) ACHR; (b) ARD; (c) ASL.

Figure 3(a) illustrates that ACHR of all policies has an increasing trend with growing Zipf parameter α. This is because user requests are more focused and cached content is more likely to fulfill user requests. Only a small amount of popular content needs to be cached to achieve a high hit rate. The TSCCS strategy outperforms other caching strategies by reasonably selecting caching nodes and improving the probability of caching popular content through the probabilistic caching scheme. Other caching strategies lack the ability to sense the hotness of the cached content, resulting in most of the cached content being non-hot content with low request rates and lower hit rates. Figure 3(b) illustrates that ARD of all policies gradually reduces as the Zipf parameter α grows. The reason is that the proportion of subscriber requests responded to at the routers is increased, which saves the transmission delay between the routers to the server and results in a more timely response to user requests. The TSCCS strategy employs the probabilistic caching scheme to promote diverse storage of cached content on cache nodes, avoiding cached data being substituted frequently and outperforming other caching strategies throughout the range. The LCE, LCD, and Prob policies have poor cached content diversity and are forwarded out of the domain when the content request does not hit the current domain, resulting in increased transmission delay. Figure 3(c) illustrates that ASL of all policies continues to decrease with the rising Zipf parameter α. This is owing to the increased proportion of cache nodes that respond to user requests, which reduces the server's burden of processing interest packets. The TSCCS strategy allocates popular content to cache nodes reasonably and enhances the diversity of cached content to improve the response ratio of content requests at cache nodes, which is superior to other policies in the caching effect. The on-path caching strategies do not distinguish between cached contents, resulting in part of the cache space being occupied by non-popular contents and an increased number of content requests responded to by the server. The Betw policy caches all the content at critical nodes, which increases the load on the server due to frequently replacing cached content on the cache nodes and the decrease in the proportion of content requests responded to.

5.3.2 Impact of Node Cache Capacity

Figure 4 assess the effect of node cache capacity on cache performance from the perspective of ACHR, ARD, and ASL, respectively.

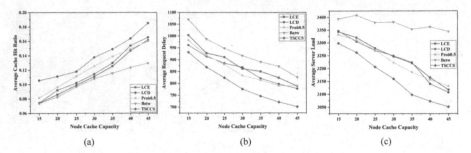

Fig. 4. Impact of node cache capacity. (a) ACHR; (b) ARD; (c) ASL.

Figure 4(a) illustrates that ACHR of all policies rises as the node cache capacity rises. The main cause is that the number of cached contents rises as the cache capacity of the nodes rises, making the percentage of cache nodes hitting content requests increase. With the probabilistic caching scheme, the TSCCS strategy effectively increases the diversity of cached content, thus responding to more content requests and improving the cache hit ratio. Although the on-path strategies promote cached content to be constantly close to users, they generate a huge amount of duplicate cache in the transmission path, and the cached content is not sufficiently diverse to respond to only some of the requests. The Betw policy stores cached content at critical nodes, whose high replacement rate becomes a particular drawback, leading to frequently replacing cached content and overall performance degradation. As shown in Fig. 4(b), ARD of all policies gradually declines as the node cache capacity rises. The reason is that more content is cached in the caching system and more and more content requests are responded to at the cache nodes, which shortens the access path of user requests and reduces the access delay. The TSCCS strategy shortens the access path of content requests with time slot correlation to obtain the appropriate set of cache nodes and also stores different content copies differentially in the cache space through the probabilistic caching policy to improve the chance of popular content being cached near users and reduce the access delay. Although the Prob and LCD policies accelerate the move of cached content to the edge nodes, they ignore content popularity, making cached content replace frequently and reducing cache performance. The LCE policy caches everywhere, which results in excessive redundancy of cached content, and most content requests need to be responded to at the server. The Betw policy only stores content copies at critical nodes, which results in the content originally fetched at the cache nodes still being responded to by the server, raising the content access latency. ASL of all policies trends downward as the node cache capacity rises, as shown in Fig. 4(c). This is because the number of cached contents rises as the node cache capacity rises, which causes the probability of content requests being responded to at the cache node to rise and the number of requests responded to by the server to decline. It is clear that the TSCCS policy prevails over the other policies. This is because the TSCCS strategy takes into account both cache location and cache content, thus fully improving cache space utilization. The on-path strategies have better caching performance than the Betw policy. The Betw policy does not show significant performance improvement during the cache capacity increase.

6 Conclusion

To overcome the problems of lack of reasonable planning of cache locations and redundancy of cache contents in the existing caching strategies in ICN, the TSCCS policy is suggested. By constructing the DSAM network model, the time-varying features of the satellite networks are effectively depicted. With the goal of selecting appropriate cache nodes, the set of cache nodes is dynamically filtered out with the cache node selection algorithm based on the eigenvector centrality. Lastly, the differentiated probabilistic caching scheme is designed for content with different popularity to reduce cache redundancy and achieve reasonable placement of cached data. Simulated experiments illustrate that the TSCCS policy has advantages over the comparison scheme in the aspects of cache hit rate, request delay, and server load.

References

1. Fu, S., Gao, J., Zhao, L.: Collaborative multi-resource allocation in terrestrial-satellite network towards 6G. IEEE Trans. Wirel. Commun. **20**(11), 7057–7071 (2021)
2. Jia, Z., Sheng, M., Li, J., Han, Z.: Toward data collection and transmission in 6G space-air-ground integrated networks: cooperative HAP and LEO satellite schemes. IEEE Internet Things **9**(13), 10516–10528 (2022)
3. Zhang, X., et al.: Data-driven caching with users' content preference privacy in information-centric networks. IEEE Trans. Wirel. Commun. **20**(9), 5744–5753 (2021)
4. Jacobson, V., Smetters, D.K., Thornton, J.D., Plass, M.F., Briggs, N.H., Braynard, R.L.: Networking named content. Commun. ACM **55**(1), 117–124 (2012)
5. Laoutaris, N., Che, H., Stavrakakis, I.: The LCD interconnection of LRU caches and its analysis. Perform. Eval. **63**(7), 609–634 (2006)
6. Zhang, M., Luo, H., Zhang, H.: A survey of caching mechanisms in information-centric networking. IEEE Commun. Surv. Tutor. **17**(3), 1473–1499 (2015)
7. Man, D., Lu, Q., Wang, H., Guo, J., Yang, W., Lv, J.: On-path caching based on content relevance in information-centric networking. Comput. Commun. **176**, 272–281 (2021)
8. Chai, W.K., He, D., Psaras, I., Pavlou, G.: Cache "less for more" in information-centric networks (extended version). Comput. Commun. **36**(7), 758–770 (2013)
9. Zheng, Q., Kan, Y., Chen, J., Wang, S., Tian, H.: A cache replication strategy based on betweenness and edge popularity in named data networking. In: 2019 IEEE International Conference on Communications (ICC), Shanghai, China, pp. 1–6 (2019)
10. Wu, H., Li, J., Zhi, J., Ren, Y., Li, L.: A hybrid ICN caching strategy based on region division. In: CoNEXT 2019 Companion, Orlando, FL, USA, pp. 78–79 (2019)
11. Zhang, Z., Lung, C., St-Hilaire, M., Lambadaris, I.: An SDN-based caching decision policy for video caching in information-centric networking. IEEE Trans. Multimedia **22**(4), 1069–1083 (2020)
12. Yang, Z., Li, Y., Yuan, P., Zhang, Q.: TCSC: a novel file distribution strategy in integrated LEO satellite-terrestrial networks. IEEE Trans. Veh. Technol. **69**(5), 5426–5441 (2020)
13. Li, J., Xue, K., Liu, J., Zhang, Y., Fang, Y.: An ICN/SDN-based network architecture and efficient content retrieval for future satellite-terrestrial integrated networks. IEEE Netw. **34**(1), 188–195 (2020)
14. Zhu, X., Jiang, C., Kuang, L., Zhao, Z.: Cooperative multilayer edge caching in integrated satellite-terrestrial networks. IEEE Trans. Wirel. Commun. **21**(5), 2924–2937 (2022)

15. Ngo, Q.T., Phan, K.T., Xiang, W., Mahmood, A., Slay, J.: Two-tier cache-aided full-duplex hybrid satellite-terrestrial communication networks. IEEE Trans. Aero. Elec. Sys. **58**(3), 1753–1765 (2022)
16. Liu, S., Hu, X., Wang, Y., Cui, G., Wang, W.: Distributed caching based on matching game in LEO satellite constellation networks. IEEE Commun. Lett. **22**(2), 300–303 (2018)
17. Taylor, D., Myers, S.A., Clauset, A., Porter, M.A., Mucha, P.J.: Eigenvector-based centrality measures for temporal networks. Multiscale Model. Sim. **15**(1), 537–574 (2017)
18. Hu, G., Xu, L., Xu, X.: Identification of important nodes based on dynamic evolution of inter-layer isomorphism rate in temporal networks. Acta Phys. Sin. **70**(10), 108901 (2021)
19. Zhu, X., Jiang, C.: Integrated satellite-terrestrial networks toward 6g: architectures, applications, and challenges. IEEE Internet Things **9**(1), 437–461 (2022)

Design and Implementation of a Pipeline-Based Data Scheduling Method for Spacecraft with Multiple Data Buses

Sheng Yu[✉], Duo Wang, Zejing Lv, Dan Wang, Zhenhui Dong, and Xiongwen He

Beijing Institute of Spacecraft System Engineering, CAST, Beijing, China
Yusheng86@outlook.com

Abstract. The MIL-STD-1553B data bus is widely used in modern spacecraft. Since a 1553B bus can support 31 remote terminals (RT) at most, a complex spacecraft possibly has multiple 1553B buses, and these buses need to work simultaneously. How to efficiently manage multiple 1553B buses by a single bus controller (BC) is a challenging problem for such spacecraft. To solve this problem, we design and implement a pipeline-based data scheduling method. First, we introduce the procedure of data transmission and the concept of preemptive scheduling. Second, we break the procedure into modules and propose the pipeline-based data scheduling method. Third, we implement scheduling software based on the method and evaluate the performance of the method through experiments. We successfully applied the software on the Tianhe core module and achieved good performance.

Keywords: 1553B data bus · Pipeline · Data management · On-board network

1 Introduction

Data bus is the key part of the On-Board Data Handling (OBDH) system of a spacecraft, and the MIL-STD-1553B data bus is widely used in modern spacecraft [1]. The 1553B bus is fault-tolerant and highly reliable, and it can respond to data transmission command in real time. These features make the 1553B bus very suitable for building spacecraft on-board network [2, 3]. The maximum data transmission rate for a 1553B bus is 1M bit/s. To achieve the maximum capacity of a 1553B bus, it is important to design an effective data scheduling scheme.

The 1553B bus has two different work modes: the time synchronization mode and the time asynchronous mode. The time synchronization mode requires strict time synchronization between BC and RTs, and divides a transmission period into time slices [4]. In each time slice, specified types of data transmission are arranged, so that data transmission delays are strictly bounded. The time asynchronous mode does not require strict time synchronization, and does not use time slices. BC can start data transmission whenever necessary, thus the time asynchronous mode is more flexible [5]. However,

R. Li et al. (Eds.): MOBILWARE 2022, LNICST 507, pp. 57–61, 2023.
https://doi.org/10.1007/978-3-031-34497-8_5

it cannot guarantee data transmission delay. The technique of priority queue and pre-emptive scheduling can be used to improve the efficiency and delay of the asynchronous mode.

According to the MIL-STD-1553B standard, one 1553 bus can support 31 RTs at most. The number of devices on a spacecraft is increasing rapidly, so one bus cannot satisfy the need of the information system of a complex spacecraft, and multiple 1553 buses need to work simultaneously. For example, the Tianhe core module uses 6 first-layer 1553 buses and one BC (the central unit) is in charge of all 6 buses. To achieve time synchronization of BC between RTs on 6 buses is very difficult, so the time synchro-nization mode is not suitable and the asynchronous mode should be used. The biggest challenge is to effectively schedule data transmission task on 6 buses by a single BC, and to achieve minimum transmission delay for time critical missions.

In this paper, we propose and design a pipeline-based scheduling method for multiple 1553 buses. First, we introduce the procedure of data transmission and the concept of preemptive scheduling. Second, we break the procedure into modules and propose the pipeline-based scheduling method. Third, we implement scheduling software based on the method and evaluate the performance of the method through experiments. We successfully applied the software on the central unit of the Tianhe core module and achieved good performance.

2   Data Transmission Procedure

According to the MIL-STD-1553B standard, there are 10 types of data transmission and 5 out of the 10 types are frequently used. The 5 types of data transmission are listed below:

- BC to RT data transmission: BC sends a receiving command word and several data words to RT, and RT replies with a status word.
- RT to BC data transmission: BC sends a transmission command word to RT, and RT replies with a status word, followed by several data words.
- RT_a to RT_b data transmission: BC sends a receiving command word to RT_b, and sends a transmission command word to RT_a, then RT_a sends data words to RT_b.
- Mode command with data word: BC sends a transmission command word to RT, then RT replies with a status word and a data word.
- BC to RT broadcast transmission: BC sends a receiving command word (RT address is 0x1F) to all RTs, followed by several data words. RTs with broadcast function reply with a status word.

To increase the data transmission efficiency, we adopt the preemptive scheduling method. All data messages are assigned with priority 1 to 4, and they are put into 4 separate FIFO (First In First Out) queues according to priority type. Priority 1 is the highest priority, and BC always uses area B of the 1553 bus to send priority 1 messages. Priority 4 is the lowest priority, and BC uses area A to send messages with priority 2 to 4. The transmission of messages in area B can interrupt messages in area A, so data messages with priority 1 are transmitted in a real-time mode. Telecommand data, time stamp, and attitude control data are typical data with the highest priority. The preemptive scheduling method is illustrated in Fig. 1.

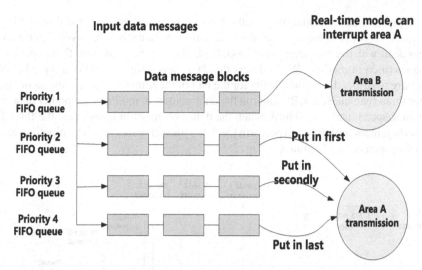

Fig. 1. The preemptive data scheduling method of a 1553 bus

Each bus has 4 FIFO data message queues. Thus, for a BC controlling 6 buses, there are 24 data message queues to manage. Within each data transmission period, the data transmission procedure of each bus can be divided into 4 modules. The first module is called data organizing module. In this module, BC organizes all data messages needed to transmit within this time period, assigns data message type and priority, and puts these messages into FIFO queues. The second module is called data write-in module. In this module messages in FIFO queues are written into the area A or area B of the 1553 bus RAM. Since the RAM size of 1553 bus is limited, only a certain number of messages can be written at a time. In our case, the number is 64, if the number of messages to send exceeds 64, then these messages need to be transmitted multiple times. The third module is data transmitting module. The 1553 bus chip transmit all data messages in its RAM according to their types, and each time at most 64 data messages can be transmitted. The module does not require the CPU of BC to process. The last module is data processing module. After data messages are transmitted, BC checks the status of transmission, and if transmission result is successful, BC saves the received data and processes or further transmits the data.

3 The Pipeline-Based Data Scheduling Method

To efficiently manage multiple data buses, we propose a pipeline-based bus data messages scheduling method based on the 4 modules of the data transmission procedure. A very important resource of a BC is the CPU time of the BC, and our target is to minimize the occupation of the CPU time for all bus data transmissions. The idea is based on the observation that the data transmitting module of each bus does not require the CPU time of BC, so BC can parallel process the data transmitting module of all buses.

The pipeline-based scheduling method uses a process and multiple threads. First, BC creates a process to manage bus data transmission. In each transmission period, the process deals with the data organizing module of all buses. Second, each thread performs the data written-in module. When enters the data transmitting module, a thread uses a semaphore to suspend itself and waits for the end of the transmission. At the same time, another thread can take the CPU and run the data written-in module for another data bus, and then suspend itself too. Third, when the data transmission is finished, the thread is activated again and continues to perform the data processing module. The pipeline-based scheduling method is illustrated in Fig. 2.

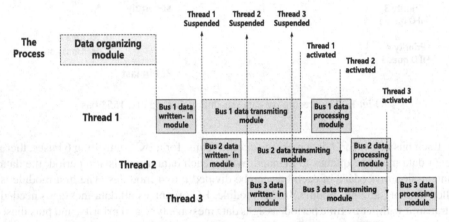

Fig. 2. The illustration of the pipeline-based scheduling method

4   Performance Evaluation

We implemented the BC scheduling software based on the proposed method and evaluate the performance of the method through experiments. The performance of the pipeline-based scheduling method is compared to the sequential schedule method that all 4 modules of each bus are process by CPU of the BC sequentially and the performance is evaluated by CPU occupied time of each method within a typical transmission period.

In our experiments, we use BM3803 as the CPU of the BC, and the main frequency of the CPU is 100 MHz. CPU cache is disabled. On each 1553B bus, the BC transmits 4K bytes data to a RT in every transmission period. The data length of each message over 1553B is 64 bytes, so each bus transmits 64 data messages. The same version of BC software is used in each experiment. We increase the number of 1553B bus controlled buy the BC, and we track the average time used by the CPU to send all data messages We compare the time used in two methods and the result is showed in Fig. 3. The results show that as the number of 1553B bus increases, the pipeline-based method can achieve better performance.

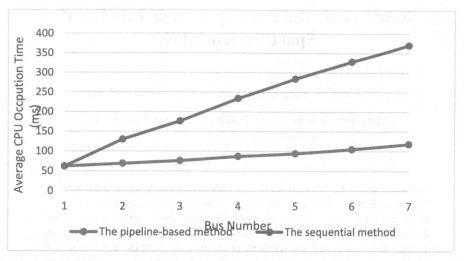

Fig. 3. The performance of the pipeline-based scheduling method vs the sequential method

5 Summary

In this paper, we design and implement a pipeline-based data scheduling method for spacecraft with multiple buses. The method is used on the Tianhe core module of the Chinese space station. We introduce the procedure of data transmission and the concept of preemptive scheduling. We break the procedure into modules and propose the pipeline-based scheduling method. Finally, we implement scheduling software based on the method and evaluate the performance of the method through experiments, and the results show that the proposed method can achieve good performance.

References

1. Yu, S., Zhou, B., Niu, J., et al.: Design and implementation of a high efficiency space packet routing algorithm on a spacecraft. In: 12th International Conference on Wireless and Satellite System (WISATS) (2021)
2. Lan, L., Liu, X., Sheng, Y., et al.: Research on routing mechanism for Inter-spacecraft 1553B bus network of space station system. Spacecraft Eng. **29**(2), 95–101 (2020)
3. Lan, L., Sun, Y., He, X., et al.: Optimization method of command management between equipment of large spacecraft. Spacecraft Eng. **30**(4), 85–90 (2021)
4. Zhang, Y., Yang, P., Yang, Z.: Design of a kind of 1553B bus communication protocol based on time synchronization. Spacecraft Eng. **30**(2), 88–95 (2021)
5. Dong, Z., Qiang, M., Mao, L., et al.: RAM fault tolerant design of 1553B bus chip for HXMT satellite. Spacecraft Eng. **27**(5), 107–113 (2018)

Research on the Development of Intelligent Space System (ISS)

Dan Wang$^{(\boxtimes)}$, Fang Dong, Sheng Yu, and Luyuan Wang

Beijing Institute of Spacecraft System Engineering, Beijing, China
wangdan_ict_hit@163.com

Abstract. First, the research scope of Intelligent Space Systems (ISS) is clarified, and then the domestic and foreign development of intelligent space systems in three directions is investigated, including intelligent information processing, autonomous task planning and intelligent information interconnection. By comparing and investigating, the scientific problems existing in the development of intelligent space system at present are put forward, and the analysis of the development trend of key technologies of intelligent space system in the future is finally formed.

Keywords: Intelligent Space System · Artificial Intelligence · intelligent information processing · autonomous mission planning · intelligent information interconnection

1 Introduction

Intelligence and networking are the development trend of future space systems. The United States, Europe and other countries and regions have intensively released a number of strategic plans, and regard intelligent technology as a strategic and basic key technology to reshape the space system, drive technological innovation, achieve leapfrog development, and drive the development of new industries. The next generation space architecture of the United States attaches great importance to the integration of advanced technologies with artificial intelligence as the core and the space field. There is a risk that China's space technology and its gap will be further widened. The white paper "2016 China's Aerospace" issued by the State Council Information Office clearly stated that we should accelerate the deep integration of industrialization and informatization, and realize the transformation of aerospace industry capabilities to digitalization, networking and intelligence. It shows that China is accelerating the construction of intelligent space systems and improving the comprehensive capabilities of space equipment.

At present, there is no unified definition of the concept of intelligent space system at home and abroad, but "automation, autonomy and intelligence" is the main vein of spacecraft technology development, which has become the consensus in the industry [1]. In 2006, the Space Operation and Support Technical Committee (SOSTC) of the American Institute of Aeronautics and Astronautics (AIAA) investigated and analyzed

R. Li et al. (Eds.): MOBILWARE 2022, LNICST 507, pp. 62–73, 2023.
https://doi.org/10.1007/978-3-031-34497-8_6

the industrial level of spacecraft autonomy and intelligence at that time, and divided it into six levels [2], from low to high, including manual operation, automatic notification, manned ground intelligent reasoning, unmanned ground intelligent reasoning, on orbit intelligent reasoning and autonomous thinking spacecraft. Chinese Academician Yang Jiachi also discussed the connotation of autonomous system in the article "Development of intelligent autonomous control technology in China's space program" [3] published in 1995: "Autonomous or semi autonomous operation means that no one participates in the control loop of the system completely or partially. Highly autonomous system is a system that can operate in an uncertain environment without external interference for a long time. More advanced autonomous system has the basic elements of intelligence and learning, and can adapt to a wider range of unpredictable environmental changes".

Combined with the research description and consensus on space intelligent technology in the domestic and international space industry, this paper defines the intelligent space system as a intelligent spacecraft, a ground intelligent control center and an intelligent user terminal, as shown in Fig. 1. It is a space-ground integrated intelligent system with autonomous perception, prediction, decision-making and collaboration capabilities. Space intelligent spacecraft has a strong ability of intelligent autonomous execution, self-management and self-learning. The ground intelligent control center has strong computing power and is responsible for large-scale data processing tasks and training tasks of intelligent information processing models, while the intelligent user terminal can provide an intelligent human-computer interface to support users to put forward task requirements or control commands through text, voice, gesture, etc.

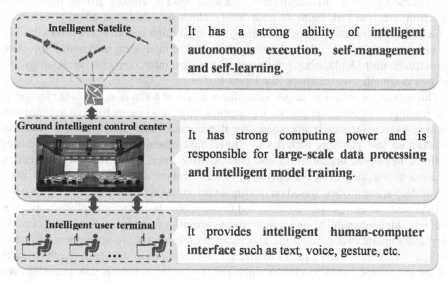

It has a strong ability of intelligent autonomous execution, self-management and self-learning.

It has strong computing power and is responsible for large-scale data processing and intelligent model training.

It provides intelligent human-computer interface such as text, voice, gesture, etc.

Fig. 1. Composition of Intelligent Space Systems

Figure 2 shows the concept of space intelligent spacecraft. Its basic components include intelligent processors, multiple sensors, intelligent algorithms and models, and hardware components supporting its operation. Under the condition of limited on-board

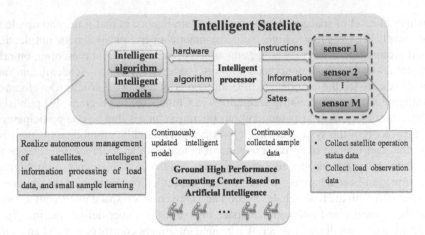

Fig. 2. Composition of Intelligent Spacecraft

resources, a large number of data processing and model training are completed on the ground; With the enrichment of on-board resources, the satellite will have stronger intelligent processing and learning capabilities.

At present, the overall technical level of spacecraft has basically achieved automation. However, the operation management mode based on the "big loop of heaven and earth" relies heavily on the ground station. From user demand proposal, ground planning, instruction upload, to satellite task execution, data download, ground information extraction, etc., the task delay is hour level, which is difficult to adapt to information assurance requirements such as strong real-time, high security and reliability [4]. The effective way to solve these problems is to realize intelligent information processing, autonomous task planning, intelligent information interconnection technology and improve the intelligence of space intelligent system.

Through target detection, target recognition, situation awareness and other technologies, intelligent information processing enables satellite systems to have autonomous situation awareness, greatly improving the timeliness of user information acquisition. Autonomous task planning includes intelligent task planning of agile remote sensing satellites, intelligent organization and collaborative planning of multiple spacecraft, autonomous planning of space operation tasks of robots and autonomous path planning of deep space probes. Based on intelligent information interconnection technology, multiple satellite agents can be connected into a space space system collaborative network with high adaptability and anti damage capability to ensure information connectivity under operational conditions. This paper focuses on the space segment of intelligent space system, namely, space intelligent spacecraft, and conducts in-depth research in three directions: intelligent information processing, autonomous task planning, and intelligent information interconnection. It sorts out the problems and key technologies in all directions, and analyzes the future technology development trend.

2 Development of Intelligent Space Systems Abroad

The United States has always been at the forefront of artificial intelligence research in the world. In the 2016 National Strategic Plan for Research and Development of Artificial Intelligence, the United States has identified the development of artificial intelligence as a national strategy; In February 2019, the Department of Defense's Strategic Outline of Artificial Intelligence issued by the U.S. Department of Defense clearly stated that the Joint Artificial Intelligence Center (JAIC) should take the lead to promote national security and prosperity by using AI; In March of the same year, the US Department of Defense established the Space Development Agency (SDA), proposed a seven tier architecture of the National Defense Space Architecture (NDSA), and expected to establish a distributed and AI supported operational management capability. In addition, the European Union, Germany, France, Britain, Japan, Canada, Russia and other governments and defense departments have also introduced AI development strategies.

2.1 Development of Foreign Intelligent Information Processing

As early as 2009, the military tactical star - 3 (Tacsat-3) satellite [7] launched by the United States carried the "Advanced Rapid Response Tactical Military Imaging Spectrometer" (ARTEMIS), which is based on on-board hyperspectral image processing technology and has the capability of automatic identification of on-board targets to send target information to combat users or portable terminals. In 2018, the European Space Agency (ESA) proposed to develop an Earth observation satellite equipped with an artificial intelligence processor, through which the satellite can autonomously study and judge the imaging target and the data content transmitted to the ground. Through on orbit intelligent processing technology, effective information is directly sent from the satellite to the operational users, which shortens the information acquisition time of "from sensor to shooter" in military applications.

In May 2016, NASA installed a set of onboard intelligent software AEGIS for the Curiosity Mars Probe, which can identify scientific targets from the navigation camera images and immediately measure them without going through round-trip communication with the Earth. The autonomy of AEGIS has been rapidly adopted as a tool for scientists to explore, and has affected the planning of the Curiosity exploration mission. In 2020, Lockheed Martin will launch its first intelligent satellite, carrying a payload named Pony Express 1, which has strong space-based computing and in orbit data analysis capabilities and provides strong flexibility.

In general, in terms of intelligent information processing technology, foreign space intelligent spacecraft have realized the transplantation and application of some mature ground algorithms. Its main purpose is to extract and recognize targets in images under various backgrounds through on-board data processing, retain only the extracted effective information, reduce the occupation of transmission bandwidth, and improve the image download speed.

2.2 Development of Foreign Autonomous Mission Planning

In terms of autonomous task planning, some technical experiments of autonomous task planning management with simple planning and decision-making algorithms have been carried out on the satellite. The United States loaded the autonomous planning package on the EO-1 satellite launched in 2000, realizing the autonomous planning capability of the satellite [8, 9]. The "Behavior Planning, Scheduling, Execution and Re planning" (CASPER) program of EO-1 satellite generates task planning based on the data of the on-board scientific analysis module, and can take the initiative to shoot when returning to the disaster point again according to the preliminary judgment of the load. The automatic reasoning system was studied in the launch management test of the "Tactical Sat-3" (TacSat-3) launched in 2009. In order to improve the target recognition capability and verify the target recognition algorithm based on statistical principles, NASA launched the "Intelligent Payload Experiment" (IPEX) technology test satellite in 2013 to improve the technical maturity of the HyspIRI satellite's intelligent payload module (IPM) in NASA's ten-year earth science survey mission, and improve the technical level required for the generation of near real time, low delay autonomous products related to future Earth observation missions. IPEX was launched on December 6, 2013 and stopped operating on January 30, 2015.

In 2018, the Japanese Falcon 2 probe achieved a fully autonomous landing of asteroids based on terrain recognition [10]. ESA has developed an interstellar trajectory planner for the Rosetta comet detector. Using the Monte Carlo tree search strategy, the optimal skimming and circling trajectories of multiple target comets are finally obtained [11]. DeepSpace 1 (DS-1) of the United States has achieved some autonomous technologies, including autonomous navigation technology, autonomous remote decision-making technology, autonomous software testing technology and automatic code generation technology [12, 13], and completed the exploration mission of crossing asteroids, Mars and comets.

In terms of autonomous mission planning, foreign countries have carried out some on orbit technology experiments with simple planning and decision-making algorithms, which are still at the exploratory stage and cannot replace the unified and centralized mission planning process on the ground. The development prospects of the ground unified mission planning and multi satellite distributed autonomous mission planning are not clear. The refined autonomous task planning and management oriented to onboard resource capability is a hot spot of future technology development.

2.3 Development of Foreign Intelligent Information Interconnection

Until July 2022, the "Starlink" system led by SpaceX has launched more than 2750 satellites and will reach 42000 low orbit satellites in the future, providing high-speed broadband services worldwide and laying a network foundation for collaborative planning and implementation of multi satellite missions. As early as 2006, the United States demonstrated formation flying and on orbit autonomy technology based on TechSat21. In 2018, the "BlackJack" project was launched to verify the on-board computer and processing system through the development of an on-board processor test called "pitboss", so as to achieve the collaborative management of low orbit large-scale constellations. In 2019, the US Space Development Agency (SDA) proposed a seven tier architecture of the National Defense Space System (NDSA), which uses a large LEO constellation composed of hundreds of satellites to build a next-generation space-based information network system. Star Link and Black Jack will be the important foundation of their tracking layer and operation management layer. They will provide automatic space-based operation management capabilities through command and control, task allocation, task processing and distribution to support the closure of the time sensitive kill chain of campaign scale and provide support for the warfighters to deal with various emerging threats. Since 2020, Lockheed Martin has launched satellites to verify SmartSat technology. At present, it has verified space-based computing and network communication technology through carrying loads.

The space information system of the US military has experienced a "spiral" development of "single satellite system → space satellite earth network → S&C4ISR integration". At present, the space system has achieved unified and comprehensive systematic development, and the "Star Earth Network" has been adopted to realize mutual connection, mutual visit and information integration. In the future, we will gradually promote the construction of S&C4ISR system and the continuous integration to GIG (Global Information Grid), realize the seamless connection and organic integration of space system and US military combat information system, and lay a physical foundation for the scheduling of multi satellite resources, the connection and integration of multi-source information.

3 Development of CHina's Intelligence Space System

The development of intelligent space system in China is still in its infancy. Intelligent technology is mainly embodied in intelligent information processing, autonomous task planning, intelligent information interconnection, etc.

In July 2017, the State Council issued the Development Plan for a New Generation of Artificial Intelligence, which proposed to build an autonomous unmanned system intelligent technology system and support platform, systematically layout artificial intelligence at the national level, deploy and build the first mover of China's artificial intelligence development, and clearly pointed out the strategic goal of the development of a new generation of artificial intelligence in three steps, so that by 2030, China's artificial intelligence theory, technology and application will generally reach the world's leading level, Become a major AI innovation center in the world. From the "Made in China 2025" issued by the State Council in 2015 to the government work report of the State Council in March 2019, AI has been upgraded to "Intelligence Plus". The Chinese government continues to pay attention to and attach great importance to the development of AI, and has upgraded AI to a national strategy.

3.1 Development of Intelligent Information Processing in China

The "Aerospace Tsinghua No.1" microsatellite launched in 2000 has realized a set of on-board image processing system and adopted cloud detection technology; In 2009, a satellite was equipped with an ocean target detection and processing device, and its ship detection rate was more than 90%, which can be processed in real time, reducing the original data rate from 1Gb/s to about 12Mb/s; Jilin No. 1 Spectral 01, 02 and 03 satellites launched in 2019 are equipped with automatic identification, search and positioning of forest fire points and sea ships by applying artificial intelligence technologies such as deep learning. In addition, a satellite of space infrastructure is equipped with real-time data processing equipment, which can complete the radiation correction, cloud judgment, region extraction, region splicing, geometric correction and other processing functions of high-resolution original images on orbit, generate image products, and quickly distribute image products to users. In addition, in terms of chip research and development for intelligent information processing, currently, the market has launched high energy efficiency and low delay artificial intelligence chips for ground reasoning, such as Nvidia Tesla P series GPU chips, Xilinx and Intel led FPGA chips, Xilinx FPGA architecture of the new multi-core heterogeneous computing platform ACAP, etc., but no aerospace chip products with long-term on orbit application capabilities have been formed.

In general, the spacecraft has good measurement, calibration, data acquisition and other capabilities, has carried out in orbit verification of processing technologies such as ocean target detection and recognition, cloud detection of optical remote sensing satellites, and is carrying out preliminary research on multi-source information feature level fusion processing technology for visible, infrared, and SAR images, but lacks the perception and cognitive ability for in orbit data.

3.2 Development of Autonomous Mission Planning in China

"Chang'e-3" and "Chang'e-4" [14, 15] detectors use active and passive optical sensors (laser radar and optical camera) to achieve autonomous obstacle detection and avoidance (HDA) operation [16, 17]. At a distance of 2.4 km from the lunar surface, the optical camera is used to take pictures of the lunar surface to obtain a large range of gray-scale images of the lunar surface. According to the texture, gray-scale and light and dark information in the images, identify and extract rocks, craters and other features to obtain a rough distribution map of obstacles. After that, the safe landing area is comprehensively determined according to the mobility of the detector and other factors; At a distance of 90~100 m from the lunar surface, the detector hovers and uses the lidar to obtain accurate lunar surface elevation information. Based on the elevation information, obstacles are identified and safe landing points are determined. The "Yutu" lunar rover in the "Chang'e 3" and "Chang'e 4" missions can autonomously achieve navigation, attitude determination and positioning, environmental awareness, obstacle avoidance planning, emergency obstacle avoidance, motion coordination control and safety monitoring before and during the movement, so as to ensure that the inspector can safely drive to the target point according to the requirements of the ground instructions [18, 19].

In terms of mission planning, China's satellite ground intelligent mission planning technology has been relatively mature [20–23], and has been applied in satellite user units for a long time. At present, the reconnaissance, operation, measurement and control, and management of domestic on orbit satellites are conducted under the guidance of human beings. The operation management scheme [24], which is formulated on the ground and uploaded for execution, is adopted. The on orbit flight process and mission process are highly dependent on ground operation control. Compared with the explosive development demand of future satellite mission scale, we still have a big gap in the basic research and engineering application realization of satellite autonomous mission planning; At present, the spacecraft only has the basic functions of "meta task" analysis, instruction arrangement and execution, and does not have relatively advanced autonomous planning capabilities [25–27].

3.3 Development of Intelligent Information Interconnection in China

The development of China's space-based information network, Internet and mobile communication network is uneven, showing the characteristics of "weak in the sky and strong in the earth". Each satellite system is built autonomously, with obvious segmentation. The number of satellites is seriously insufficient, and the type of satellites is relatively single. What is more striking is that the satellite did not realize spatial networking, and could not play the integrated networking effectiveness of space-based information system. At present, the space-based network lacks unified planning and design, has not yet achieved the advantages of integrated networking, and has not formed the system service capability to support the joint use of informatization.

The Beidou Global System is the core of China's space-based space-time reference network. Beidou-3 is the largest constellation system built in China. It has provided global users with all-weather, all-weather, high-precision positioning, navigation and time service. Beidou-3 adopts inter satellite link technology, designs reasonable network protocols and task planning, realizes autonomous operation management of the navigation constellation, and ensures long service life, high reliability and high precision measurement of the inter satellite link of the navigation constellation [28]. Without the support of the ground station, the Beidou Global Navigation Satellite System has the capability of 60 day autonomous navigation service.

However, the Beidou 3 information system cannot support the application requirements of the constellation network flexible management and control, and its network management and control can only adopt the full static management mode, relying entirely on the ground instructions. Under the control mode of "one satellite, one tube", the operation efficiency is limited, and there are still problems such as fault free adaptability, inability to meet emergency/burst transmission tasks, and failure to support random access.

4 Development Trend of Key Technologies of Intelligent Space System

4.1 Development Trend of Intelligent Information Processing Technology

Most of the on-board data of spacecraft are transmitted to the ground for processing, which cannot meet the requirements of high timeliness such as emergency disaster reduction or operational applications. The improvement of intelligent information processing capability on board can greatly shorten the system loop, reduce the system delay, improve the accuracy of information extraction, and improve the application efficiency of space-based systems. At present, a few satellites have successfully achieved in orbit disaster monitoring, marine target detection, extraction and positioning, but their detection accuracy is not high enough to support practical applications. On orbit intelligent information processing technologies such as infrared, spectrum and radar are still in the research stage. The future on orbit information processing system needs to complete the information extraction of on orbit load data and measurement and control data, and has the capabilities of environment autonomous perception, intelligent target discovery, type recognition, target tracking, etc.

The main scientific problems faced by intelligent information processing include: 1) Multi-target alignment in multi view scenes: in complex battlefield environment, due to different loads, orbits and satellites, the data from different views of the same target have large differences in shape and appearance, which leads to the decline of information processing accuracy; 2) Limited sample problem: The amount of load, state and other data obtained through sensors is large, but the effective samples for specific targets and space-time are limited, which belongs to small sample data, and it is difficult to learn accurate models from them; 3) On-board computing and storage resources are severely limited, and conventional complex and advanced intelligent algorithms need to consume a lot of resources, so the problem of algorithm lightweight must be solved. In addition, due to the constraints of satellite scale and time-space relationship, the available resources of medium and low orbit spacecraft for target reconnaissance in a single area in a specific time are very limited, and the task needs must be met through intelligent coordination and planning of constellation and cluster spacecraft. In order to solve these problems, it is necessary to focus on intelligent automatic induction, information extraction and knowledge reasoning of limited sample data in the follow-up research; Carry out research on light-weight deep learning network model under limited resources, carry out model sharing based on migration learning, light-weight deep learning network model, multi-source heterogeneous data association and intelligence generation and other key technologies.

4.2 Development Trend of Autonomous Mission Planning Technology

Due to the complexity of space flight mission process, tight TT&C resources and high requirements for reliability and safety, the rationality of mission planning is an important factor for the successful completion of space missions [29]. At present, the operation management mode of spacecraft relies heavily on the ground station, and the delay from user demand to satellite task execution is too long, which is difficult to adapt to the requirements of strong real-time information assurance [30, 31]. In the future, intelligent spacecraft will have the ability of optimal autonomous trajectory planning for the points of interest, and can autonomously realize task decisions such as staring at static targets and active tracking of moving targets; It is capable of intelligent organization and collaborative planning of multiple spacecraft, realizing intelligent organization and autonomous task collaboration of multiple satellites on orbit, and completing orderly division of labor and collaborative work. Taking the intelligent detection robot as an example, the system will reduce the difficulty of autonomous operation of the robot and avoid the impact of extreme terrain conditions on the surface of the detection body through autonomous path planning.

The scientific problems faced by autonomous task planning include: 1) With the increase of the scale of satellite task planning and scheduling, its solution space expands explosively, which makes it extremely difficult to solve; 2) The dynamic adjustment of task planning may cause resource conflicts, so resource constraints and resource utilization of original planning tasks should be fully considered; 3) The spacecraft needs to make task decisions in high dynamic and strong real time according to the changes of sensing information, and must solve the fast computing problem of intelligent task planning technology. In order to further improve the accuracy and autonomy of autonomous task planning, key technologies such as dynamic task planning for multi-target tracking under complex boundary conditions, rapid multi task conflict resolution and intelligent optimization technology need to be tackled in the follow-up research.

4.3 Development Trend of Intelligent Information Interconnection Technology

At present, the space system nodes have not yet achieved interconnection, which is not conducive to flexible scheduling and collaborative use of resources. The future intelligent space system supports the integration of heaven and earth and intelligent information interconnection. Users can obtain the required information in real time, and multiple spacecraft can work together. For example, high orbit census satellites can provide target guidance for low orbit detailed survey satellites through inter satellite networks to achieve collaboration. In addition, in the future, intelligent space systems will have a huge amount of sensors and communication resources. They need to have efficient control over space-based network nodes, computing nodes and routes, and have highly adaptive and damage resistant intelligent information interconnection capabilities to ensure flexible networking and information connectivity; On this basis, the integration of communication, navigation, remote sensing and other space-based nodes into a network can be realized, and satellite resources can be configured in real time to cope with dynamic changes.

The scientific problems faced by intelligent information interconnection include: 1) Dynamic changes in link bandwidth and large differences in bandwidth; 2) Large space link distance range, long delay and strong intermittency will cause the problem of not being able to connect frequently; 3) Self repair of damaged network nodes and links; 4) Intra satellite and inter satellite resources are difficult to share on the network. The key technologies that need to be studied in depth to solve the above problems include: 1) Intelligent routing technology oriented to the characteristics of space-based networks; 2) Node dynamic access management technology; 3) Network topology dynamic adjustment technology adapting to dynamic link; 4) Network congestion management and fault self recovery mechanism; 5) Information sharing mechanism based on asynchronous message transmission.

5   Conclusion

In this paper, intelligent space system is studied from three aspects: intelligent information processing, autonomous task planning and intelligent information interconnection. Based on the research on the development at home and abroad, combined with the development status of relevant technologies of intelligent space system, the existing scientific problems are analyzed, and the development trend of key technologies of intelligent space system is summarized.

After nearly half a century of development, intelligent space systems in various countries have gradually achieved different degrees of autonomous control, and are still accelerating the pace of space intelligence technology research. At present, our country has preliminarily verified the intelligent data processing capability through deep learning and other artificial intelligence technologies on Jilin No.1 and Tianzhi No.1. In the future, China should vigorously develop fast and accurate on-board intelligent technology, and promote its application in intelligent space systems as soon as possible. At the same time, it should speed up the transformation of applications. It can consider the combination of industry, education and research to promote strategic cooperation between the aerospace industry and domestic technological advantaged institutions. We should make choices and reasonable arrangements in basic algorithm research, hardware product development, and mature algorithm engineering, so as to launch models and practical applications as soon as possible.

References

1. Wang, D.Y., Fu, F.Z., Meng, L.Z., et al.: Research of autonomous control technology for deep space probes. J. Deep Space Explor. **6**(4), 317–327 (2019)
2. Lavallee, D.B., Jacobsohn, J.: Intelligent control for spacecraft autonomy-an industry survey. California:AIAA Paper-7384, in: Space2006 (2006)
3. Yang, J.C.: Development of intelligent autonomous control technology for the Chinese space program IFAC Conference on Intelligent Autonomous Control in Aerospace. Beijing: IFAC (1995)
4. Wang, D.Y., Fu, F.Z., Liu, C.R., et al.: Connotation and research status of diagnosability of control systems:a review. Acta Automatica Sinica **44**(9), 3–19 (2018)
5. Zhukov, B., Lorenz, E., Oertel, D., et al.: Space-borne detection and characterization of fires during the bi-spectral infrared detection(BIRD) experimental small satellite mission. Remote Sens. Environ. Interdisc. J. **100**(1), 29–51 (2006)
6. Verfaillie, G., Pralet, C., Lemaitre, M.: Constraint-based modeling of discrete event dynamic systems. J. Intell. Manuf. **21**(1), 31–47 (2010)
7. Xiao, Z.: Tactical star project in operational responsive space program. Aerospace Shanghai **28**(4), 37 (2011)
8. Sherwood, R., Chien, S., Tran, D., et al.: Autonomous science agents and sensor webs: eo-1 and beyond. In: IEEE Aerospace Conference, New York, IEEE (2006)
9. Chien, S., Sherwood, R., Tran, D., et al.: The EO-1 autonomous science agent. In: Proceedings of the 3rd IEEE International Joint Conference on Autonomous Agents and Multiagent Systems. New York, pp. 420–427. IEEE (2004)
10. Yoshimitsu, T., Kawaguchi, J., Hashimoto, T., et al.: Hayabusa-final autonomous descent and landing based on target marker tracking. Acta Astronaut. **65**, 657–665 (2009)
11. Davies, P., Barrington-Cook, J.: The impact of autonomy on the on-board software for the Rosetta mission In: Proceedings of the DASIA 97 Conference on'Data Systems in Aerospace, pp. 133–139 (1997)
12. Nayak, P., Kurien, J., Dorais, G., et al.: Validating the DS-1 remote agent experiment C. In: Proceedings of the 5th International Symposium on Artificial Intelligence, Robotics and Automation in Space, vol. 349 (1999)
13. He, X.W., Li, N., Xu, Y.: Requirements analysis of intelligent spacecraft avionics system and discussion of its architecture. Spacecraft Eng. **04**(27), 82–89 (2018)

14. Chen, D., Cheng, W., Gao, Y.C., et al.: Research on self-organization mission planning for multi-spacecraft coordination. Comput. Measur. Control **27**(5), 221–229 (2019)
15. Wang, D.Y., Tu, Y.Y., Liu, C.R., et al.: Connotation and research of reconfigurability for spacecraft control systems: a review. Acta Automatica Sinica **43**(10), 1688–1695 (2017)
16. Sun, Z.Z., Zhang, T.X., Zhang, H., et al.: The technical design and achievements of chang'E-3 probe. Scientia Sinica Technologica **44**(4), 331–343 (2014)
17. Ye, P.J., Sun, Z.Z., Zhang, H., et al.: Mission design of chang'e-4 probe system. Scientia Sinica Technologica **49**(2), 138–146 (2019)
18. Ye, P.J., Sun, Z.Z., Zhang, H., et al.: An overview of the mission and technical characteristics of Chang'E-4 lunar probe. Sci. China Technol. Sci. **60**(5), 658–667 (2017)
19. Wu, W.R., Wang, Q., Tang, Y.H., et al.: Design of chang'E-4 lunar farside soft-landing mission. J. Deep Space Explor. **4**(2), 111–117 (2017)
20. Wang, D.Y., Tu, Y.Y., Fu, F.Z., et al.: Autonomous diagnosis and reconfiguration technology of spacecraft control system. Control Theory Appl. **36**(12), 1966–1972 (2019)
21. Williamsonw, R., Speyer, J.L., Dang, V.T., et al.: Fault detection and isolation for deep space satellites. J. Guid. Control. Dyn. **32**(5), 1570–1584 (2009)
22. Xiang, S., Chen, Y.G., Li, G.L., et al.: Review on satellite autonomous and collaborative task scheduling planning. Acta Automatica Sinica **45**(2), 252–260 (2019)
23. Xing, L.N.: An autonomous mission planning name work for the new remote sensing satellite. In: Proceedings of the 3rd China High Resolution Earth Observation Conference, China, Beijing, IECAS (2014)
24. Xie, J., Wang, G.: Innovation and technology characteristics of Beidou-3.Space Int. **467**(11), 6–9 (2017)
25. Zhao, Y., Li, F., Wu, B., et al.: Precise landing site selection and evaluation system design for Chang'e-4 probe. Spacecraft Eng. **28**(4), 22–30 (2019)
26. He, Y.Z., Wei, C.L., Tang, L.: A survey on space operations control. Aerospace Control Appl. **40**(1), 1–8 (2014)
27. Cao, J.F., Zhang, Y., Chen, L., et al.: Orbit determination of Chang'E-4 lander using doppler measurement. J. Astronaut. **41**(7), 920–932 (2020)
28. Feng, X.E., Li, Y.Q., Yang, C., et al.: Structural design and autonomous mission planning method of deep space exploration spacecraft for autonomous operation. Control Theory Appl. **36**(12), 2035–2041 (2019)
29. Xi, Z.: Study on mission planning of spaceflight applying artificial intelligence. Acta Aeronautica ET Astronautica Sinica **28**(4), 791–795 (2007)
30. Williamson, W.R., Speyer, J.L., Dang, V.T., et al.: Fault detection and isolation for deep space satellites. J. Guid. Control. Dyn. **32**(5), 1570–1584 (2009)
31. Wu, H.X., Hu, J., Xie, Y.C.: Spacecraft intelligent autonomous control: past, present and future. Aerospace Control Appl. **42**(1), 1–6 (2016)

Integrated Satellite-Terrestrial Information Network

Features Extraction of Reconstruction Model Using in Augmented Reality System of Teleoperation Mobile Robots

Zhang Dongpu[1]([✉]), Xu Fang[2], Chen Huimin[3], Wu Wen[1], Cui Zhaojing[1], and Guo Weiguo[1]

[1] Beijing Institute of Spacecraft System Engineering, Beijing 100094, China
zhangdongpu@163.com
[2] Beijing Lenovo Software Ltd., Co., Beijing 100085, China
[3] Sifang College, Shijiazhuangt Tiedao Unverisity, Shijiazhuang 051132, China

Abstract. In manned deep space exploration, teleoperation robot can cooperate with or even replace astronauts to perform various dangerous tasks in unfamiliar environment. By combining augmented reality system with teleoperation robot, the higher reliability and accuracy required by teleoperation robot can be obtained. The real-time tracking algorithm is one of the key and difficult points in the realization of on orbit teleoperation augmented reality system. Feature extraction based on reconstruction model is the basis of real-time tracking of the system. This paper studies the feature extraction algorithm based on reconstruction model, analyzes the feature points extraction of Harris and sift from the principle level combined with the task characteristics, studies the relationship among the time, image size and number of feature points of the two kinds of feature extraction through experiments, and tests and analyzes the practical application effect of the selected feature extraction methods in the system, and obtains the SIFT The conclusion is that feature point extraction is more suitable for on orbit augmented reality teleoperation system, and the future work is prospected.

Keywords: augmented reality · teleoperation mobile robots · reconstruction model · SIFT · features extraction

1 Introduction

Teleoperation robot is an intelligent robot that can perform scientific tasks such as remote inspection and detection of harsh environment, sampling and analysis, and material handling under remote control. [1] Operators monitor or control remote robots to complete various tasks, so as to achieve the purpose of carrying out tasks in inaccessible or dangerous environments. In manned deep space exploration missions, for unfamiliar, dangerous or inaccessible environments, teleoperation robots can be used to perform rich tasks [2]. It is imperative for robots to land on unknown celestial bodies such as the moon and asteroids or engage in dangerous work instead of humans, so as to prevent humans from

R. Li et al. (Eds.): MOBILWARE 2022, LNICST 507, pp. 77–90, 2023.
https://doi.org/10.1007/978-3-031-34497-8_7

being hurt during deep space exploration and protect people's lives. In order to accurately teleoperate the robot, it is first necessary to obtain the surface environment of the celestial body where the robot is located, and judge the moving range and distance according to the environment [3–5]. Because the unknown celestial environment is strange and complex, the two-dimensional environment model is not enough to express the real situation of its surface, and it is impossible to accurately judge the distance in the environment. In the previous research, we used Metashape software to reconstruct the 3D environment model based on the collected 2D images, which laid a technical foundation for the subsequent 3D environment reconstruction and 3D model reconstruction for deep space exploration teleoperation tasks [2]. By developing the augmented reality simulation control system of teleoperation robot based on ARToolKit, the augmented reality control platform is built at the remote control end of the robot, which improves the working efficiency of teleoperation robot. [6] Real-time tracking algorithm suitable for on-orbit teleoperation augmented reality system is one of the key and difficult points to realize this system, and feature extraction based on reconstruction model is the foundation to realize real-time tracking of this system. In this paper, the feature extraction algorithm based on reconstruction model is studied, which lays the foundation for real-time tracking of on-orbit teleoperation augmented reality system.

2   Principle and Experiment

2.1   Principle of Point Application

In the manned space exploration mission, due to the particularity of the environment, the augmented reality system applied to the on-orbit teleoperation robot must realize two important functions: one is to reconstruct the three-dimensional environment based on two-dimensional images; The second is to realize real-time tracking based on the reconstructed model. Figure 1 is the system flow chart of real-time tracking in the augmented reality system of on-orbit teleoperation robot based on ARToolKit As shown in the figure, in the implementation process, the 3D environment reconstruction based on 2D images provides a reconstructed 3D model for the follow-up tracking process, which can be attributed to an offline process, and will not be described in detail in this article. The real-time tracking algorithm based on the reconstructed model is to use the reconstructed three-dimensional model provided by the offline process for real-time tracking. Among them, the useful information of the prior model includes: the original image used for reconstruction, the matching relationship between the two-dimensional feature points of the reconstructed image and the three-dimensional points of the model, etc. Because of the use of the relevant information of the reconstructed 3D model, the real-time tracking algorithm can effectively avoid the influence of external conditions, such as the change of illumination or the change of scene.

For the tracking algorithm, how to establish the correspondence between the three-dimensional target and the two-dimensional image sequence is the key point of the tracking algorithm. In the real-time tracking algorithm adopted in this system, the following methods are adopted: firstly, the k-d tree of the reconstructed model is established, and this k-d tree contains the three-dimensional point information of the model; Then, in the online tracking stage, the feature points of each frame in the input image sequence are

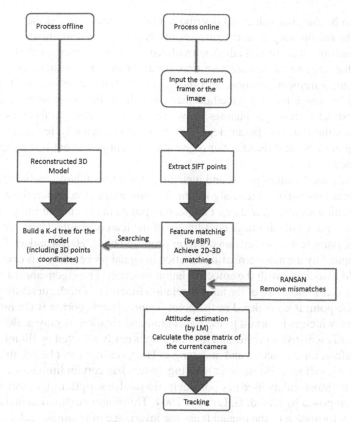

Fig. 1. System Flow Chart

searched by BBF, so as to find the 2D-3D matching relationship. Only after the matching relationship between the three-dimensional points and the two-dimensional feature points of the image is established can the current camera matrix, that is, the P matrix of the camera, be obtained. In the off-line process, the prior model includes the 3D points of the original image and model used for reconstruction and the corresponding 2D points of the image, and the k-d tree of the model is established by using these information. At this time, the established k-d tree already contains the coordinates of three-dimensional points, which can be well used for feature matching in the following tracking process.

2.2 Feature Point

To use 2D images for 3D reconstruction, the first step is to extract the feature points in the images. Feature extraction is not only used for 3D reconstruction, but also used in real-time tracking of the system. Therefore, the process of feature point extraction and matching is the basis of online process, which is related to the final effect of the whole on-orbit teleoperation augmented reality system.

Features can be corner, junetion, edge point, sometimes called edge pixels and points extracted by other interest operators. The attribute parameters or descriptive features of a feature can be the gray value and distribution of the image around the feature point, as well as the relationship with the surrounding feature points, moment invariants and angles. Similarity measure can adopt normalized correlation coefficient (for example, the gray values around the feature points are used as matching entities), or it can adopt a designed measurement function, and then combine with other constraints. Feature matching is an image matching method that takes the points with some local special properties extracted from two pictures or two images in a video sequence as conjugate entities, takes the attribute parameters of feature points, namely feature description, as matching entities, and realizes the registration of conjugate entities by calculating similarity measures.

Commonly used feature points and matching algorithms mainly include Harris feature algorithm and SIFT feature algorithm. Feature extraction generally uses Harris feature extraction algorithm to extract the feature points in the current image frame and obtain the two-dimensional image coordinates of the feature points. Harris operator is a signal-based point feature extraction operator proposed by C. Harris and M. J. Stephens in 1988. Inspired by the autocorrelation function in signal processing, this operator gives the matrix M associated with the autocorrelation function. The eigenvalue of the matrix m is the first-order curvature of the autocorrelation function. If both curvature values are high, then the point is considered as the point feature. Harris corner is the most classic feature point, which is invariant to the translation and rotation of gray scale. However, Harris corner is sensitive to scale, and its matching is easily affected by illumination and scale. Therefore, the extraction and matching of Harris corner can't be suitable for large visual changes, and its application in tracking system has certain limitations.

SIFT is the most widely used key point detection and description algorithm at present. It was first proposed by David. G. Lowe in 2004. This feature extraction makes full use of the local information of the image. It has the invariance of rotation, scale, translation, viewing angle and brightness, which is conducive to the effective expression of target feature information. In addition, it is robust to parameter adjustment. When describing features, the number of appropriate feature points can be adjusted according to the needs of the scene for feature analysis. The main features of this feature point are as follows: a) It is a local feature of the image, which is invariant to rotation, scaling and brightness changes, and stable to a certain extent to angle of view changes, affine transformation and noise. B) Good uniqueness and rich information, which is suitable for fast and accurate matching in massive feature databases. C) Quantity, even a few objects can produce a large number of feature vectors. D) High speed, and the optimized matching algorithm can even meet the real-time requirement.

2.3 Experiments

From the foregoing, it can be seen that feature point extraction is the basis of real-time tracking in on-orbit teleoperation augmented reality system, and its feature point extraction effect is directly related to the success or failure of on-orbit teleoperation task. In order to find a method to extract the feature points of the reconstructed model which is suitable for the on-orbit teleoperation augmented reality system, we carried out related experiments on Harris feature points and SIFT feature points extraction. The experiment is based on a computer with Windows XP operating system. The computer configuration is Intel Pentium 4, 2.8GHz CPU, 512MB memory and GeForce 6600 graphics card. The algorithm is implemented by third-party development packages, including OpenGL, OpenCV and VXL. From the foregoing, it can be seen that feature point extraction is the basis of real-time tracking in on-orbit teleoperation augmented reality system, and its feature point extraction effect is directly related to the success or failure of on-orbit teleoperation task. In order to find a method to extract the feature points of the reconstructed model which is suitable for the on-orbit teleoperation augmented reality system, we carried out related experiments on Harris feature points and SIFT feature points extraction. The experiment is based on a computer with Windows XP operating system. The computer configuration is Intel Pentium 4, 2.8GHz CPU, 512MB memory and GeForce 6600 graphics card. The algorithm is implemented by third-party development packages, including OpenGL, OpenCV and VXL.

3 Results and Discussion

3.1 Analysis of Algorithm and Discussion of Experimental Results

From the angle of algorithm principle, Harris feature point was put forward earlier, which is the most classic feature point. It is invariant to the translation and rotation of gray scale, but Harris feature point is sensitive to scale, and its matching is easily affected by illumination and scale. SIFT feature point is an image local feature description operator, which is based on the feature detection method of invariant technology and is invariant to image scaling, rotation and even affine transformation. The descriptor of this feature point is a 128-dimensional vector. SIFT points keep certain deformation for image change factors such as rotation, scaling, affine transformation, angle of view change, illumination change, etc., and also keep good matching for factors such as object movement, occlusion, noise, etc., so that feature matching between two images with big differences can be realized. The tracking schematic diagram based on SIFT feature points is shown in Fig. 2.

The construction process of the 128-dimensional descriptor of SIFT points is as follows: for any key point, in its scale space (i.e., a layer of Gaussian pyramid structure), take the neighborhood with the key point as the center, then divide the neighborhood evenly into sub-regions (each sub-region has a size of), and calculate the gradient direction histogram for each sub-region (the histogram is evenly divided into 8 directions). Then, the gradient histograms of eight directions in the sub-regions are sorted in turn according to their positions, thus forming a one-dimensional vector, which is the descriptor of the feature points with constant scale. The first dimension corresponds to the first gradient direction of the first subregion, the second dimension corresponds to the second gradient direction of the first subregion, and the ninth dimension corresponds to the first gradient direction of the second subregion, and so on.

Theoretically, the scale invariant feature is a similar invariant, that is, it is invariant to the scale change and rotation of the image. However, due to the special treatment of many details in the construction of this feature, it has strong adaptability to the complex deformation and illumination changes of the image, and at the same time, the operation speed is faster and the positioning accuracy is higher. This feature point has the following

Fig. 2. Tracking based on SIFT points

properties: Theoretically, the scale invariant feature is a similar invariant, that is, it is invariant to the scale change and rotation of the image. However, due to the special treatment of many details in the construction of this feature, it has strong adaptability to the complex deformation and illumination changes of the image, and at the same time, the operation speed is faster and the positioning accuracy is higher. This feature point has the following properties:

(1) Stability. This feature is a local feature of the image, which is invariant to rotation, scaling and brightness changes, and also stable to a certain extent to angle changes, affine transformation and noise.
(2) Accuracy. Accurate positioning of key points not only improves the accuracy, but also greatly improves the stability of key points. But also rich in information, and is suitable for fast and accurate matching in massive feature databases.
(3) Quantity. Even a few objects can produce a large number of feature vectors.
(4) High speed. DoG(Difference of Gaussians) operator is used to detect key points in multi-scale space. Compared with the traditional detection method based on LoG(Laplacian of Gaussian) operator, the operation speed is greatly accelerated, and the optimized matching algorithm can meet the real-time requirements.
(5) Adaptability. When constructing descriptors, the statistical characteristics of sub-regions are taken as the research object instead of single pixel, which improves the adaptability to local image deformation. For the sub-regions of the neighborhood sum of the key points, the gradient amplitude is weighted like Gaussian function, which strengthens the central region and weakens the influence of the edge region, thus improving the adaptability of the algorithm to geometric deformation. This feature is not only invariant to the general linear illumination model, but also adaptable to complex illumination changes.

(6) Scalability. It can be easily combined with other forms of feature vectors.

Firstly, SIFT algorithm performs feature detection in scale space, and determines the position and scale of key points. Then, the main direction of gradient in the key point field is used as the directional feature of the point, so as to realize the independence of operators on scale and direction. The algorithm is mainly composed of the following four steps:

(1) Detecting extreme points of scale space: determining the positions of image features in all possible scale spaces of the image, and these positions are the selected positions in subsequent processing. The location of image features in the scale space is determined by a Gaussian difference filter, and the image features obtained by this Gaussian difference filter are well invariant to the rotation and scaling operations of the image.
(2) Accurate location of extreme points is the key points: after a large number of alternative positions are obtained, more detailed screening and filtering are needed to ensure that the remaining features have sufficient stability. These screened image feature positions are called key points.
(3) Specify main direction for key points: Based on the direction of the gradient of image grayscale near the key points, one or more directions are assigned to the key points. All subsequent processing is based on the direction, scale and position of key points.
(4) Generating key point description sub-vector: according to the scale of each key point, calculate the gradient of the gray level of the points in the image in the neighborhood of the key point, and then establish the multi-dimensional information description of the key point, so as to ensure that the obtained key point description is not very sensitive to local image distortion and illumination changes.

In the actual calculation process, in order to enhance the robustness of matching, Lowe suggested using 16 seed points to describe each key point, so that 128 data can be generated for one key point, that is, a 128-dimensional feature vector can be finally formed. At this time, the influence of geometric deformation factors such as scale change and rotation has been removed from the feature vector, and the influence of illumination change can be further removed by further normalizing the length of the feature vector.

In order to verify the above theoretical analysis, we simply compare the actual operation effects of the two feature point detection and matching processes, and preliminarily select the feature extraction scheme of the reconstruction model suitable for the on-orbit teleoperation augmented reality system. The actual photos are used for simple experimental comparison, and the scene photos, Harris algorithm detection map and SIFT algorithm detection map are shown in Fig. 3 below.

According to the actual operation results, we can see that the number of Harris feature points is small, and the matching relationship is simple, so the calculation time is relatively short. Without considering the accuracy requirement, the matching process of Harris feature points is simpler, and the calculation amount is relatively low, so it is suitable for the scene where the calculation ability is constrained. In order to ensure the normal realization of various functions in the space environment with strong radiation, most spacecraft use aerospace-grade components. Under the same power consumption, weight, volume and other conditions, their computing power is not the same as that of

a Scene shooting picture

b SIFT algorithm detection chart   c Harris algorithm detection chart

Fig. 3. Preliminary experiment of feature point extraction method of figure

civil devices used daily on the same scale. From this point of view, Harris feature points are more suitable than SIFT feature points for feature extraction of reconstruction model of on-orbit teleoperation augmented reality system.

However, as mentioned in the previous analysis of Harris algorithm, Harris feature points are sensitive to scale, and their matching is easily affected by illumination and scale. In the manned deep space exploration mission, the task of on-orbit teleoperation robot is to be able to perform scientific tasks such as long-distance inspection and detection of harsh environment, sampling and analysis, material handling, etc. under remote control, and its environment is mostly unknown celestial bodies such as the moon and asteroids that have no atmosphere around it. In such an environment, because there is no atmosphere for reflection and scattering, the natural light from the outside or the illumination light from the extravehicular floodlighting equipment carried by the spacecraft itself will be more direct, and the contrast between light and dark will be stronger. Therefore, it is extremely unfavorable for Harris feature point matching process which is easily influenced by illumination and scale. In addition, the manned deep space exploration mission belongs to the deep space exploration mission with people involved, and the implementation process is costly in all aspects, and human life cannot be lost, so the reliability of the system is extremely high. Harris algorithm is not as good as SIFT algorithm in terms of stability and reliability, although it requires less computing power of devices. From the point of view of the requirements of manned deep space exploration mission on the accuracy, stability and reliability of the system, it is found that the more SIFT feature matching points are, the more advantageous it is to match feature points based on 3D scene reconstruction model, and even to some extent, it has a relatively stable feature tracking ability for images taken from any angle. From the point of view of maximizing the stability and accuracy of the system, SIFT feature matching points are more suitable.

3.2 Experiment and Discussion of SIFT Feature Point Extraction

Traditional visual tracking systems often use Harris corner to track and extract features, but the change of visual angle will block Harris corner, or the extraction will fail due to the influence of illumination. The extraterrestrial environment is full of various unknown factors, such as obstacles, light changes, harsh environment and so on. In order to avoid the influence of occlusion, illumination change and environment, the feature extraction of reconstruction model applied to on-orbit teleoperation augmented reality system is realized by SIFT algorithm. As the result of the previous experiment shows, the number of SIFT feature points is more, the calculation is more and the time is longer. In order to further analyze the feasibility of applying SIFT algorithm to feature extraction of reconstructed model of on-orbit teleoperation augmented reality system, and to study the influence of image size and image texture on the number and time of extracting SIFT feature points, the following two groups of experiments were carried out in this paper.

(1) Comparative analysis of Harris feature points and SIFT feature points extraction time

Harris points and SIFT points of images with the same size and different textures are extracted respectively. The size of each image is 256×256, but the texture information of each image is different. The image of the experiment is shown in Fig. 4. The experimental data are shown in Table 1.

The data in Table 1 shows that for images of the same size, regardless of the complexity of the image texture or background, the time taken to extract Harris points is about 0.74 s; Even if the image size is the same, the time and the number of feature points used to extract SIFT points are different due to different textures. Images of Harris point and SIFT point are extracted as shown in Fig. 4 and Fig. 5 respectively. The experimental results are shown in Fig. 5.

Figure 4 and Fig. 5 show that the time taken to extract Harris feature points is basically independent of the richness of image texture; However, the time taken to extract SIFT feature points is closely related to the richness of image texture. The richer the texture of the image, the more SIFT feature points are extracted, and the longer it takes.

(2) Experiment on extracting time of SIFT points of different sizes in the same image

The SIFT points of the same image with different sizes were extracted to study the relationship between extraction time and the number of feature points. The original image of the experiment is shown in Fig. 3. The experimental data are shown in Table 2. For the same image with different sizes, extract the relationship curve between the number of SIFT points and the time taken and the image size, as shown in Fig. 6.

It can be seen from Fig. 6 that for images with the same texture, when the image size increases, the time taken to extract SIFT points and the number of extracted SIFT points also increase. From the results of the above two groups of experiments, it can be concluded that the image size and texture information both affect the time taken to extract SIFT points and the number of SIFT points extracted. On the one hand, with the increase of image size, the time for extracting SIFT points also increases; On the other hand, from the comparative experiment, it can be seen that the extraction of Harris feature points is basically not affected by image texture, while the extraction of SIFT feature points is closely related to the richness of image texture. If the texture of the image is richer, the number of extracted SIFT feature points will be more, and the corresponding time will be more.

Table 1. Time for extracting Harris points and SIFT points

No	Time to select Harris point (s)	Time to extract SIFT points(s)	Number of SIFT points
1	0.76	1.87	339
2	0.74	1.90	345
3	0.74	3.15	888
4	0.68	1.28	204
5	0.74	2.23	494
6	0.76	2.02	396
7	0.81	1.59	225
8	0.73	1.76	272
9	0.77	1.06	93
No	Time to select Harris point (s)	Time to extract SIFT points(s)	Number of SIFT points

Fig. 4. Original picutre of 256 × 256

a Extract Harris points   b Extract SIFT points

Fig. 5. Comparison between extraction results in 256 × 256 image.

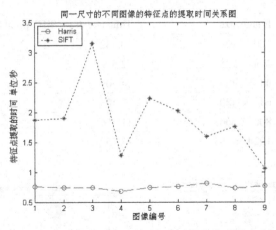

Fig. 6. Time relations of feature points extracted from 256 × 256 images

This characteristic of SIFT point is not ideal for tracking system, especially for real-time tracking system, which will affect the real-time performance of tracking system. However, considering the high stability of SIFT point, it can well solve the influences of occlusion, illumination and environment, which is very important for tracking system. On the other hand, the tracking system doesn't need too many feature points, as long as it can track the target object. Therefore, in the tracking algorithm studied in this paper, SIFT feature points can effectively track features (Figs. 7 and 8).

Fig. 7. Image of the experiment

Table 2. Relationship between extraction time of SIFT feature points and image size

No	Image size	Time to extract SIFT points(s)
1	160 × 120	0.532
2	314 × 235	2.5
3	448 × 336	4.609
4	640 × 480	7.40
5	800 × 600	11.656
6	1024 × 768	23.25

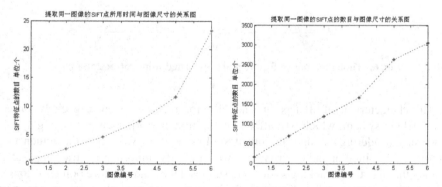

Fig. 8. Relationship between the time taken to extract SIFT feature points of the same image and image size

3.3   Analysis of Practical Application Effect

Combined with the above analysis results, we apply SIFT algorithm to the reconstruction model feature extraction experiment in the augmented reality system of on-orbit teleoperation, and further analyze and verify its feasibility. In the experiment, a 640 × 480 stone table image was used as the experimental image. The test input image is shown in Fig. 9a. The experimental results after extracting SIFT feature points are shown in Fig. 9b.After many experiments, it takes about 5–6 s to extract SIFT points from a single image with the size of 640 × 480, and the number of extracted SIFT points is about 1200. The result of extracting SIFT points from the current frame image in Fig. 9a is shown in Fig. 9b The number of SIFT points in the current frame image is 1221, and the consumed time is 5.265 s.

a   b

Fig. 9. Image input by experiment and image after feature extraction

The experimental results show that there are more than 1000 SIFT feature points extracted from the image, which takes about 5–6 s. For the real-time tracking algorithm, the speed of extracting feature points is slow, which has two impacts on the tracking algorithm: on the one hand, the more features that can be tracked, the easier it is to find the feature matching between images, thus providing accurate 2D-3D matching point pairs for camera attitude estimation in the following tracking process in the whole system process, so as to ensure the tracking accuracy; On the other hand, the more features that can be tracked, the greater the amount of data, and the slower the computing speed. In the follow-up, it is still necessary to improve and perfect the feature point extraction algorithm. On the premise of ensuring the accuracy and stability of feature point extraction, the running amount is further reduced and the extraction speed is increased.

4 Summarize and Prospect

Man-machine cooperation can give full play to the respective advantages of man and machine, and man-machine cooperation mode is an important feature of people participating in deep space exploration missions in the future. Based on the requirements of human-machine cooperation tasks such as on-orbit augmented reality teleoperation in unknown celestial environment, this paper analyzes the extraction process of Harris feature points and SIFT feature points through research and experiments, and compares the number and time of feature points extracted by two different algorithms in combination with the actual working background and environmental requirements of feature extraction in the reconstruction model of on-orbit teleoperation augmented reality system. After the corresponding conclusion is drawn, the relationship between the extraction time and number of SIFT feature points in different image sizes is analyzed, and it is actually applied to the further experiment of reconstruction model extraction in orbital teleoperation augmented reality system. Through research, the following conclusions are drawn:

(1) For the same feature extraction target picture, Harris algorithm can be used when the number of feature points extracted is small and the time is short, and the accuracy requirement is not considered. The SIFT algorithm extracts a large number of feature points and takes a long time. However, considering the requirements of the manned deep space exploration mission for the accuracy, stability and reliability of the system, SIFT feature points are more suitable for the feature extraction process of the reconstruction model of the on-orbit teleoperation augmented reality system.

(2) Compared with Harris feature points, with the increase of image size, the extraction time of SIFT feature points increases. This is because the extraction of SIFT feature points is greatly affected by the degree of image texture, which is closely related to the richness of image texture. The richer the image texture is, the more SIFT feature points are extracted, and the longer it takes. Considering that the system requires high stability and accuracy, SIFT feature points can be selected as the feature extraction method of the reconstruction model of this system.

(3) In the practical application verification of the system, both the size and texture information of the image affect the extraction of more than 1000 SIFT feature points, which takes about 5–6 s. For the real-time tracking algorithm, the speed of extracting feature points is still slow. In the follow-up research work, it is necessary to study the improvement of feature point extraction algorithm, further improve the extraction speed of SIFT points, improve the visual tracking performance of augmented reality on-orbit teleoperation system, and improve the human-computer interaction experience in the process of on-orbit teleoperation as a whole.

References

1. Jiwu, W., Zixin, L., Shijie, Y., et al.: Research on reconstruction of three-dimensional environment for the mobile lunar exploration based on Metashape. Robot Explor. **21**, 263–269 (2015)
2. Dongpu, Z., Lin, T., Kewu, H., et al.: Vision tracking algorithm reality system of teleoperation mobile robots. In: Proceedings of 2020 3rd International Conference on Unmanned System, pp.1047–1052 (2020)
3. Azuma, R., Baillot, Y., Behringer, R., Feiner, S., Julier, S., MacIntyre, B.: Recent advances in augmented reality. IEEE Comput. Graphics Appl. **11–12**, 34–47 (2001)
4. Guangchao, Z., Tianmiao, W., Wusheng, C., et al.: Research on augmented reality based teleoperation system. J. Syst. Simul. **5**, 943–946 (2004)
5. Skrypnyk, I., Lowe, D.: Scene modelling, Recognition and tracking with invariant image features. IEEE (2004)
6. Szeliski, R., Kang, S.: Recovering 3D shape and motion from image streams using non-linear least squares. Technical report, Cambridge Research Laboratory (1993)

Research on Rapid 3D Reconstruction for Teleoperation in Manned Lunar Exploration Mission

Lin Tian[1(✉)], Yinuo Sheng[1], Xisheng Li[1], Pengcheng Wang[1], and Jiwu Wang[2]

[1] Beijing Institute of Spacecraft System Engineering, Beijing 100094, China
lucksonner@163.com
[2] Beijing Jiaotong University, Beijing 100044, China

Abstract. Teleoperation can greatly improve the whole mission benefits of manned lunar exploration, while it is necessary to provide a real and effective environment for astronauts through rapid 3D reconstruction. The requirements of teleoperation and the characteristics of the operated objects in the future manned lunar exploration mission are analyzed. According to the characteristics of the lunar environment, a 3D rapid reconstruction scheme based on the combination of motion structure recovery and binocular vision is proposed, and the proposed scheme and its accuracy are verified through ground tests.

Keywords: Manned Lunar Exploration · Lunar Teleoperation · Rapid 3D Reconstruction · Structure From Motion · Binocular Vision.

1 Preface

1.1 A Subsection Sample

Lunar has already become the primary target of human deep space exploration since the new century, and several countries and institutions have declare their lunar exploration plans. Teleoperation means controlling robots remotely to complete relatively complex operations in a site far away from the operator. In the manned lunar exploration mission, teleoperation can support astronauts controlling robots to reach dangerous sites and carrying out deep exploration works. For large-scale exploration, high-intensity and repetitive works, astronauts can focus on the control operation for a long time in a safe and comfortable environment with good mental state. Meanwhile, this can help avoiding time consumption and risks of pressure cabin entry and exit, which reducing the requirements of astronauts' personal characteristics. Teleoperation can also support multiple operators to cooperate at different levels, which greatly improves the whole benefits of mission. In order to support teleoperation, it is necessary to build a 3D environment of the operation site through VR technology to provide operators with a strong sense of immersion and comprehensive and systematic task information.

© ICST Institute for Computer Sciences, Social Informatics and Telecommunications Engineering 2023
Published by Springer Nature Switzerland AG 2023. All Rights Reserved
R. Li et al. (Eds.): MOBILWARE 2022, LNICST 507, pp. 91–105, 2023.
https://doi.org/10.1007/978-3-031-34497-8_8

Rapid 3D reconstruction of environment is the basis of high-quality and high-efficiency lunar teleoperation. It needs to provide effective environment and information of lunar robot and environment for astronauts with limits of computing and communication resources. This paper investigates and analyzes the situation of lunar teleoperation missions. Following the analysis of the teleoperation requirements of manned lunar exploration missions, a fast 3D environment reconstruction method suitable for the characteristics of lunar environment and the operation of lunar robots is proposed, while the accuracy is tested and verified by ground tests. The study can provide a useful reference for mission applications in the future.

2 Development of Lunar Teleoperation Technology

2.1 American Lunar Rover

In 1967, the U.S. 'Surveyor-3' lunar probe successfully landed on the lunar. It completed the lunar soil collection tasks under the control of the ground station, and realized the earliest space robot teleoperation in human history.

The Apollo-15/16/17 missions utilized the non-pressurized manned lunar rover (LRV), with a maximum distance of 36 km. The LRV was manually controlled by the astronauts. At the same time, the ground control center was remotely controlling at different berths based on TV images. The ground control personnel were divided into three task groups: task command and control, system operation and status monitoring. In addition, there were support groups such as lunar surface experiments (Fig. 1).

Fig. 1. Manned lunar rover in Apollo program.

2.2 Former Soviet Union Lunar Rover

The 'Lunar-17' lunar probe launched by the former Soviet Union in 1970 carried the lunar rover'Lunokhod-1', which is the first lunar surface exploration activity carried out in the world. Lunar-17 worked for 11 months, and the walking distance of Lunokhod-1 reached 10.54 km, while the inspection area was 80000m2. In 1973, the Lunar-21 lunar probe with the Lunokhod-2 lunar rover was successfully launched. Lunokhod-2 carried out patrol and exploration activities, and its total walking distance was 37 km.

Both Lunokhod-1 and Lunokhod-2 adopted the ground teleoperation. Four panoramic cameras were used to collect high-resolution images. During the teleoperation from ground, five controllers sat in front of the television of ground control center, and the image of lunar surface returned by the lunar rover was displayed on the screen. According to these images, the driver sent commands to the lunar rover for moving slowly and avoiding from craters and obstacles. The camera protruding from the front of the rover body transmitted an image to the ground every few seconds. Although the quality was not so high, it could ensure that the 'driver' can avoid obstacles and move to the target position. When the lunar rover was in the 'wandering' state and unable to determine the subsequent moving path, it obtained higher resolution images through four panoramic cameras (Fig. 2).

Fig. 2. Lunokhod lunar rover of the former Soviet Union

2.3 Chinese Lunar Rover

In December 2013, the Chang'e-3 (CE-3) lander successfully achieved a soft lunar landing. On December 15, the Yutu lunar rover realized the separation and mutual shooting of the two, which marked the success of the Chang'e-3 mission and became China's first remote operation to patrol and detect an extraterrestrial object. The Yutu lunar rover worked in an unknown and complex environment on the lunar surface, and had two working modes: autonomous operation and remote operation. The ground mission support and teleoperation control system was the main system to realize the teleoperation, which was composed of 3D terrain construction, whole mission planning, detection cycle planning and other functional modules. The Yutu lunar rover restored and established 2D panoramic images and 3D topographic maps through a variety of algorithms, and realized task planning such as behavior sequence and travel path based on environment module, kinematics module and multi-constraint optimization algorithm. The Yutu lunar rover was equipped with panoramic camera, navigation camera and

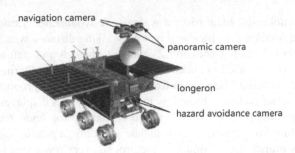

navigation camera

panoramic camera

longeron

hazard avoidance camera

Fig. 3. Overall configuration of Chang'e-3 lunar lander with lunar rover 'Yutu'3

obstacle avoiding camera for imaging at different distances. In order to achieve stereo vision, all cameras used a dual camera configuration (Fig. 3).

In 2014, the CE-4 mission realized the first human landing on the back of lunar. The 'Yutu-2' lunar rover carried by it was optimized for ground teleoperation software based on CE-3, and the interactive interface was simplified through improving the level of automation. The CE-5 mission has realized the first lunar surface automatic sampling and return mission in China. Its surface sampling manipulator system mainly included two parts: lunar surface execution and ground remote operation, which were used for the ground test, test verification and on orbit operation of the surface sampling device (Fig. 4).

Fig. 4. CE-4 lunar surface moving traces of the rover Yutu-2

2.4 Summary

The problem of teleoperation delay on lunar surface is more serious. Considering the communication delay, information processing and transmitting, operator decision-making and other delays, the teleoperation delay is generally in the order of more than ten seconds. The continuous teleoperation of the lunar robot by ground operators in early missions is difficult, and the 'move wait' strategy can only be used. Although the system stability under large time delay is achieved, the system efficiency is greatly reduced.

In order to achieve continuous teleoperation under large time delay, prediction display and other technologies have been gradually developed, but the decision-making of operators needs the support of realistic 3D environment, and the immersion of operators is enhanced through virtual reality to improve the efficiency of teleoperation.

3 Requirement Analysis of Teleoperation for Manned Lunar Exploration

3.1 Teleoperation Task Analysis

According to the mission design of future manned lunar exploration mission, three types of teleoperation requirements can be summarized:

(1) Unmanned lunar exploration activities in manned lunar exploration

In the early stage of manned lunar exploration mission, it is necessary to carry out pre-exploration activities on the lunar surface through lunar robots, such as detailed exploration of candidate landing sites for manned lunar landing, in-depth exploration of the site selection of manned lunar research station or manned lunar base, and large-scale mobile exploration of the lunar surface. Remote operation the lunar robot can be done through a lot of ways, which not only ensures the efficiency and coverage of lunar exploration, but also reduces the cost and risk of subsequent manned lunar exploration missions.

(2) Human-machine joint detection in high risk areas

When astronauts carry out exploration activities on the moon, they will be threatened by the complex terrain, vacuum, extreme high and low temperatures, space radiation and other environmental threats on the moon. The man-machine joint working mode of astronauts in the pressured cabin + lunar robots can be utilized to reduce the risk of astronauts carrying out extravehicular activities.

(3) Large scale extravehicular operations centered on astronauts

When in the stage of large-scale system level lunar surface exploration or lunar resource development and utilization, it is necessary to establish a set of support system for large-scale extravehicular operations around astronauts, and take remote operation as the main task mode. Extravehicular large-scale operations are characterized by long duration, cooperative operation of multiple astronauts, and support of various resources during operation. If the astronauts are located in a suitable environment, the remote operation mode can avoid the inconvenience of fine operation when wearing extravehicular clothing, and can also establish a friendly and more convenient human-computer interaction channel through the mixed reality with the support of rich resources in the cabin.

3.2 Characteristic Analysis of Teleoperation Object

According to the results of teleoperation tasks and requirements analysis, the lunar teleoperation objects can be divided into two kinds: mobile type and operation type.

The mobile type mainly refers to the interaction between the operated object and the lunar terrain environment. The point of teleoperation is to measure and determine the relative pose relationship between the lunar robot and the surrounding terrain, and select the correct and safe mobile path (Fig. 5).

Fig. 5. Lunar surface moving robots

The operation type mainly refers to the interaction between the manipulator and the operated object. The key point of teleoperation is to measure the relative pose relationship between the manipulator and the operated object, and form the motion command of the manipulator (Fig. 6).

Fig. 6. Task types of single arm and double arm of lunar surface manipulators

4 Research on Rapid 3D Environment Reconstruction Method for Lunar Teleoperation

4.1 Comparative Analysis of Three-Dimensional Lunar Surface Reconstruction Methods

As an important branch of computer vision, 3D reconstruction technology can be divided into active acquisition and passive acquisition. The qualitative comparison of various 3D reconstruction methods is as follows (Table 1).

According to the characteristics of the lunar environment, binocular vision (BiV) and Structure from motion (SFM) are used for 3D reconstruction:

(1) When there are many feature points, SFM based method is used for 3D reconstruction;
(2) When there are few feature points, BiV is used for 3D reconstruction.

Table 1. Comparison of 3D reconstruction methods

Method	Automation level	Reconstruction effect
Shading method	Fully automated	The reconstruction effect is poor, vulnerable to illumination, and the robustness is poor
Photometric stereoscopic visual method	Can achieve a certain degree of automation	The reconstruction effect is good, affected by the light source, and the robustness is poor
Texture method	Fully automated	The reconstruction effect is poor, insensitive to light and noise, and has good robustness
Contour method	Fully automated	Depends on the number of contour images
Focusing method	Difficult to realize automatic reconstruction	It can calculate the depth of each point, and the reconstruction effect is better
Structure from motion method	Fully automated	The reconstruction effect is better. The more images, the better the reconstruction effect
Binocular vision	Fully automated	The reconstruction effect is better in the case of weak texture scene
Time flight method	Fully automated	The reconstruction effect is quite good
Structured light method	Fully automated	The reconstruction effect is quite good

4.2 3D Reconstruction Based on Moving Structure Restoration

SFM is a method to restore camera parameters and 3D information using numerical methods by detecting matching feature points in multiple uncalibrated images. The method has very low requirements for images, and can use video or even random image sequences for 3D reconstruction; At the same time, image sequences can be used to realize the self-calibration of the camera in the reconstruction process, which eliminates the pre-calibration steps of the camera; Moreover, due to the progress of various feature point extracting and matching technology, the robustness of method is also very strong.

Considering the limited field of view of a single monitoring camera, we can introduce the PTZ monitoring camera technology with target tracking, which can ensure that the robot is always within the effective range of the monitoring camera. At the same time, according to the new workspace of the mobile robot, we can control the scanning of the PTZ left, right and pitch, and provide a model for 3D environment reconstruction (Fig. 7).

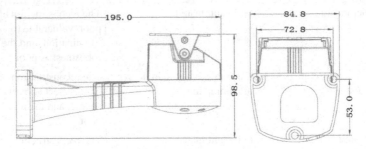

Fig. 7. Structural dimension and physical object of PTZ1

4.3 3D Reconstruction Based on Binocular Stereo Vision

Binocular stereo vision is a method to obtain depth information based on the parallax principle. It observes the same object from multiple perspectives and obtains images, then matches the images from different perspectives, calculates the depth information through the triangulation principle and the offset between corresponding points. This can obtain the distance between the object and the camera, and finally obtain the 3D information of the object. This method simulates the process of stereoscopic imaging of human eyes, and can achieve good results with low cost and simple system structure. It is widely used in product detection and quality control, and can collect images in an instant, so it is more effective for the measurement of moving objects.

5 Experiment and Accuracy Analysis of Rapid Reconstruction of 3D Environment

5.1 3D Reconstruction Test Based on Structure from Motion

The robot head pan tilt camera collects 2D images of the surrounding environment, imports the 2D images into the Meta-Shape software, and generates a 3D model through the process of aligning photos, establishing dense point clouds, generating meshes, generating textures. So the format is exported, and the ruler is placed in the environment. The scene accuracy is detected by the robot walking through a specified distance. Secondly, the model is imported into Unity 3D software for mapping, physical configuration and other operations. Finally, HTC vive glasses are configured to observe the scene (Fig. 8).

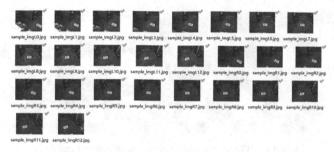

Fig. 8. Laboratory image collected by PTZ camera

The Meta-Shape software is imported for 3D reconstruction and accuracy analysis (Fig. 9).

Fig. 9. Meta-Shape reconstruction diagram

3D environment is successfully reconstruct and observed with HTC Vive. By measuring the error between the grid distance detection of the calibration plate and the real environment, the test error is less than 1%, which can fulfill the requirement that the error of 10m scale 3D environment reconstruction of the lunar surface teleoperation task is less than 1% (Figs. 10, 11 and Table 2).

Fig. 10. 3D environmental map

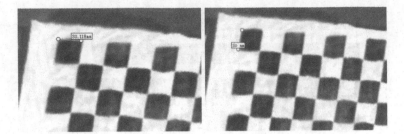

Fig. 11. 3D reconstruction error measurement results

Table 2. Accuracy error of 3D reconstruction

Line segment number	Direction	Measured value /mm	Software measurements /mm	Relative error /mm	Relative error	Average error
1	level	30	30.118	0.118	0.393%	0.271%
2	level	30	30.235	0.235	0.783%	
3	level	30	29.891	-0.109	-0.363%	
4	vertical	30	30.001	0.001	0.003%	0.089%
5	vertical	30	29.841	-0.159	-0.530%	
6	vertical	30	30.238	0.238	0.793%	

Considering the task characteristics of no-obvious-features such as poor light and less texture information in the lunar environment, the meeting room and corridor area is selected as the on-site test environment with dark light and weak ground texture information. The 3D environment model is successfully reconstructed, as shown in the following figure (Fig. 12).

Fig. 12. 3D reconstruction of meeting room and corridor scene

5.2 3D Reconstruction Test Based on Binocular Vision

SFM 3D reconstruction is not good for weak texture scene with few feature points.

According to the characteristics of less lunar terrain environment texture and no obvious prominent features, binocular vision method is used to reconstruct the 3D model, and the model is accurately measured and monitored. Ranging experiment is carried out as following:

(1) A binocular stereo vision system with parallel optical axis is constructed by using two cameras of the same model;
(2) The binocular stereo vision system is calibrated to determine the internal and external parameters of the two cameras;
(3) Use both left and right cameras to shoot the fixed calibration plate scene at the same time (the obtained image pairs are shown in the figure);
(4) In the self-developed human-computer interaction interface, the captured image pairs are imported, while the matching corresponding points in the left and right images are manually selected. Then the 3D coordinate information of the obtained image points in the world coordinate system is calculated by using the principle of triangular ranging.

Fig. 13. Human-computer interaction interface and image pair display

In order to effectively verify the accuracy of 3D reconstruction, the gray image of calibration plate is selected for ranging. The actual size of the calibration plate is 30 mm × 30 mm. In order to verify the accuracy of distance measurement, 8 corners in the first row and 6 corners in the first column of the calibration plate are selected, and the absolute and relative error of the measurement distance are obtained (Fig. 13).

Absolute error calculation: $\Delta = (L' - L)/L$, where L' is the measured value and L is the true value;

Relative error calculation: Δ is the absolute error and L is the true value, $\delta = \Delta/L \times 100\%$ (Fig 14).

It can be seen from the data in the table that the reconstructed environment size is basically the same as the real size. With the increase of measurement distance, the absolute error and relative error are reduced, and both arrive below 1%. The best working distance of the camera is within 5m. In the ranging test, it can be seen from the table that there is no significant difference in the y-axis coordinates with the increase of the

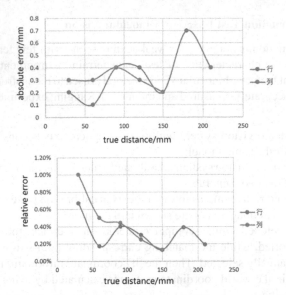

Fig. 14. Absolute and relative error of 3D reconstruction

measurement distance, which indicates that the measured points are at the same height. These verifies the accuracy of the measurement.

5.3 3D Reconstruction Experiment of Typical Lunar Teleoperation Mission

The simulation of virtual scene is based on Unity3D software. Unity3D is a cross plat-form, fully integrated professional virtual simulation engine that provides rich scene management functions (Fig. 15).

Fig. 15. Unity3D operation interface

Based on a campus environment, 3D reconstruction and robot walking control in virtual reality is simulated (Fig. 16).

The requirement of 3D reconstruction based on Metashape software is very low. Video or even random image sequences can be used for 3D reconstruction. At the same

(a) Scene of robot in position 1

(b) Scene when the robot moves to position 2

Fig. 16. Description of 3D simulation control based on VR

time, image sequences can be used to realize the self calibration of the camera in the reconstruction process and eliminate the pre-calibration steps of the camera. With the progress of various feature point extraction and matching technology, the robustness of SFM is also very strong. However, the shortage of 3D reconstruction based on software is mainly due to the large amount of computation. Because the reconstruction effect depends on the density of feature points, the reconstruction effect of weak texture scene with fewer feature points is poor.

In order to test the matching accuracy between the size of the environment model in Unity3d and the size in the real scene, the method of walking and rotating the robot is used to verify the accuracy of the model. The matching accuracy of the model has a great impact on the subsequent tests. First, a graph is drawn in OpenGL, which is composed of several concentric circles (green) and rays (red) divergent from the center of the circle. The spacing of several concentric circles is set to a value, and the angle between the rays is set to a value. Then place the robot's walking starting point in the center of the drawing, and verify the dimensional accuracy of the model (Fig. 17).

In OpenGL, we set the radius of the first concentric circle as 2.5m, the radius of the second concentric circle as 5m, and set the angle between several red rays to 30°. Then we add a walking program for the robot in Unity3D. The starting point is the center of the concentric circle, so the robot can move 2.5m and 5m from the starting point respectively. Running the program shows the robot has reached the concentric circle of 2.5m and 5m. Editing the program (let the robot rotate 30° and walk), we can see the robot walking along the rays separated by 30° (Fig. 18).

Fig. 17. Starting point of robot placement

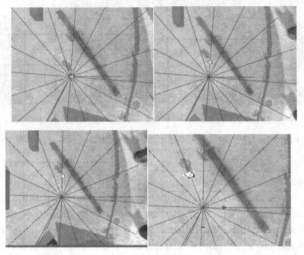

(a) robot starting point (b) robot walking 2.5m (c) Robot walking 5 meters (d) robot rotating
30 °

Fig. 18. Robot walking and rotating control2

With simulation verification, it is proved that the size of the environment model in Unity 3D is consistent with that in the real scene, which lays the foundation for the subsequent experiments.

6 Summary

According to the requirements of 3D environment reconstruction in the future manned lunar exploration teleoperation mission, the structure from motion + binocular vision method was selected, and the 3D reconstruction test is successfully carried out in the laboratory environment. The 3D environment reconstruction and motion control test including robot is successfully realized in the outdoor environment, and the 3D reconstruction accuracy is better than 1%, which can meet the requirements of lunar surface teleoperation for manned lunar exploration.

References

1. Zhang, D., Tian, L., Huang, K.: Jiwu wang Vision tracking algorithm for augmented reality system of telecommunications mobile robots. In: 2020 3rd International Conference on unmanned systems (2020)
2. Wang, J., pei, X.: Distance measurement system based on binocular stereo vision. In: The 2021 International Conference on artificial life and Robotics (icarob2021) (2021)
3. Wang, J., zeng, W.: Research on realization method of augmented reality based on unity3d. J. Robot. Netw. Artistic life **6**, 195 (2019)
4. Shengyi, J., Haifei., L., Song, P., Bo, W., et al.: Design of tele operation ground support system for chang'e-4rover. Spacecraft Eng. **28**(4), 116–124
5. Xin, Z., Aiguo, S., Yonghui, Z., huijun, L.: Design of a virtual human machine system for manipulator tele operation. Manned spaceflight **26**(3), 353–362 (2020)
6. Chang, L., Jianggang, C., Ning, H., et al.: Research on space understanding method in mixed reality for astronaut training. Maned Spaceflight **26**(1), 26–33
7. Huang, Q.: Research on multi modal mixed reality system based on hololens and haptic rendering. Thesis of Nanjing University of Aeronautics and Astronautics, (2019)
8. Xinlei, G.: Mixed reality framework based on visual positioning. Thesis of Xidian University (2019)
9. Xiaoong, X.: Research on Key Technologies of ground tele operation for space robot. Thesis of Southeast University (2017)

Onboard Software Maintenance Design and Implementation for Networking Satellites

Wei Wu[✉], Liang Qiao, Hongcheng Yan, Cuilian Wang, Yong Xu, and Xiaorui Yang

Beijing Institute of Spacecraft System Engineering, Beijing, China
18610104602@163.com

Abstract. A design method of onboard software automatic update for networking satellites is proposed. Using the inter-satellite link, the hand-in-hand satellites with each other transmit the version numbers of the software and FPGA that can be updated and the applicable satellites to each other. When the version numbes of a software item between hand-in-hand Sat-A and Sat-B is inconsistent (Sat-a is higher than Sat-B), Sat-B can automatically initiate the request to update. Then Sat-A can automatically read out the software data from the Nandflash memory with splitting and re-framing and send it to Sat-B, according to the dedicated parameters of Sat-B and the inter-satellite link data transmission format. The updated software data is received and verified by Sat-B, and then stored in Nandflash memory and program store Norflash or EEPROM memory. After the update is completed, Sat-B will transmit the latest software version information to other hand-in-hand satellites, and support the software update Correspondingly. If this scheme can complete the software update of one of the group networking satellites on the ground, it can automatically upgrade the satellites software of the whole network, reduce the ground operation, and greatly improve the efficiency of onboard software maintenance. The method has been demonstrated with two space network routers for Compass Navigation Satellites in laboratory. A Virtex-5 FPGA configuration data in one router is updated by terrestrial injection and the corresponding Virtex-5 FPGA configuration data in the other router is updated automatically with Inter-Satellite Link.

Keywords: Networking Satellites · Software Maintenance · Automatic Updating

1 Introduction

With the rapid development of space industry, the types and functions of satellites are also expanding, while the development cycle of satellites is constantly shortening. In order to adapt to the expansion of the complexity of satellite functions and the compression of the development cycle, the satellite functions trends to be more and more defined and implemented by software. Therefore there are more and more embedded software and FPGA items in a satellite (hereinafter referred to as software without distinction). At present, a large satellite has hundreds of software items, and even one electronic unit with complex functions has more than a dozen.

R. Li et al. (Eds.): MOBILWARE 2022, LNICST 507, pp. 106–116, 2023.
https://doi.org/10.1007/978-3-031-34497-8_9

Function based-on-software brings great flexibility to the realization of satellite functions [1]. An important feature is that some core function can be maintained onboard, that is, after the satellite is launched into orbit, the satellite functions can also be modified by changing the software code. Onboard software maintenance mainly has the following three design necessities or requirements: First, correcting software errors. Due to the shortening of satellite development cycle and the enlargement of functional complexity, many software functions are not fully tested on the ground, and cannot be debugged completely. The second is to adapt to the space operation environment. Due to the radiation characteristics of space environment, the software program carrier may have errors caused by memory bit reversal. In order to correct these errors, the software needs to be maintained onboard. Third, software functions upgrading. With the advancement of satellite in orbit operation, it may be necessary to add some new functions or upgrade the original functions, which also requires the software to have the function of onboard maintenance [2–4].

Onboard software maintenance needs to be considered in the system design. The software items that need to be maintained need to be supported in the hardware design. For example, the software program memory needs to be designed into EEPROM or flash that can be rewritten many times. At the same time, the satellite OBDH software needs to be able to support the data receiving and distribution processing of satellite software program data.

At present, the design of onboard software maintenance is mostly for a single satellite. The ground TT&C system uploads the data of a software program into the OBC frame-by-frame according to the format of special data frame. The program data are analyzed and distributed by OBC and finally received and stored by an electronic unit where the software item is located. These operations are executed and written into the memory with one-by-one instruction. The data go through multiple steps, and the slowest step will become the bottleneck of the maintenance system, resulting in low efficiency and high complexity of onboard maintenance operations.

As many satellites add inter satellite links for networking operation, the efficiency will not meet the requirements of simultaneous maintenance of many satellites while the above method is used to maintain the satellite software program one by one.

2 Single Satellite Onboard Software Maintenance

The design of single satellite onboard software maintenance is relatively mature. The operation mainly uploads the software data from the ground TT&C station frame by frame into the memory of the target software program. Figure 1 shows the maintenance path diagram of an electronic unit on a satellite, which is a common software onboard maintenance scheme of the current satellite. The electronic unit has an SRAM-based FPGA that needs to be maintained. The ground system needs to cut the configuration data of the FPGA into data blocks continuously and organize them into telecontrol frames. The ground TT&C system uploads these frames into the satellite one by one through the TT&C channel. The frames will reach the CMD receiving block of the OBC through transponder, and parsed and distributed to the maintenance-needed electronic unit through the corresponding interface (1553B bus interface in the example). After received by electronic unit, the maintenance data frame will be written into program memory by the FPGA control block, which is generally realized by a highly reliable anti-fuse FPGA or a special AISC.

In the single satellite maintenance scheme [2], the telecontrol data frames are directly written into the program memory frame by frame, without corresponding collection, storage, processing and distribution. For example, the OBC only takes instruction decoding and forwarding. The correctness of the configuration item data is mainly guaranteed by the target electronic unit itself, while the transponder and OBC only guarantees the correctness of channel decoding and the verification of the instruction data frame, respectively. In this mode, the efficiency of onboard software maintenance is determined by the slowest of the three links: first, the rate of the TT&C channel (① in Fig. 1); The second is the bus data transmission rate from the OBC to the electronic unit (② in Fig. 1); The third is the rate at which the FPGA control block writes data to the program memory (③ in Fig. 1). For example, if the rate of uploading from TT&C channel is 100kbps, the transfer rate allocated by the bus is only 10kbps, and the write rate of program memory is 50kbps, then the effective rate of software maintenance can only be 10kbps. Therefore, the efficiency of onboard software maintenance is greatly reduced, and the cost of updating operation is increased accordingly. This problem will become more prominent as the satellite is configured with a higher-speed TT&C channel.

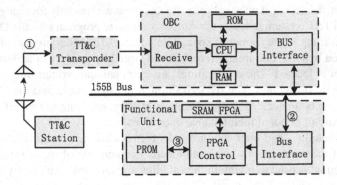

Fig. 1. Onboard software maintenance diagram for single satellite

Table 1. Configuration data size of common SRAM-based FPGAs

NO	FPGA	Configuration data size (bit)
1	XC2V3000(V2)	10,494,368
2	XC4VSX55(V4)	22,744,832
3	XC5VFX130T(V5)	49,234,944
4	XC7K325T(K7)	91,548,896
5	XC7VX690T(V7)	229,878,496

In order to solve the problems of low efficiency, the OBC can be configured with a large RAM to cache the maintenance data frames quickly uploaded from the ground into RAM, and then distribute them according to the corresponding rate [5]. With the increasing scale of FPGAs used on satellites, the amount of configuration data of some FPGAs has reached 30 Mega-bytes (see Table 1), and the SRAM configured by the OBC has been unable to meet the cache requirements of maintenance data frames, so it is necessary to deploy large-capacity SDRAM memory.

3   Networking Satellite Onboard Software Maintenance

3.1   Characteristics of Networking Satellites and Software Items

All satellites operating in a network have exactly the same or similar functions, such as one certain generation of GPS navigation satellites. Each satellite has the same software list, and the functions of the given software programs are also the same. For example, inter-satellite link data processing FPGAs, which are allocated on each satellite, are given the same functions.

Are all the software program data with the same functions on networking satellites consistent? It is needed to be divided into two cases: embedded CPU software and FPGA.

For embedded CPU software program with identical functions, the program data may also be inconsistent, mainly manifested in the inconsistency of some parameters, such as SCID. Storing these parameters as important data in the nonvolatile memory can achieve the consistency of program data. When the software is initialized and running, it loads the corresponding parameters to complete the configuration of the software function. Some embedded CPU software with different functions can be processed with different branches, and the control of which still uses state parameters. For example, the different functions of the two satellites are A and B, which are controlled by the state parameter S. If $S = 0$, execute the A function, otherwise $S = 1$, execute the B function, and the S parameter needs to be saved as an important parameter.

The configuration data of FPGA with the same function is almost consistent in networking satellites, and the configuration of some different parameters can be set by CPU software. Some satellites within networking constellation have inconsistent functions. For example, some satellites are configured with two inter satellite links, while others are configured with five inter satellite links, so the functions of inter satellite link data processing FPGA are different. Under this situation, different status satellites can be identified by making different settings on the peripheral pins of FPGA. For example, pulling down a pin (logic level is 0) and pulling up (logic level is 1) indicate the satellite configured with two and five inter satellite links respectively.

Therefore, the software program data of networking satellites with the same function can be the same, which makes it possible to realize the all networking satellites onboard software maintenance with one-time data uploads by TT&C systems. When the program data of one satellite are successfully updated in orbit, there is no need to upload data into other satellites. Sending the corresponding "copy" and "paste" commands to the satellites that have completed the update can achieve all the networking satellites software maintenance. This can greatly reduce the workload of maintenance operation.

3.2 System Design of Networking Satellites Onboard Software Maintenance

The network topology of satellites is usually divided into hybrid network and single network. The satellites of a single network are all located at the same orbital altitude. The satellites in the hybrid network are at different orbital altitudes, and interconnected by inter satellite links in the same and different orbits. For example, the BeiDou-3 Navigation Satellite System includes satellites with GEO–MEO orbital altitudes.

The maintenance design of networking satellites needs to select one satellite as the software maintenance server, which receives the uploading data from TT&C system to complete the software maintenance function of the satellite, and supports the sending of program data to other satellites through the inter satellite link.

For hybrid network satellites, the observation and control of higher orbit satellites has a long visible time, which is suitable as software maintenance server. For example, for the satellite network containing GEO orbiting satellites, GEO satellite is always visible from ground, and there are also visible arcs between GEO orbiting satellites and LEO satellites. Therefore, selecting one or more GEO as software maintenance servers can realize the software updates of the whole networking satellites.

For a single network, the design and hardware configuration of each satellite are the same, and the visibility from ground is basically the same. The visibility between satellites is related to the network topology.

Generally, it is impossible to maintain the software of the whole networking satellite with one satellite as the software maintenance server. Therefore, in a single network satellite system, each satellite can be used as a software maintenance server. After each satellite completes the reception and procession of the maintenance data, it can realize the distribution and transmission of the program data to the adjacent chain satellites.

4 Design Technologies of Software Maintenance Server

The software maintenance server is the core to realize the software updating of all the networking satellites. It has the functions of receiving, verification, storage and distribution of the uploaded data from TT&C system.

4.1 Receive and Verification of Reconstructed Data Annotation

Software maintenance server function is generally located in OBDH subsystem. Before sending the reconstructed data frame, one maintenance start instruction, which includes the software program identification, the number of maintenance data frames, is sent prior to data frames themselves. While receiving the instruction, the OBDH subsystem is ready to start receiving the maintenance data frames, which are uploaded from the ground TT&C system. The data frame format is generally virtual channel data unit (VCDU) [6], whose format is shown in Fig. 2.

The VCDU adopts the standard CCSDS format. The version number is a fixed value. The spacecraft identifier(SCID) is a unique identifier of the satellite. The virtual channel identifier (VCID) will be allocated according to the data type, and the maintenance data frame will be given a specially defined identifier. The symbol field and insertion field are fixed values, and each spacecraft will be designed and determined according to requirements. The data field contains a header and a segment of program data. The header contains the sequence information of frames and the characteristic information of the segmented program data. One software program data need to be divided into several same size data segments, which are placed in the VCDU data zone.

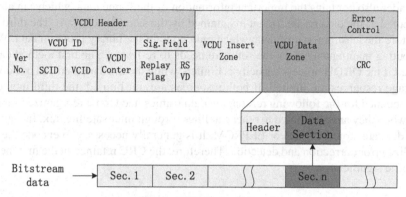

Fig. 2. VCDU data frame

After receiving the VCDU frame, the OBDH subsystem completes the CRC verification of each frame of data and temporarily stores each frame of data in RAM. When there is CRC error or frame loss according to the frame continuity interpretation, the corresponding frame will be re-uploaded from the ground. Then all frames of data are received correctly. The continuity of frames can be judged according to the VCDU counter or the frame sequence information in the header of data zone.

A program data verification instruction, which contains the verification code of the software data is sent from ground while all maintenance data frames are received correctly and completely. Then, the OBDH subsystem verifies the program data. If the verification code is consistent with the verification code in the verification instruction, it indicates that the program data uploading is correct, otherwise it needs to be uploaded again on the ground.

4.2 Maintenance Data Processing and Storage

As a software maintenance server, all uploaded maintenance data need to be stored for subsequent writing into memory or distribution to other satellites. Program data can be stored in RAM or flash. RAM is not suitable for long-term storage of maintenance data due to data loss of power failure. After receiving maintenance data, the OBDH subsystem can temporarily cache it in RAM. Flash or EEPROM is suitable for long-term data storage, because data in which can be saved even when it is powered down. Therefore, the maintenance data needs to be stored in high-capacity flash or EEPROM after receiving and checking.

According to the way of storing data, it can be divided into three ways. The first is to store the whole VCDU frame, the second is to store the VCDU data containing the header in Fig. 2 (striping the VCDU Head, VCDU Insert Zone and CRC), and the third is to store only program data (striping Header of data zone after the second way). The first way needs the most storage space. Its advantage is that it includes CRC verification, which can be used as checking code. In addition, if the configuration items of the local satellite are maintained, the format of the data frame sent and output can be VCDU format, which can reduce the re-framing expense. The second way is to store less data. At the same time, the header also contains the important information of the frame data, which can also be distributed as the data frame format maintained by the satellite software. The third way is to store the least amount of data, which only contain the binary program data. When distributing maintenance data, the software needs to re-frame. The first method can be adopted if the OBDH process capacity is limited, while the third method can be adopted if storage resources are limited. If both resources are not limited, the third method is recommended for the following reason: the data frames need to be reorganized for both ways when they are distributed to other satellites through inter satellite link. In addition, when data are stored in flash or EEPROM, it is generally necessary to encode the data to realize error correction and detection. Therefore, the CRC retained in the first method is of little significance.

4.3 Maintenance Data Distribution

When receiving the ground command to start the maintenance of a software program on the local satellite, the OBDH subsystem reads the maintenance data from flash and completes the verification, and then re-frame the data according to the local data transmission protocol to distribute the data to the destination electronic unit, which completes the receiving, storage and processing of the maintenance data. The process of software maintenance of local satellite is shown in Fig. 3.

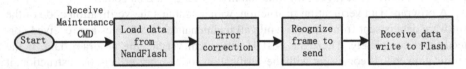

Fig. 3. Software maintenance data distribution process for local satellite

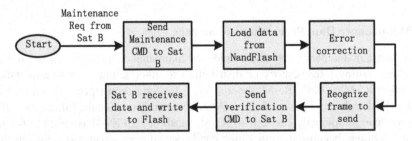

Fig. 4. Software maintenance data distribution process for slave satellite

When the local satellite receives the maintenance instructions sent by the ground to other satellites, the local satellite needs to send the following commands autonomously through the inter satellite link: a). Send the maintenance start instruction so that the destination satellite begins to prepare to receive maintenance data; b). Read out the maintenance data from flash and complete the verification, reorganize the frame according to the data frame format of the inter satellite link and send it to the destination satellite frame by frame. The destination satellite will return some telemetry information of the received maintenance frame. The local satellite can reissue the lost frame and wrong frame information according to the telemetry judgment until all data frames are correctly sent to the destination satellite; c). Send the maintenance data verification command. After the verification is correct, the destination satellite writes the data into flash to complete the receiving process of maintenance data. The whole distribution process is shown in Fig. 4.

If data frame format also adopts AOS for inter satellite link, the frame format is also mainly VCDU, which may have the following differences from the VCDU frame format uploaded to the local satellite from the ground: a). Frame length of VCDU; b). Spacecraft identifier in VCDU leader; c). VCDU insertion field; d). CRC check.

4.4 Design of Automatic Updating of Networking Satellite Software

According to the data distribution design in above section, it is necessary to send control instructions from the ground and maintain the software program one by one. The advantage of this updating method is high reliability. The designer confirms the necessity and feasibility of software updating. However, the workload of manual updating will be unbearable when the scale of networking satellites increases to hundreds.

At present, most of the ground consumer electronic product supports automatic software update. When it is detected that its software version is lower than the software version of the server, it can send an update application to the server and then update the software to the latest version with the user authorization. The software server of ground consumer electronic products has strong performance and can support all users' software update applications. The performance of the software maintenance server of the networking satellites is not much different from that of other satellites, and it is difficult to support the same automatic update method as the ground system.

In order to reduce the link length of software maintenance data transmission, it is more reasonable to use the hand-in-hand software automatic update method, which means that the data updated by the satellite software come from the adjacent satellites with established connections. All adjacent satellites regularly send version information of all their software to each other. When the software version is consistent, it does not need to be updated; otherwise, satellites with older software versions can send software update requests to "hand in hand" satellites. The specific operation process is as follows: a). The ground injects the software update program as well as version information and the applicable satellite lists into the software maintenance server Sat-A through the satellite ground link. b). Sat-A sends the software version information to "hand in hand" Sat-B through the inter satellite link. When Sat-B finds that the software version is higher than the current version itself and the applicable satellite list includes Sat-B, it sends the software update request to Sat-A. c). After receiving the software update request, Sat-A will send software update data to Sat-B according to the method in above section. d). While updating all data and runs successfully, Sat-B will send the updated software version information to the other satellites. When the version of other satellites software "hand in hand" with Sat-B is lower than this version, the same method to send a software update request to Sat-B can be achieved.

In the above method of automatic software update, there are two problems to be solved: a). When a satellite has multiple "hand in hand" satellites with software versions higher than its own, which one should it send a software update request? b). In the process of software update, the link time cannot meet the completion of data update. Should it wait until the next link building or switch to obtain software update data from other satellites?

For the first problem, in the case of non automatic, the ground selects a link to complete the software update at one time according to the satellite link conditions (such as link availability time and link rate). Under automatic conditions, after knowing all the "hand in hand" satellites currently available for software update, the target satellite needs to select a "hand in hand" satellite with the highest bandwidth for software update according to the link building planning table of the whole networking satellite. The bandwidth here is the link available time multiplied by the link rate.

For the second problem, Sat-A sends updated data to Sat-B. After finishing a part of updating, the link is interrupted. If waiting for the next link between Sat-B and Sat-A, it may take.

a long time, while the implementation is relatively simple. If there is a "hand-in-hand" Sat-C that can also send updated data, Sat-B can send a data software update request to Sat-C. At this time, the request information also includes the data package information that needs to be updated. The data package that has been received through Sat-A does not need to be re-transmitted. This implementation method is more complex. In the latter way, after rebuilding the available link between Sat-B and Sat-A, it is necessary to inform Sat-A that it is no longer necessary to send software update packets, unless B sends a software update request to Sat-A again.

5   Verification of Onboard Software Maintenance

Two space routers [7] were used for relevant maintenance tests in the laboratory. These two routers are used for one GEO and one MEO orbiting satellite respectively. The GEO satellite contains five high-speed inter satellite link ports, and the MEO satellite contains two ports. The high-speed forwarding blocks of the two routers are implemented with Virtex FPGA. The situation of the two FPGAs conforms to that described in section III and can be distinguished by setting of hardware pins. Pulling up the external pin of the FPGA of GEO satellite indicates that the FPGA has five high-speed inter satellite link ports, and pulling down the corresponding external pin of the FPGA of MEO satellite indicates that the FPGA has two ports.

The basic structure of the router for GEO satellites is shown in the Fig. 5. The difference between routers used for MEO satellites is that the ST pin of FPGA is pulled down to the ground through resistance, and there are two external high-speed inter satellite link interfaces. The on-board router includes CPU system, FPGA system and solid-state storage system. The CPU system includes processor, program memory PROM and data memory SDRAM, and the interface with FPGA system and storage system is

IO Bus. The FPGA system includes Virtex FPGA, controlling ASIC circuit and FPGA program memory Norflash. The CPU system can receive maintenance data from TT&C Circuits and write it into the program memory Norflash of FPGA through the controlling ASIC. The router can also receive maintenance data through the high-speed inter satellite link interface, forward it to the on-board CPU, and then write it into the program memory Norflash. Solid state storage system includes storage management circuit and solid state memory Nandflash (Fig. 6).

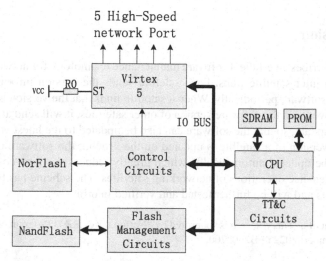

Fig. 5. Logical composition of GEO satellite on-board router

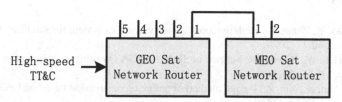

Fig. 6. Software maintenance test of networking satellites

According to one link state of the satellite in orbit, GEO satellite high-speed port one is connected with MEO satellite high-speed port one by cable, indicating that the two satellites are linked in orbit. In the initial state, the Virtex FPGA version number of both routers is 0x00, and then the program of GEO satellite router Virtex FPGA is updated to 0x01 version through the satellite ground high-speed TT&C system. At the same time, the configuration data are stored in the solid-state memory Nandflash. The version information is transmitted to the MEO satellite space router through the inter satellite link. When the MEO system finds that the program version of Virtex FPGA is lower than the FPGA program version of the GEO satellite, it immediately initiates an update application. After GEO orbiting satellite receives the request, its CPU software reads out the configuration data of version 0x01 in the solid-state memory into SDRAM and completes the verification. Then it is re-split and packaged to form maintenance data frame to send to MEO satellite, according to the inter satellite link data frame format between the two satellites. The MEO satellite stores all the configuration data in SDRAM when it receives the maintenance data frames through the inter satellite port one. After the data frames are collected completely, all the configuration data are written into the program memory Norflash of FPGA. The whole maintenance process takes about half an hour without manual intervention.

6 Conclusion

This paper describes an efficient software maintenance technology for networking satellites by using inter satellite links. Each satellite sends the version information of its maintainable software periodically. When a satellite finds that the version of a software program is lower than the software version of other satellites, it will send an application for software update, so that the software can also be updated to the latest version. After the software version of a satellite is updated on the ground, the software of the whole network can be updated automatically, which greatly reduces the time cost of ground manual maintenance operations of networking satellites. The scheme has been verified by ground tests and will be further tested and verified in orbit.

Acknowledgments. This research is sponsored by "National Key R&D Program of China" with its research number: 2022YFB2902700.

References

1. Zan, P., Cao, Y., Zhang C.: High functional density avionics system for satellites. Chin. Space Sci. Technol. **40**(1) (2020)
2. Pang, B., Hao, W., Zhang, W.: Scheme of SRAM-FPGA On-orbit reconfiguration. Spacecraft Eng. **26**(5), 51–56 (2017)
3. Wang,W., Yan, X., Xiu, Z.: Design method of online reconstruction based on FPGA. Comput. Meas. Control **28**(12) (2020)
4. Yuan, S., Qu, Z., Shao, Y.: A low cost and high reliability FPGA on orbit reconfigurable load management scheme. Space Electron. Technol. **28**(12) (2017)
5. Xiong,H., Yan, G., Li, G.: Design of on-orbit software reconfiguration system of small satellite based on minimum system. J. Telemetry Tracking Command **41**(3) (2020)
6. Zeng, L., Yan, C.: Design and hardware implementation of virtual channel link control unit and VCDU multiplexing unit. Chin. Space Sci. Technol. **27**(2), 17 (2020)
7. Wu, W., Zhou, D., Yan, H.: Desing and implementation of high-speed space router. In: Six National Space Data System Conference (2019)

Model Based Development of Spacecraft OBDH Software

Zhenhui Dong$^{(\boxtimes)}$, Yahang Zhang, Peiyao Yang, Yiming Liu, and Xuan Chu

Institute of Spacecraft System Engineering, Beijing, China
564760683@qq.com

Abstract. In view of the difficulties faced by the current document driven development mode of software, this paper systematically introduces the research work of the model driven development mode of spacecraft OBDH(On-Board Data Handling) subsystem software. The business requirements of the OBDH subsystem software are modeled by Simulink, forming the OBDH subsystem software model architecture. After completing the model design of the basic functions such as remote control, telemetry, bus management and satellite time management, the model is simulated and verified, and the code is automatically generated. Finally, the hardware in the loop test is completed. This research has established a complete business chain of "requirement design - requirement modeling - model design and model in the loop - code automatic generation - hardware in the loop" for the spacecraft OBDH subsystem software, which has laid a foundation for model driven development of future OBDH software expansion functions.

Keywords: Model · Software · Spacecraft · OBDH

1 Introduction

In the traditional software development process, the design results of each stage are presented in the form of documents and transferred between stages, thus forming the document-based software development mode. However, with the increasing complexity of spacecraft software, the traditional document-based software development mode is facing more and more obvious difficulties, including backward representation, lack of early verification means, and difficulty in reuse.

For the above reasons, model driven software development has gradually attracted attention in recent years. Model Based Development (MBD) [1] refers to a software development method that takes Model Driven Architecture (MDA) [2] as the guiding ideology, takes models as the core of software development, and guides software understanding, design, construction, development, operation, maintenance and modification. Model driven development also makes the information transfer between each stage of software development process from the past documents to models, avoiding the huge pressure and island phenomenon caused by the need to synchronize design documents in software development.

© ICST Institute for Computer Sciences, Social Informatics and Telecommunications Engineering 2023
Published by Springer Nature Switzerland AG 2023. All Rights Reserved
R. Li et al. (Eds.): MOBILWARE 2022, LNICST 507, pp. 117–124, 2023.
https://doi.org/10.1007/978-3-031-34497-8_10

2 Design Idea

The functions of the OBDH subsystem software include managing the whole satellite bus network, telemetry, remote control, program control and satellite management [3]. The software is generally a multi process software based on the real-time operating system [4]. The OBDH subsystem is a typical discrete system and a strong real-time multitask system. Operations with high real-time requirements usually need to be handled in the interrupt processing program.

There are two main goals for the development of model driven OBDH software: 1) Build a universal spacecraft OBDH software architecture model and model the main business requirements. At the same time, the trusted model library is accumulated on the basis of software components to form organizational assets; 2) Find a model-based software development process suitable for spacecraft OBDH software, open up the whole process development link of model-based software development, build a prototype system of model-based software development mode, and objectively evaluate the impact of model-based software development mode on spacecraft OBDH software development efficiency and quality.

The overall design idea is divided into the following four parts. Each research content is progressive in order. The above research content is used as input, and the results are provided to the next research content, thus forming a research process of progressive and clear research purpose.

2.1 General Functional Requirements Modeling

The goal of conventional functional requirements modeling of spacecraft OBDH software is to quickly determine the logic and basic functions of the requirements object, establish the connection between the requirements and the model, and do not need to go deep into the internal details of the model. At this stage, it is required to quickly verify whether the data interface, input and output between the requirements and the complete system are reasonable, and determine the main business functions. Conventional function requirement modeling of spacecraft OBDH software mainly completes the abstraction and definition of business functions, and serves as the input and basis for subsequent modeling. The specific business logic and model architecture will be implemented in the subsequent stages after the rationality of the system layer is verified.

2.2 Model Architecture Design

After completing the modeling of the conventional functional requirements of the spacecraft OBDH software, this research starts the design and development of the spacecraft OBDH software model architecture, and develops a universal OBDH software architecture model that includes telemetry, remote control, bus communication management, satellite time management, memory read and other functions common to the spacecraft OBDH software. Based on the actual project needs and the technical characteristics of OBDH software, this research has built three different forms of software architecture models: 1) general software architecture model, in which component software can be integrated. The architecture has complete functions, and the model is simulated and verified. During the process of building the model architecture, the special model library for OBDHs is extracted and generated; 2) The general software architecture model and the self-developed general test software are connected through TCP/IP network, supporting telemetry downlink, receiving remote control commands, and supporting bus data simulation; 3) The general software architecture model and the underlying driver and operating system interface are jointly compiled through Makefile, and then the binary executable file can be directly downloaded to the hardware device or virtual simulation test software (such as the software test platform) for running.

2.3   Function Module Encapsulation and Model Library Construction

Model library organizes many functional models according to a fixed structure, and effectively manages and uses each functional module through a unified model base management system. From the perspective of software, each functional model in the model library is a model architecture that can be reused and assembled into an application system [5, 6]. It can be seen that the common model base is an important achievement of unified standardization construction. Through the modeling of business function requirements and the transformation of the component interface of OBDH software, a universal model library of OBDH software is formed. In the subsequent modeling work, the model library can be directly used in Simulink or call module encapsulation through C Caller to facilitate users to build new OBDH software architecture models.

2.4   Automatic Generation of Software Code

After building the spacecraft OBDH software model, the model-based spacecraft OBDH software code generation is carried out. Specifically, code generation based on Simulink model can use Simulink's own RTW tool to generate intermediate files in TLC format first, and then generate target C or C + + files according to the target file type configured by the user. At the same time, combined with the compiler set by the user, the target file can be compiled to generate an executable file [7].

During the code generation process of Simulink, for the configuration of peripheral models, some options in the sub model need to have the same configuration, such as optimization options and code generation format. However, for the configuration in Code Generation, such as whether to generate reusable code, and the way to generate reusable code peripheral interfaces, you only need to configure in the peripheral model, while the configuration in the internal sub model has no impact on the results. To ensure the consistency, effectiveness and efficiency of generated code, the generated code needs to be configured locally and follow certain configuration specifications. It includes simulation configuration, hardware environment configuration, overall configuration, report generation configuration, code annotation format configuration, interface configuration, etc. At the same time, in order to improve the readability, migration and reusability of generated code configuration, code style configuration, code template configuration, data type replacement configuration, and memory configuration are also required.

3 Model Based Development of OBDH Software

3.1 Software Requirements Modeling

This work adopts the architecture design tool System Composer in Simulink software, which is used for requirements modeling in the early stage of the project. First, use the Requirement Editor to sort and decompose the requirements, then use System Composer to model the software requirements, and establish the link between the requirements and the model. The correspondence between the requirement model and the design model can be realized by dragging the requirement items directly, and the completeness of the requirement realization can be verified. Figure 1. Shows the requirement model framework design and interface design.

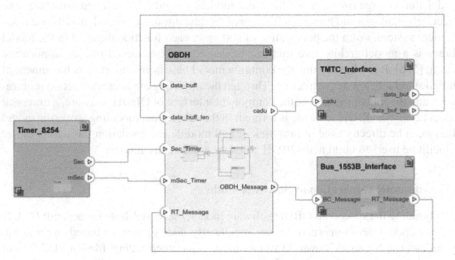

Fig. 1. Requirements model framework and external interface

3.2 Functional Model Architecture

The universal software function model architecture of OBDH is implemented by using Simulink/Stateflow toolbox, Simulink model library and Matlab M function. This research only models and generates code for the application layer of the OBDH software, and conducts some special processing and integration for the underlying hardware driver and the interface between the application software and the operating system. In addition, considering that spacecraft OBDH software has generally established an organizational asset library of software components, this part of code can be directly integrated into the entire software model without modeling and code generation. The general software architecture model includes telemetry, remote control, bus communication management, satellite time management, memory read and other requirements. Figure 2. Shows the overall architecture of OBDH model.

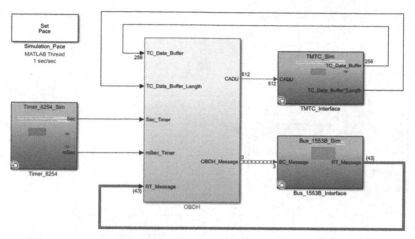

Fig. 2. Overall architecture of OBDH software model

3.3 Generate Code

Model driven software development needs to establish code generation configuration items according to the requirements of code generation. In this research, two different configuration sets are established, namely, the configuration set for simulation and the configuration set for code generation, so that the functions of model simulation and code generation are realized in a set of models. Users can browse and modify the contents of these two configuration sets through the Model Explorer tool.

After the simulation and verification of the OBDH software model is completed, C code can be generated. The generated C code can view the generated report and track the relationship with the model, as shown in Fig. 3. After the source code is generated according to the user's needs, the generated source file can be packaged, which facilitates the generation of source code to other compilation environments for compilation, running and debugging operations.

The automatically generated code is integrated with some handwritten codes (including software components, general library functions, and hardware drivers). By specifying and setting the main functions generated by different subsystems to achieve multitask scheduling, configuring Makefile files, adding macros required for compiling models, and finally jointly compiling the automatically generated code and handwritten code and downloading them to the hardware environment or virtual software testing environment for running.

In this study, the C code generated by model driven method totaled 5813 lines, including 12 C source files and 16 header files. There were 82 function modules in total, accounting for 21% of the engineering code (about 22000 lines of component, hardware driver and other handwritten code). There are two reasons why the code generated by the model accounts for a relatively low proportion in the total code. One is that this research mainly aims at technical verification, so only some software functions are used as examples for modeling and code generation. The other is that some models in this research are only used for model simulation and verification, not for code generation.

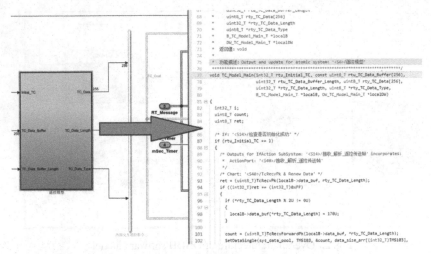

Fig. 3. Model code tracking

4   Simulation Verification

The spacecraft OBDH software model is based on the Matlab/Simulink standard model development environment. Through the Intermediate communication model, the interface between the spacecraft OBDH software model and the traditional ground test software is connected. Based on the existing mature ground test software, the rapid verification of the model in the loop and hardware in the loop of the spacecraft OBDH software model is realized, and the entire model-based development process is fully connected. The environment of the spacecraft OBDH software based on this method is shown in Fig. 4.

This research establishes a complete process from requirements management, model architecture, model design, code generation and simulation testing for spacecraft OBDH software. The model test environment is built, and the model closed-loop simulation test is carried out, and the consistency between the automatically generated code and the running results of the model is verified. The technical indicators achieved in this study are shown in Table 1.

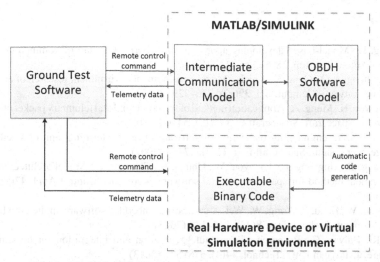

Fig. 4. Model-based development environment of OBDH software

Table 1. Technical indicators reached.

Index name	Achievement of indicators
Functional items covered by the model	A general model of OBDH software is established, which covers 5 types of OBDH software models and 3 types of software interface models
Automatically generate code	Automatic code generation time is within 30 s
Execution efficiency of automatically generated code	The SRAM used by the automatically generated code in the running process does not exceed 500KB; The average running time of the software after time equalization is less than 50 ms

5 Conclusions

This research changed the development mode of spacecraft OBDH software from the traditional handwritten coding development mode to the model driven development mode, and verified various technologies such as software requirement modeling, general architecture model, general model library, model simulation and verification, and software automatic generation. By connecting the existing general software test platform with the model, the efficiency of model simulation verification is improved. After model simulation verification, embedded software code is automatically generated, which can be directly run on the OBDH hardware equipment or virtual simulation platform after compilation. The simulation and verification of model can reuse existing organizational assets. This research has formed a complete model driven business chain of spacecraft OBDH software, laying a foundation for the subsequent model-based development of complex functions of OBDH software in the future.

References

1. Furong, L.: Model-based developing approach for airborne software of commercial engine. Process Autom. Instrum. **38**(6), 26–30 (2017)
2. Li, Y., Shenglin, G., Geng, C., Lei, L.: Model development environment research of embedded real-time software. Comput. Sci. **39**(z3), 226–229 (2012)
3. Xiaongwen, H., Meng, Z.: Application method of telecommand and telemetry packet utilization standard in spacecraft. Spacecraft Eng. **21**(3), 54–60 (2012)
4. He, X., Sun, Y.: engineering realization of software in central terminal unit of satellite data management system. Spacecraft Eng. **16**(5), 47–53 (2007)
5. Xiaogang, D., Jingsong, L., Dianyou, W., Chuan, L., Chaohui, C.: Model architecture based development method for spacecraft control software. Aerospace Control Appl. **47**(2), 55–62 (2021)
6. Wenquan, W., Kepu, S., Yong, W., Wei, X.: Airborne embedded software application based on MDA. Comput. Technol. Dev. **8**(23), 145–148 (2013)
7. Jiali, R., Haiyan, C.: Research of code auto-generation and integration for the embedded software. J. Taiyuan Univ. Technol. **44**(4), 518–521 (2013)

Design of Aerospace Cloud Computing Server Based on Docker Cluster

Zhenhui Dong[1]([✉]), Luyuan Wang[1], Bowen Cheng[1], Zhihong Xu[1], and Chaoji Chen[1,2]

[1] Beijing Institute of Spacecraft System Engineering, Beijing 100094, China
564760683@qq.com
[2] School of Mechanical Engineering, Tongji University, Shanghai 201804, China

Abstract. To solve the problems of different space-based application platforms, lack of unified specifications and poor real-time performance, this paper proposes a design scheme of space-based cloud server based on Docker cluster, drawing on the container technology and cloud native architecture used by ground cloud computing. The computing module of the space-based cloud server realizes network communication through the route switching module, and integrates a high-capacity storage module to complete data access. The real-time operating system running integrated container services on the computing module and the lightweight container cluster management framework realize the dynamic deployment and orchestration of space-based container applications. The design framework has been verified in the space-based cloud server prototype, and the test results show that the framework achieves universal high-performance computing, virtual resource integration scheduling, and autonomous task migration. In the future, it can be deployed to space-based satellite clusters to provide users with space-based cloud information services, including universal high-performance computing, information intelligent processing, etc.

Keywords: Docker · Cluster · Cloud Computing · Server

1 Introduction

After years of construction and development, although the ground-based information acquisition, transmission, processing and application systems with professional applications as the main goal have been initially built, these systems are distributed in different regions, belong to different management departments, and have different development platforms and lack of unified specifications, forming a pattern of "chimney development", resulting in low efficiency of resource use, difficulties in information sharing, poor timeliness of task response, etc. It restricts the full play of the resource efficiency of the entire space-based information system.

With the continuous deepening of the space based network demonstration, the space-based network information system with the ability of "super computing, fast storage, massive transmission and flexible reconstruction" is the core system that needs technical

R. Li et al. (Eds.): MOBILWARE 2022, LNICST 507, pp. 125–131, 2023.
https://doi.org/10.1007/978-3-031-34497-8_11

breakthrough. At the same time, in recent years, research institutions in various countries have carried out research on space-based high-performance computing technology, gradually exploring subversive computing methods, and steadily improving the computing efficiency of spacecraft. Under the background that satellite network has become a global hotspot, new technical requirements such as integrated satellite-terrestrial, satellite Internet, artificial intelligence applications, and on-board information processing pose serious challenges to satellite electronic information systems, which are facing a profound technological transformation. The future space-based network satellite information service system needs to break through the traditional architecture, and realize the leapfrog development of system capabilities and the fundamental transformation of product model through a new architecture design.

Cloud computing system, with its good universality, scalability and high reliability, provides a strong technical support for improving the service capability of spatial information service system [1]. In cloud computing, software and hardware are virtualized into logical resources. No matter what kind of device the terminal is, it can access services on demand through the network without paying attention to its internal structure and operation mode. The emergence of cloud computing technology provides a new idea for the implementation of spatial information services. The "space-based cloud" can directly provide service guarantee for users, and can also be used as a supplement and enhancement to the "ground-based cloud" to make up for the shortcomings of the "ground-based cloud" in terms of coverage, emergency support and mobile support capabilities.

2 Container Technology and Cloud Native Architecture

Virtualization refers to simulating physical hardware resources into multiple logical devices through software, and programs can run on independent logical devices without affecting each other. In virtualization technology, Docker plays an important role as an open-source container engine. Compared with traditional virtual machines, Docker containers are relatively lightweight. Docker daemons can directly communicate with the main control system, allocate resources to containers, and isolate containers from the main system and containers from each other [2]. Customized and integrated Docker operating system has the following advantages: 1) small size, fast startup; 2) The CPU does not need to support virtualization, and the hardware requirements are low; 3) Easy migration: Docker's image includes a complete environment that supports application operation, ensuring the consistency of the operating environment and facilitating migration; 4) Isolation: Docker applications are independent of the underlying infrastructure.

Cloud native technology is a collection of a series of technologies, including containers, container orchestration, microservices, DevOps and intelligent operation and maintenance technologies, among which containers are the core technologies of cloud native infrastructure [3, 4]. Cloud native is designed to deploy to the cloud. To ensure the successful operation of container applications, the operating system needs to support relevant services. Cloud Native widely adopts the Docker + Kubernetes technical architecture. Users can create application images based on needs and run them directly on the cloud.

The space-based cloud native technology adopts an open computing-storage-network architecture, and is based on the advantages of high-speed interconnection, space-time benchmark, and multi satellite global coverage of space-based networks to build a highly reliable and high-performance cloud native computing system architecture. Carry out system business analysis and function definition, have the ability of modularization, scalability, plug and play, flexible reconfiguration, realize the sharing and on-demand allocation of computing, storage, network resources, support the dynamic migration of tasks, the migration process is uninterrupted, users are not aware of it, the single machine in a single satellite processes the task load balance, and the satellite in a constellation processes the task load balance.

In view of the requirements for information security, fault isolation and recovery, reliability and real-time of the future space-based information service system, the physical hardware resources are simulated as multiple logical devices through container virtualization technology, and programs can run on mutually independent logical devices without mutual influence, thus providing a lightweight isolation environment for software development, deployment and operation. Based on the lightweight container management platform, the integration of container application development and operation and maintenance is realized, and the intelligent model is rapidly deployed to the space-based network environment. When a computing node in the system fails, the container instance will be automatically scheduled to other redundant nodes to ensure the continuous operation of the business.

3 Design of Space-Based Cloud Computing Server

The space-based cloud native high-performance processing platform system requires a high degree of intelligence, networking and systematization. The traditional space-based information system cannot meet the requirements in terms of computing capacity, storage capacity, communication speed and distributed collaboration. In order to achieve high-speed transmission, intelligent processing, mass storage and other space-based distributed cloud information services, the space-based cloud computing server is designed based on the SpaceVPX standard. Based on the SpaceVPX standard, the hardware modules with different functions are assembled to form a combined application product. The hardware modules are connected through backplane buses at different levels, so as to achieve a high degree of flexibility and scalability in the information interaction between the modules in the whole machine. The prototype of the space-based cloud server is internally integrated with high-performance computing module, high-capacity storage module and routing switching module, realizing the integration of computing, storage and network resources.

The layered design of the Docker based cloud server system is shown in Fig. 1. It consists of five elements: high-performance computing module, customized lightweight on-board operating system, container cluster management middleware, container application, and Rancher monitoring system. After integrating the virtualization container technology on the customized lightweight operating system and realizing the application service containerization, the container applications can be scheduled and deployed through the container cluster management middleware, so as to achieve the resource virtualization and balanced scheduling of multiple physical computing units in the satellite, provide a unified standard virtual operating environment for various users and applications, and achieve on-demand resource allocation and elastic computing.

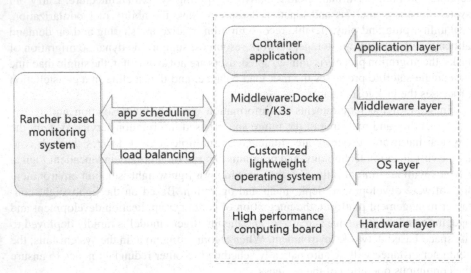

Fig. 1. Layered design of space-based cloud server system

3.1 Design of Real-Time Operating System for Integrated Container

The traditional embedded real-time operating systems such as VxWorks and RTEMS are not completely suitable for the application scenarios of space-based cloud services after being customized. The reason is that space-based cloud services require the operating system to support virtualization, cloud native, AI and other technologies in addition to the high real-time requirements of the operating system. However, the early embedded real-time operating systems in the aerospace field have limited functions and poor software ecology. At present, Linux operating system is widely used in cloud computing servers on the ground. Although it is not a hard real-time operating system, the real-time performance can be greatly improved to microseconds by inserting RT-patch into the Linux kernel, which can meet the requirements of real-time processing on the satellite.

Integrating Docker services into the Linux operating system depends on the Yocto project [5], which requires the support of multiple components such as meta-virtualization, meta-networking, meta-filesystems, and meta-python. The above components can be obtained from the Internet and added to bblayers.conf file through the bitbake-layers add-layer command. After that, the local.conf file is configured and the system is compiled during the system configuration. After the compilation is successful, the QEMU tool integrated by Yocto can be used for simulation testing to verify the availability of Docker services. It should be noted that the Linux kernel layer needs to be customized to support Docker to work in bridge mode. The Docker image created after the kernel configuration is completed can work normally.

3.2 K3s Based Container Cluster Management

The onboard operating system integrating Docker obtains the application image from the Docker's official public repository by default. Due to the special operating environment of the onboard computer, it cannot connect to the public repository, so you need to configure a private image source. Select a node in the cluster as the private repository of the container image. The user uploads the image of the satellite application to the private warehouse. When deploying K3s, specify each node in the cluster to obtain the image from the private repository.

K3s is a lightweight cloud native framework based on Kubernetes [6]. A single node can be selected as the single node architecture of the server side. The K3s cluster of the single node architecture can theoretically meet all the task requirements. The architecture is shown in Fig. 2. In a single node architecture, the cluster has only one K3s server node and embedded SQLite database. Each agent node is registered to the same server node. The administrator of the K3s cluster can directly allocate all node resources in the cluster through the cluster API functions on the K3s server node.

Deploying K3s in the on-board computer environment can facilitate the management of container applications on multiple computing cells to achieve load balancing and resource integration among computing cells, thus further realizing multi cell collaborative computing. In addition, K3s can realize the migration of cluster content application, so as to ensure the reliable operation of applications in the K3s cluster.

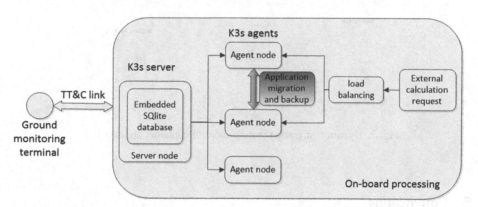

Fig. 2. K3s based container cluster management

4 Instance Verification

On the prototype of the space-based cloud server, the K3s based container cluster management is verified by an example. In order to facilitate the deployment and management of containers, the container management platform Rancher is installed on the space-based cloud servicer. The Rancher Server can be deployed in one of the high-performance computing modules. The ground-based monitoring terminal can intuitively monitor the health status and capacity of the container cluster through the browser, and perform elastic resource allocation.

Three high-performance computing modules are deployed in the prototype computer. One of them is selected as the server node of K3s, and the other two are selected as agent nodes (agent1 and agent2 respectively). The Rancher Server is deployed on the server node. Figure 3 shows the dynamic migration management of container applications in cloud computing services. In the case test process, after the initial deployment of 10 container applications, the three nodes ran multiple container applications according to the equilibrium strategy. The agent2 node was manually isolated from the system. The container applications originally running on the agent2 node were automatically migrated to the server node and agent1 node. After the agent2 node is rejoined to the system, after deleting multiple container applications from the server node and agent1 node, some of the deleted container applications will be automatically migrated and deployed to agent2 node according to the load balancing policy.

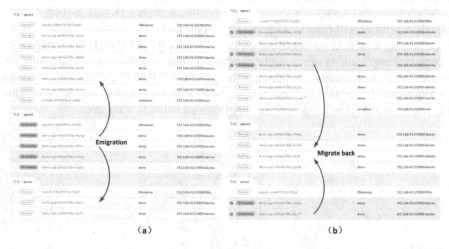

(a)   (b)

Fig. 3. Dynamic migration management of container applications

5   Conclusions

To improve the business carrying capacity of on-board computer, on the one hand, it depends on the improvement of hardware computing power, and on the other hand, it needs the support of on-board computer application software. The current on-board application software has some compatibility problems when running on cross platform systems. At the same time, the special software ecological environment of on-board computers adds inconvenience to software deployment. Running the application software on the on-board computer in the form of a container can not only solve the compatibility problem during software deployment, but also improve the security of on-board applications through resource isolation between containers. At the same time, the container cluster management method is used to deploy satellite applications on multiple computing cells. The container application can be deployed on multiple computing cells with one click only once. After the application of container technology, the development and maintenance efficiency of on-board software will be greatly improved.

Acknowledgment. This research is sponsored by "National Key R&D Program of China" with its research number:2022YFB2902700.

References

1. Straub, J., Mohammad, A.:Above the cloud computing: applying cloud computing principles to create an orbital services model. In: The 6th Proceeding on Sensors and Systems for Space Applications. Washington D. C., pp. 879–879. SPIE (2013)
2. Bo, P., Peng, Y., Zhicheng, M., Jianguo, Y.: Performace measurement and analysis of ARM embedded platform using Docker container. J. Comput. Appl. **37**(S1), 325–330 (2017)
3. He, Z., Huang, D., Yan, L., Lin, Y., Yang, X.: Kubernetes based converged cloud native infrastructure solution and key technologies. Telecommun. Sci. **36**(12), 77–88 (2020)
4. Lu, G., Chen, C., Huang, Z., Huang, Z.: Research on intelligent cloud native architecture and key technologies for cloud and network integration. Telecommun. Sci. **36**(9), 67–74 (2020)
5. Du, D., Hu, A., Li, L., Zhang, Y.: Customizing Linux distribution based on the Yocto. Microcomput. Appl. **35**(14), 68–70 (2016)
6. Qiuxia, Y., Bin, Z., Lin, L., Yingying, W., Le, C.: Analysis of cloud native based edge computing products and projects. Inf. Commun. Technol. **15**(4), 71–78 (2021)

Integrated Satellite-Terrestrial Intelligent Information Processing, Decision and Planning (1)

Analysis and Simulation of High Orbit Weak Signal Tracking Algorithm

Xiaojiang Yang, Qian Yu$^{(\boxtimes)}$, and Dongbo Pei

Space Star Technology Company Limited, Beijing 100195, China
yuqian818@126.com

Abstract. Autonomous navigation technology of high orbit spacecraft is one of new aerospace techniques that are badly in need of development in China. It is widely used in communication, navigation, meteorology, early warning and other fields. High orbit navigation receiver provides a convenient and effective means for autonomous navigation and positioning of high orbit spacecraft. In the high dynamic environment, the carrier frequency, phase and pseudo code phase change greatly along with the supporter motion. Because the influence of Doppler frequency change introduced by supporter dynamics on pseudo code tracking loop can be eliminated by carrier assistance, the dynamic performance of receiver mainly depends on the carrier tracking module. The increase of propagation path and high dynamic signal of high orbit leads to problems of large loss of received signal path and weak signal of high orbit navigation receiver. Through carrying out special research on high orbit weak signal tracking technology, several simulations and analyses, reasonable design of loop noise bandwidth, adjustment of pre-integration time and other measures, the navigation weak signal of −173 dBw can be effectively and stably processed and traced. The algorithm has been applied to Chang'E-5 satellite, and provides technical guidance and index reference for deep space exploration projects, such as high orbit satellite navigation and circumlunar flying.

Keywords: High orbit spacecraft · Autonomous navigation · Weak signal · Loop · Integral time

1 Introduction

High earth orbit satellite includes geostationary orbit (GEO) satellite and highly eccentric orbit (HEO) satellites whose maximum orbit altitude is generally higher than 20,000 km. Currently, high orbit satellites are playing an increasingly important role in communication, navigation, meteorology, early warning and other fields. Autonomous navigation technology of high orbit spacecraft is one of new aerospace technologies needing to be developed urgently in China, and the use of navigation receivers in high orbit spacecraft has become the mainstream of engineering applications [1]. The biggest difference between the application of high orbit spacecraft navigation receivers and the terrestrial

© ICST Institute for Computer Sciences, Social Informatics and Telecommunications Engineering 2023
Published by Springer Nature Switzerland AG 2023. All Rights Reserved
R. Li et al. (Eds.): MOBILWARE 2022, LNICST 507, pp. 135–149, 2023.
https://doi.org/10.1007/978-3-031-34497-8_12

receivers is that the former needs to receive navigation satellite signals from the opposite side of the Earth. The increase in signal propagation path leads to the problem of large loss of path and weak received signal. Research on navigation with weak GPS signals started at the end of the 20th century and has been carried out on HEO, MEO, and GEO satellites for several on-orbit applications, verifying the availability of weak signals of sidelobes of GPS navigation satellites in high orbit [2, 3]. For example, the U.S. TEAMST-YES and Falcon Gold missions confirm that GEO transfer orbit satellites can successfully track GPS signals at an altitude of 26,000 km and send back GPS sampling data for ground processing; German Equator-S project operated in HEO orbit and successfully tracked the GPS sidelobe signal at an altitude of 61,000 km; in China, the GNSS high orbit receiver developed by Space Star Technology Company Limited was successfully applied to Chang'E-5 flight test vehicle, which completed GPS/GLONASS navigation signal reception and realized real-time navigation and positioning orbit determination algorithm in 50,000 km transfer orbit, and obtained high orbit GNSS signal characteristics with real-time orbit determination position accuracy of 15.8 m during 48 h continuous navigation tracking (3-axis, 1 σ). With the further development of navigation technology, China has realized the global network of Beidou-3 satellite navigation system. In order to adapt to the rapidly developing navigation market and the further demand of high orbit navigation tasks, it is necessary to carry out the research of high orbit GPS/BD2/GLONASS multi-system combined high-precision orbit determination [4–9] and its weak signal capture and tracking technology, among which the solution of long-term tracking without frequency loss is the key to stabilize the subsequent positioning algorithm.

The algorithm studied in this article is applied to the Chang'E-5 GNSS high orbit receiver. Based on the theory of weak signal tracking in high orbit and high dynamic environment, we analyze the loop tracking error and combine with the actual engineering application requirements, to simulate the weak signal tracking algorithm, verify the effectiveness of the algorithm, and derive the minimum limit of weak signal that can be tracked in the loop under the algorithm. In order to explore the application feasibility of the deep space navigation devices such as circumlunar flying, we conduct in-depth research on the combination of multiple systems, such as Beidou-3, GPS, GLONASS and other devices and carry out multi-fusion high orbit high precision navigation, so as to provide theoretical and engineering basis.

2 Tracking Principle of Weak Signal

There have been many studies on the principle of weak signal capture and tracking [10–15], among which, two processing methods based on the Square Root of Kalman Filter with inversion of unknown navigation bits have achieved better results in tracking weak signals [16].

Since the carrier tracking loop is the weak link of stand-alone receiver, its tracking threshold determines characteristics of the latter. The scheme of carrier pre-detection integrator, carrier discriminator and carrier filter determines characteristics of the receiver carrier tracking loop. Carrier loops are usually implemented using PLL (Phase Lock Loop, PLL) and FLL (Frequency Lock Loop, FLL). The three functions of pre-detection integrator, discriminator and loop filter determine characteristics of the carrier loop. The characteristics of the carrier tracking loop of navigation receiver [17, 18] are shown in Fig. 1.

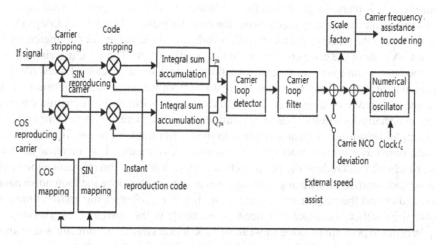

Fig. 1. Carrier tracking loop of navigation receiver

The Phase Lock Loop (PLL) aims to lock the phase of the input carrier signal. By adjusting the phase of the output signal, the phase between the output signal and the input signal can be consistent at all times [19, 20]. In practice, since the input to the PLL is not a continuous time signal, the corresponding PLL is in digital form. Considering the on-satellite dynamic effects, general onboard navigation receivers are mainly used in three-order PLL loop applications. The Costas loop has become a fairly common carrier loop for navigation receivers due to its insensitivity to 180° carrier phase shifts caused by data bit jumps.

When the discriminator of the PLL is used directly to discriminate the frequency difference between the input carrier and the copied carrier, the corresponding carrier loop becomes a frequency lock loop (FLL). Because the relative motion between the navigation satellite and the receiver causes Doppler shift, and the frequency drift of the receiver oscillator is unknown, the FLL needs to identify the frequency difference between the input carrier and the copied carrier, and adjust the copied carrier frequency output from the CNC oscillator accordingly, and achieve the same frequency with the input carrier after several adjustments. The FLL discriminator requires 2 samples in a data jump interval, and the maximum pre-detection integration time of FLL is 10 ms, and the ATAN2 discriminator is generally used as the discriminator in the case of low signal-to-noise ratio.

The main function of the code loop is to maintain the phase agreement between the copied C/A code and the received C/A code, and further to obtain the measurement of the received code phase as well as the pseudorange [21]. The settings of the programmable pre-detection integrator, code loop discriminator and code loop filter determine the characteristics of the receiver code tracking loop. During the operation of the receiver, the code loop tracking module reproduces three receiver recurrent codes, advancing, immediate and lagging, which are correlated with the carrier stripped satellite signal, and the correlated signal is then integrated into the code loop discriminator, and the recurrent code is adjusted by the adjustment variables of the control CNC oscillator, so that the recurrent code is phase-aligned with the modulated PRN code of the received signal.

Similar to the carrier loop mechanism, the code loop uses a Delay Lock Loop (DLL), which can infer the phase of the received C/A code based on the control parameters of the copied C/A code or the code numerical control oscillator, etc. The DLL discriminator is smoothed to contain a non-zero mean noise floor, especially in the case of weak received signals, where accurate measurement of the noise floor becomes more important [22].

Generally, navigation receivers use PLL for carrier tracking. For dynamic environments, especially for satellite-based navigation receivers, there are large Doppler shifts and Doppler shift rates of change, mainly in the carrier tracking loops. To adapt to the satellite-based dynamic environment, the most effective method is to increase the loop noise bandwidth and reduce the pre-detection integration time. But, to reduce the effect of noise and improve the tracking accuracy, it is necessary to reduce the loop noise bandwidth and extend the pre-detection integration time (i.e., coherent integration time). To resolve the conflict, a compromise needs to be made in the design of the carrier loop [23]. In order to perform tracking of weak signals, it is necessary to simulate and analyze the tracking error of PLL, FLL and code loop, so as to design the tracking loop and code loop accordingly.

3 Error Analysis of Loop Tracking

3.1 Error Analysis of Phase Lock Loop (PLL)

The main sources of phase errors in the PLL circuit are phase jitter and dynamic stress errors. The phase jitter is the square root of the sum of the squares of the individual uncorrelated phase noise sources, which include thermal noise and oscillator noise, which in turn contains jitter caused by vibration and jitter caused by Allan Variance. Since the 3σ phase error caused by all noise sources should not exceed 450, the corresponding 1σ empirical method is to set the tracking threshold of the PLL to 150. In addition, other PLL jitter sources may be transient or negligible, so thermal noise is usually used as the only source of carrier tracking error. PLL thermal noise jitter is shown in Fig. 2.

As can be seen in Fig. 2(a), the PLL thermal noise jitter intensity is much smaller than the tracking threshold and flat under normal signal conditions ($C/N_0 \approx 44$ dB/Hz). As the carrier noise ratio decreases, the jitter intensity accelerates and the PLL tracking error becomes larger, making the tracking loop unstable. PLL thermal noise jitter is proportional to the square of the loop bandwidth and decreases with increasing cumulative summing time. Therefore, the PLL thermal noise jitter can be reduced by increasing the cumulative summing time and reducing the loop bandwidth. It should be noted that in a general signal tracking loop, the cumulative summing time is limited by the data code length, and reducing the loop bandwidth will compromise the dynamic performance of the loop.

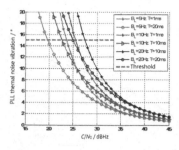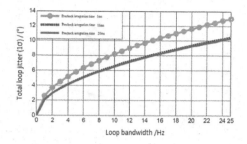

Fig. 2. Left (a): PLL thermal noise jitter, right (b): Relationship between PLL loop bandwidth and measurement error

Figure 2(b) shows the PLL loop jitter corresponding to different bandwidths at $C/N_0 = 29dB/Hz$, which can reflect the relationship between PLL loop bandwidth and measurement error.

Conduct simulation for the error of PLL tracking. Analysis of the simulation results in Fig. 2(b) shows that the pre-detection integration time of 1 ms, 10 ms and 20 ms can meet the requirement of total loop error less than 15° in the case of $C/N_0 = 29dB/Hz$ and jerk of 0 for the loop bandwidth from 0 to 18 Hz. The loop error of the pre-detection integration time of 20 ms is overall smaller than the loop error when the pre-detection integration time is 1ms, while the error of the pre-detection integration time of 10ms is not much different from the error of 20 ms.

3.2 Error Simulation and Analysis of Frequency Lock Loop (FLL)

Similar to PLL, the source of frequency measurement error of FLL also includes two parts: frequency jitter and dynamic stress error, where the frequency jitter is mainly caused by thermal noise, while the amount of frequency jitter caused by mechanical jitter and Allan Variance is neglected because it is relatively small [24]. Dynamic stress of FLL is much better at the same noise bandwidth and C/N_0. With reduced pre-detection integration time, dynamic stress performance of FLL will be improved to some extent. In addition, since the FLL discriminator requires two samples in one data jump interval, the maximum pre-detection integration time of FLL is 10 ms for C/A codes.

The main sources of FLL frequency errors are also thermal noise frequency jitter and dynamic stress errors. The effect of frequency jitter caused by base oscillator vibration and Allan Variance on FLL is small and negligible. For the FLL circuit, the empirical tracking threshold is that the jitter 3σ value caused by all loop stress sources is not allowed to exceed 90°within one pre-detection integration time t.

Figures 4 and 5 show the relationship curves of thermal noise jitter versus loop bandwidth for the same carrier noise ratio with different pre-detection times, and the relationship curves of thermal noise jitter versus loop bandwidth for the same pre-detection integration time with different carrier noise ratios, respectively.

As can be seen from Fig. 3, the thermal noise jitter of FLL is proportional to the loop bandwidth, inversely proportional to the pre-detection time and the carrier noise ratio, and independent of the spreading code rate and the loop filter order.

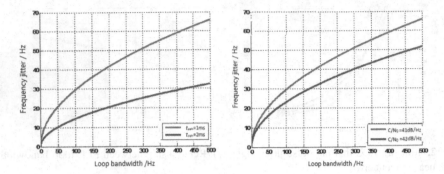

Fig. 3. Left(a): Thermal noise jitter under the same carrier noise ratio and different pre-detection time, right(b): Thermal noise jitter under the same pre-detection time and different carrier noise ratio.

Figure 4 shows the FLL loop jitter corresponding to different bandwidths at $C/N_0 = 29\text{dB/Hz}$, which can reflect the relationship between FLL loop bandwidth and measurement error.

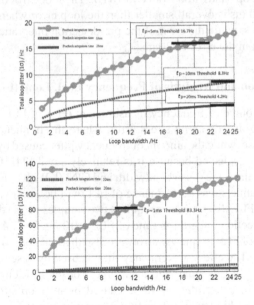

Fig. 4. Relationship between FLL loop bandwidth and measurement error, ($C/N_0 = 29\text{dB/Hz}$ Loop jitter corresponding to different bandwidths)

Analyzing the relationship between FLL loop bandwidth and measurement error, it can be seen that the FLL loop can meet the requirement that the total loop error is less than the corresponding threshold value in the case of C/and jerk of 0, pre-detection integration time of 1 ms, 10 ms and 20 ms in the case of loop bandwidth from 0 to 18 Hz.

In this case, the threshold value is calculated according to the FLL tracking threshold equation, i.e., $3\sigma_{FLL} = 3\sigma_{tFLL} + f_e \leq 0.25/t(Hz)$, where σ_{tFLL} is the thermal noise frequency jitter and f_e is the dynamic stress error in the FLL tracking loop. And the overall loop error for a pre-detection integration time t of 20 ms is smaller than the loop error for a pre-detection integration time t of 1ms.

3.3 Error Analysis of Delay Lock Loop (DLL)

Without considering multipath and other interferences, the sources of measurement errors in the code loop mainly include code phase jitter caused by thermal noise and dynamic stress errors. In the process of GPS software receiver code tracking (DLL), the main sources of error in ranging come from thermal noise distance error jitter and dynamic stress error. The DLL empirical method threshold is that the 3 σ value of jitter caused by all error sources in the loop is not allowed to exceed half of the linear traction range of the discriminator.

The carrier loop-assisted code tracking loop eliminates the effect of dynamic stress error, so as long as the carrier loop remains stable, the dynamic stress error experienced by the code loop is negligible, and only the thermal noise distance error jitter is considered in the code tracking threshold analysis. When the update time is 1ms, the thermal noise suppression performance of the second-order DLL with different parameters is shown in Fig. 5.

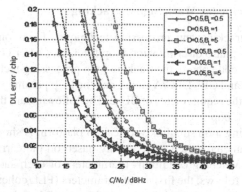

Fig. 5. Thermal noise suppression performance of second-order DLL (Loop update time = 1 ms)

It can be seen from Fig. 5: DLL thermal noise jitter increases at an accelerated rate as the carrier noise ratio decreases, making the tracking loop unstable. The DLL thermal noise jitter is proportional to the square of the loop bandwidth, and the thermal noise error becomes larger as the bandwidth is widened. Due to the carrier-assisted code technique, the dynamics in the code tracking loop are virtually removed, so the dynamic stresses experienced by the code loop are negligible as long as the carrier loop is kept stable, and this effect can be excluded from the code loop tracking threshold analysis.

Figure 6 shows the loop jitter corresponding to different code ring correlator intervals for $C/N_0 = 29dB/Hz$ and pre-detection integration time = 20 ms, which can reflect the relationship between the DLL loop bandwidth and the measurement error.

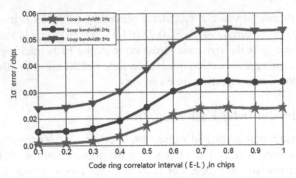

Code ring correlator interval (E-L) ,in chips

Fig. 6. Relationship between DLL loop bandwidth and measurement error, (C/N0 = 29 dB/Hz, Pre-detection integration time = 20 ms)

Analyzing the simulation results of DLL loop bandwidth and measurement error, it can be seen that DLL can meet the requirements of total loop error in the case of loop bandwidth from 0 to 18 Hz when C/N0 = 29 dB/Hz and pre-detection integration time is 20 ms, while different code loop correlator interval DLL loop error is different.

4 Simulation of Weak Signal Tracking Algorithm

4.1 Simulation Scheme for Weak Signal Tracking

Weak GNSS signal tracking and processing techniques focus on the design of frequency discriminator, phase discriminator, loop filter, etc. After considering capturing and removing the NH code phase, the tracking loop processing technology is not much different for BD-2 B1 and GPS L1 C/A codes, and the loop parameter indexes applicable to GPS can also meet the requirements of BD-2. The following are the simulation results corresponding to each loop.

The trace processing loop simulink verification platform is shown in Fig. 7.

The tracking parameter switches are mainly based on the carrier noise ratio. GPS tracking parameters switching conditions (parameters of each satellite are controlled independently) are as follows: the first set of parameters (PLL coherent integration time of 2 ms, code loop coherent integration time of 2 ms, FLL coherent integration time of 1ms, FLL bandwidth of 0.3, code loop bandwidth of 2) is used after switching from capturing channel to tracking channel. When the tracking time is greater than 1,000 ms, it is switched to the second set of parameters (PLL coherent integration time of 10 ms, code loop coherent integration time of 10 ms, FLL coherent integration time of 5 ms, FLL bandwidth of 0.4, code loop bandwidth of 0.6). When the second set of parameters is tracked for more than 500 ms and the carrier noise ratio is greater than 23, it is switched to the third set of parameters (PLL coherent integration time of 20 ms, code loop coherent integration time of 20 ms, FLL coherent integration time of 10 ms, PLL bandwidth of 8, code loop bandwidth of 1). Check the carrier noise ratio status every 0.5s under the third set of parameters tracking status, and cut back to the second set of parameters when the carrier noise ratio status is less than 20.

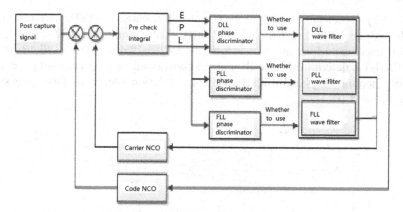

Fig. 7. Weak signal tracking loop

BD tracking parameters switching conditions (parameters of each satellite are controlled independently) are as follows: the first set of parameters (PLL coherent integration time of 1ms, code loop coherent integration time of 1ms, FLL coherent integration time of 0.5 ms, FLL bandwidth of 0.3, code loop bandwidth of 2) is used after switching from capturing channel to tracking channel. When the tracking time is greater than 1,500 ms, it is switched to the second set of parameters (PLL coherent integration time of 2 ms, code loop coherent integration time of 2 ms, FLL coherent integration time of 1ms, FLL bandwidth of 0.2, code loop bandwidth of 0.5). When the second set of parameters is tracked for more than 1,000 ms and the carrier noise ratio is greater than 22, it is switched to the third set of parameters (PLL coherent integration time of 2 ms, code loop coherent integration time of 2 ms, FLL coherent integration time of 1ms, PLL bandwidth of 14, code loop bandwidth of 0.5). Check the carrier noise ratio status every 0.5 s under the third set of parameters tracking status, and cut back to the second set of parameters when the carrier noise ratio status is less than 20. If it is less than or equal to 30 for 20 s consecutively, it switches to the fourth set of parameters (PLL coherent integration time of 2 ms, code loop coherent integration time of 2 ms, FLL coherent integration time of 1ms, PLL bandwidth of 6, code loop bandwidth of 0.5), whose tracking sensitivity is higher than the third set.

4.2 Simulation Results of Dynamic Environment

Use Matlab simulink to simulate the GPS receiver tracking loop. Figure 8 shows the top-level structure of the simulation system. The simulation system uses frame processing for the simulation of signal data.

Considering that the dynamic effect of code loop tracking has been removed from the carrier tracking loop, the simulation is actually the weak signal DLL tracking accuracy when the dynamics is 0. Select the code loop discriminator type $(I_E - I_L) \times I_P + (Q_E - Q_L) \times Q_P$ and verify the loop tracking performance corresponding to different loop bandwidths and integration times under different C/N_0 conditions.

According to the analysis of the in-satellite dynamic range of the L1-band GPS satellites received by HEO and GEO, the velocity range is ±10 km·s-1 and the acceleration range is ±2 g, which corresponds to the Doppler shift range ± 53 kHz and the Doppler shift change rate ±105 Hz·s-1. Taking −175 dBw as an example, the corresponding PLL and DLL tracking performance at −175 dBw (C/N0 = 29 dB/Hz) to −170 dBw (C/N0 = 34 dB/Hz) is determined by analyzing the corresponding loop tracking parameters, including loop tracking bandwidth Bn, loop pre-detection integration time tp, as shown in Figs. 8, 9 and 10.

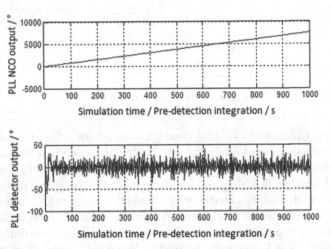

Fig. 8. Figure 10 PLL tracking performance at BnPLL = 15 Hz, t_p = 20 ms, (C/N_0=29 dB/Hz, B_n=15 Hz, Total simulation times = 1000,Correlation operation time = 20 ms, Statistics start from the 200th per detection integration cycle, σ_{PLL} (sim) = 12.261

Statistics of theoretical and simulated values of tracking loop error in dynamic environment (acceleration 2g) are performed for the loop parameters used in the above simulation. As for the BD-3 GEO satellite, its data bit rate is 500 bit·s-1, which cannot be integrated coherently for a long time and requires a non-coherent carrier loop and a non-coherent code loop, which will not be discussed too much here. The simulation analysis results are shown in Table 1.

According to the simulation results, it can be seen that PLL and DLL can complete tracking normally under pre-detection integration time of 20 ms and acceleration of 2 g, the pseudo-range measurement error is within 15m at −175 dBw, and the carrier phase measurement accuracy is about 10°.

Statistics on the GPS L1 signal power received by GEO and the corresponding reception altitude angle show that the maximum received power at GEO is about −163 dBw and the receiver sensitivity is −182 dBw, a difference of 19 dB, so there is a certain degree of mutual interference between strong and weak signals in the navigation signal processing. Similarly, the comparison between the received power of HEO orbit and the received altitude angle shows that the maximum received power of HEO is also about −163 dBw, which is more than 20 dB different from the lowest received power. Therefore, when dealing with weak signals for high-orbit navigation (−175 dBw), it is

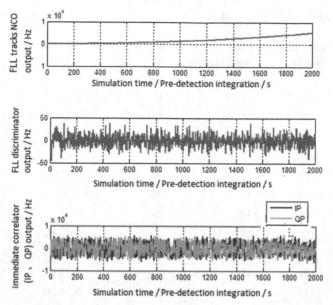

Fig. 9. FLL tracking performance at BnFLL = 10 Hz, $t_p = 5$ ms, (C/N_0=29 dB/Hz, B_n=10 Hz, Total simulation times = 1000, Correlation operation time = 5ms, Statistics start from the 500th per detection integration cycle, σ_{FLL} (sim) = 9.1251 Hz, σ_{FLL} (theory) = 7.9918 Hz)

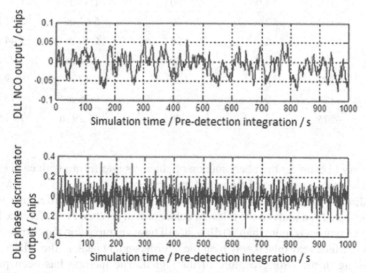

Fig. 10. DLL tracking performance when BnFLL = 2 Hz, $t_p = 20$ ms, (C/N_0=29dB/Hz, $\Delta =$ 1chips, B_n=2 Hz, Total simulation times = 1000, Statistics start from the 50th per detection integration cycle, σ_{DLL} (sim) = 0.043864chips, σ_{DLL} (theory) = 0.035003chips)

Table 1. Simulation analysis of weak signal loop tracking performance

Loop Type	Receiving Power/dBw	Loop Bandwidth/Hz	Pre-detection integration time/ms	Theoretical value	Simulation error
PLL	−160	31.38	1	2.05°	2.07°
	−170	15	1	4.45°	5.67°
	−171	15	20	4.99°	6.91°
	−172	15	20	5.62°	7.13°
	−173	15	20	6.32°	8.56°
	−174	15	20	7.10°	9.78°
	−175	15	20	7.99°	11.68°
FLL	−160	21.2	1	9.42 Hz	9.84 Hz
	−170	10	5	4.17 Hz	4.88 Hz
	−171	10	5	4.72 Hz	5.59 Hz
	−172	10	5	5.36 Hz	6.42 Hz
	−173	10	5	6.10 Hz	7.14 Hz
	−174	10	5	6.97 Hz	7.83 Hz
	−175	10	5	7.99 Hz	9.12 Hz
DLL	−160	1.06	20	1.37 m	1.69 m
	−170	2	20	5.67 m	6.22 M
	−171	2	20	6.40 m	7.44 m
	−172	2	20	7.22 m	7.99 m
	−173	2	20	8.17 m	9.19 m
	−174	2	20	9.25 m	9.73 m
	−175	2	20	11.29 m	13.15 m

also necessary to consider the phenomenon of channels interfering with each other due to the simultaneous reception of signals of higher power.

According to the simulation results, when the signal power difference is within 20 dBw, the signal can find out the relevant peak normally. When the difference between the two signal powers is more than 20 dBw, it will have an impact on the correlation peak of the signal, which may mistakenly treat the interdependent peak as the self-correlation peak, resulting in the wrong capture of the signal. The method has been proven in engineering to identify loop mis-capture tracking by demodulating the messages to distinguish between strong and weak signals.

4.3 Real-Time Orbit Determination Results

By applying the above technologies to engineering practice, the real-time orbit determination accuracy of Chang'E-5 satellite can reach 15.81 m. By sending the raw observation data downlinked from GNSS to the third party for post-event orbit calculation, and differencing the real-time bit velocity in the real-time orbit determination state in telemetry with the calculated orbit, we obtain the real-time orbit determination error, which is used to evaluate the GNSS on-orbit performance. The analysis period of the raw observation data is about 48 h. The specific conclusions are as follows: GNSS position error of the orbit determination is 15.8133 m (tri-axis, 1σ), as shown in Fig. 11(a); velocity error is 0.012108 m·s-1 (tri-axis, 1σ), as shown in Fig. 11(b).

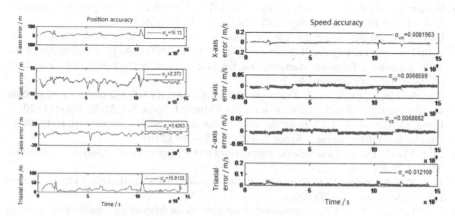

Fig. 11. Left(a): Position accuracy of the high orbit navigation receiver, right(b): Speed accuracy of the high orbit navigation receiver.

5 Conclusion

Based on the analysis of the velocity and acceleration of relative motion, it is known that the relative velocity range of the high-orbiting satellite-based navigation receiver is ±10 km·s-1 and the relative acceleration range is ±2 g, which corresponds to the Doppler shift range ±53 kHz and the Doppler shift change rate ±105 Hz·s-1. The analysis of GEO and HEO received power and received altitude angle shows that the maximum power of high orbit received GPS signal with antenna gain is −153 dBw, and it is almost able to receive the signal of the main lobe, the first sidelobe and the second sidelobe when the received power is −173 dBw.

Weak signal tracking theoretical analysis and simulation results show that the algorithm enables the receiver to handle −173 dBw navigation weak signals stably in high-orbit orbit applications, and the research results can provide theoretical support and technical index reference for real-time orbit determination of high-orbit satellites in orbit, and enhance the autonomy and real-time performance of high-orbit satellites. We will further expand the scope of simulation tests to verify the structure, conduct error analysis considering other parameters and carry out physical tests to further explore the feasibility of the application of navigation equipment in deep space such as circumlunar flying, study the feasibility of combined navigation of Beidou-2 navigation system and other navigation systems in high orbit environment, and lay the theoretical and engineering foundation for multi-fusion high orbit high precision combined navigation of high orbit navigation receivers and other equipment such as INS.

References

1. Jiang, H.: Acquisition of Beidou Weak Signal in High Orbit Environment. Hebei University of Science and Technology, Shijiazhuang (2017)
2. Winternitz, L.M.B., Bamford, W.A., Heckler, G.W.: A GPS receiver for high-altitude satellite navigation. IEEE J. Sel. Top. Signal Process. **3**(4), 541–556 (2009)
3. Unwin, M., De Vos Van Steenwijk, R., Blunt, P., et al.: Navigating above the GPS constellation – preliminary results from the SGR-GEO on GIOVE-A. In: Proceedings of the 26th International Technical Meeting of the Satellite Division of The Institute of Navigation, pp. 3305–3315. ION, Nashville (2013)
4. Guo, R., Liu, L., Li, X., et al.: Precise orbit determination for GEO satellites based on both satellite clock offsets and station clock offsets. Chinese J. Space Sci. **32**(3), 405–411 (2012)
5. Liang, M., Qin, H., Li, F.: Solving the near-far problem for positioning the high earth orbital satellite with GPS. Chinese J. Space Sci. **30**(3), 255–262 (2010)
6. Li, J., Ma, G.: Effect of ionospheric irregularities on GPS performance. Chinese J. Space Sci. **33**(2), 158–169 (2013)
7. Ji, S., Zhu, W., Xiong, Y.: Calculate and application of the GPS satellite clock offset. Chinese J. Space Sci. **21**(1), 42–48 (2001)
8. Liu, H., Wang, H.: Orbit determination of satellite on the Middle-high earth orbit based on GPS. Chinese J. Space Sci. **25**(4), 293–297 (2005)
9. Li, L., Li, C., Huang, W., Zhou, Y.: Orbit determined method of high elliptical orbit satellite based on BDS navigation and inter-satellite link. Chinese J. Space Sci. **38**(6), 915 (2018). https://doi.org/10.11728/cjss2018.06.915
10. Wu, Y.: Research on Acquisition and Tracking Algorithms for GPS Weak Signal. Chongqing University, Chongqing (2012)
11. Wie, J.: Research on Acquisition and Tracking of GPS Weak Signals under Multipath Interference. Nanjing University of Aeronautics and Astronautics, Nanjing (2014)
12. Qiu, L., Li, L.: GPS signal acquisition based on FFT. In: 2010 Second International Conference on Information Technology and Computer Science, pp. 110–113. IEEE, Kiev, Ukraine (2010). https://doi.org/10.1109/ITCS.2010.33
13. Liu, Y., Chen, Z., Guo, S.: Implement and performance analysis of pseudo code acquisition based on FFT. In: Proceedings of the 5th World Congress on Intelligent Control and Automation. Hangzhou, China (2004)
14. Dong, Z., Wu, S.: New acquisition method for DSSS with large Doppler. Syst. Eng. Electron. **30**(8), 1424–1426 (2008)
15. Hu, H., Sun, H., Ji, Z.: Study on algorithm and control strategies of GPS carrier tracking loop under high dynamic conditiong. J. Astronaut. **32**(8), 1805–1812 (2011)
16. Zhou, G.: Research and Realization of Acquisition and Tracking for Weak GPS Signals. Shanghai Jiao Tong University, Shanghai (2009)
17. Liu, W., Yuan, H., Wei, D., et al.: A new GNSS signal carrier tracking algorithm for ionospheric TEC monitoring. Chinese J. Space Sci. **34**(1), 63–72 (2014)
18. Tang, L.: Research on the Tracking Technology in GNSS. Xidian University, Xi'an (2017)

19. Song, C., Wang, X., Zhuan, Z.: Estimate algorithm for pseudo-code phase delay and its uncertainty in the assisted GPS receiver. Chinese J. Space Sci. **29**(6), 620 (2009). https://doi.org/10.11728/cjss2009.06.620
20. Wang, W.: Research on Beidou Navigation Signal Tracking Algorithms and Software Implemention. Xidian University, Xi'an (2017)
21. Hong, Y., Yao, Z., Lu, M.: Research on adaptability of satellite navigation signal code tracking theory. Comput. Simul. **29**(12), 53–56, 375 (2012)
22. Yu, Y.: Research and Implementation of GNSS Signal Tracking Technology for High-Orbit Spacecraft. Dalian University of Technology, Dalian (2018)
23. Li, Y.: Research and Implement of the Acquisition and Tracking for the New-styled Navigation Signals. National University of Defense Technology, Changsha (2013)
24. Wen, C., Yue, F., Qiu, Y., et al.: Research on tracking of high earth orbit BDS weak signal. J. Spacecraft TT&C Technol. **32**(4), 363–370 (2013)

Avionics System Architectures for Software-Defined Spacecraft

Xiongwen He[1,2], Jionghui Li[2(✉)], Fan Bai[2], Xiaoyu Jia[2], Xiaofeng Huang[2], and Mingwei Xu[1]

[1] Department of Computer Science and Technology, Tsinghua University, Beijing 100084, China
[2] Beijing Institute of Spacecraft System Engineering, Beijing 100094, China
lijionghui@126.com

Abstract. Developing upon open system architecture, Software-Defined Spacecraft, as a new generation of spacecraft, can support payload plug-and-play, application software loading as needed, and system function reconfiguration on demand. Therefore, the Software-Defined Spacecraft is able to solve the design and application limitations of traditional specific-designed spacecraft, making it become a significant developing trend of future spacecraft. Regarding to the software defined spacecraft bus, this paper analyzes the requirements for avionics system on the aspects of space field development, technology development and corresponding applications. Then, combining with the development status, the avionics system architecture of software defined spacecraft is proposed, along with the related key technologies.

Keywords: Software-Defined Spacecraft · avionics system · intellectualization · networking

1 Introduction

The concept of Software-Defined is originated from Software-Defined Radio (SDR). With the rapid development of modern computing technology, the advantages of Software-Defined are becoming more and more prominent. The scope of Software-Defined is also developing and expanding, gradually becoming an innovative architecture, an innovative design concept and an innovative design method, which has penetrated into many fields, even developing to the trend of software-defined everything. The core idea of Software-Defined is to decouple software and hardware through a unified interface. Under the premise of sufficient hardware performance, software developers are responsible for meeting different needs of different users; And hardware developers can focus on improving hardware performance under a unified standard architecture. This way of "software defined" can minimize the development cycle and cost, and can give the flexibility of system function update and upgrade.

© ICST Institute for Computer Sciences, Social Informatics and Telecommunications Engineering 2023
Published by Springer Nature Switzerland AG 2023. All Rights Reserved
R. Li et al. (Eds.): MOBILWARE 2022, LNICST 507, pp. 150–164, 2023.
https://doi.org/10.1007/978-3-031-34497-8_13

There is also a trend of Software-Defined in the space engineering. The vision is that through the Software-Defined design, the hardware bus of spacecraft can be defined as models, in order to improve the adaptability of spacecraft bus to different tasks. Then, software is used to support on-orbit reconstruction and performance upgrading. By Software-Defined method, the traditional spacecraft is transformed into a multi-purpose and network-collaborated spacecraft, which can shorten the spacecraft development cycle, and reduce the spacecraft development cost. So as to enter a new stage of systematic development and global service of spacecraft.

At present, the spacecraft architecture is mostly customized for specific mission. The spacecraft hardware and software design is closely related to the spacecraft application, with hardware as the main and software as the auxiliary. This traditional spacecraft design method has shown the following five shortcomings: (1) The hardware bus of designed spacecraft are different, and different types of spacecraft do not adapt to each other in hardware, and parts of components cannot be interchanged; (2) The software is incompatible with each other, and the application software developed for one model cannot run directly on the spacecraft of another model; (3) The spacecraft cannot achieve on-orbit performance improvement during its life cycle; (4) The development cycle is long, the cost is high, the functions are inflexible, the on-orbit reconfiguration ability is relatively weak, and it is difficult to mass produce; (5) The spacecraft software is non-accessible for third parties due to its closed architecture. In view of the above shortcomings, it is a good way to develop an open system architecture and a novel generation of Software-Defined Spacecraft that supports payload plug-and-play, application software loading on demand, and system function reconfiguration on demand. The concept of Software-Defined Spacecraft mainly includes software-defined bus and software-defined payload [1]. The avionics system is the kernel to achieve spacecraft bus software-defined. Regarding to the software-defined spacecraft bus, this paper first analyzes the requirements of avionics system for software-defined of spacecraft from the dimensions of field development, technology development and application. Then, combining the state-of-art development status, the ideas of avionics system architecture for Software-Defined Spacecraft is proposed with list of supportive key technologies.

2 Related State-of-art

2.1 Software Defined Spacecraft

At present, technologies related to Software-Defined Spacecraft are actively developing. The Eutelsat Quantum series satellites jointly developed by ESA, Eurosat and Airbus Defense and Space are experimental communication satellites carrying software reconfigurable loads. They can adjust the beam coverage, frequency band and power on-orbit, and can also change the orbit position to achieve on-orbit functional reconstruction [2]. SmartSat is a micro/nano software-defined satellite proposed by Lockheed Martin uses virtual machines and multi-core processing to form an elastic architecture, which supports the rapid assembly of various satellite platforms and enhances the rapid data processing capability. The frequency bandwidth and beam coverage can be adjusted to support mission on-orbit modification [3]. Galactic Sky, a small solid rocket company in the United States, has designed a software-defined satellite named Gsky-1, which uses Galactic Sky^{TM}, a proprietary software-defined satellite technology developed by Galactic Sky, which adds a cloud based intelligent layer to support the scheduling, deploying, monitoring and managing resources and other missions. With the support of CNES and the ESA, Thales Alenia Space Company is developing a new type of "real-time on-orbit reconstruction" satellite, called "Space Inspire", which aims to achieve real-time mission adjustment and reconfigurations on-orbit, supporting multiple services from video broadcasting to broadband connection, which maximize the efficiency and effective use of satellite hardware resources.

Research institutions in China are also carrying out research on software-defined spacecraft. The conceptual research of Software Satellite based on SDR has started from 2002, which takes the payload based on SDR and defines the payload function through software [4]. An experimental satellite for software-defined technology, called TianZhi-1 was developed by the Institute of Software Chinese Academy of Sciences, and was launched in 2018. It has successfully carried out more than 10 on-orbit experiments by means of software uploading, including intelligent measurement and operation control, intelligent data compression, intelligent information processing and other aspects [5]. In 2019, the TianXiang satellites (China Netcom 1 A and B satellites) were successfully launched. The satellite was equipped with a space-based router to perform software-defined network (SDN). Using the features of SDN, the controllers of the micro satellites which are responsible for highly complex routing calculation can be placed on the ground. However, all the mentioned software-defined spacecraft are mainly small satellites, and there is still a lack of systematic design methods and concepts of software defined spacecraft which suit for all fields from the perspective of system, technology and architecture.

2.2 Avionics System of Spacecraft

It can be seen from the relevant development of software-defined spacecraft that the core idea of software-defined spacecraft is to remove the coupling between the software and hardware of spacecraft products, so that spacecraft software can independently evolve, load on demand, and dynamically reconstruct. By this way, more functions can be realized and more missions can be fulfilled without large modification the hardware. To implement decoupled software and hardware, spacecraft avionics systems are meeting the development requirements of the next generation of spacecraft which is to transform from discrete units into integrated multi-function computing platform [6].

The concept of spacecraft avionics systems is introduced from aviation. The development of aviation avionics systems has gone through four generations, which are separated, combined, integrated and advanced integrated [7]. In 2004, Honeywell International borrowed from the architecture of integrated modular avionics system (IMA) and proposed an avionics system architecture for space-craft to implement software-hardware decoupling, aiming to provide dynamic reconfigurability and scalability for spacecraft. This architecture divides a phys-ically high throughput computer into multiple virtual machines, and each virtual machine is used as the resource of corresponding software applications, so as to realize the time division of processing resources, the space division of storage space, and the division of input/output interfaces, and improve the effective fault tolerance performance of the system. At the same time, in order to min-imize the impact of changes in user applications on the system, both software and hardware adopt hierarchical design [6], so that the architecture supports open application development.

NASA successfully launched the Orion manned spacecraft in 2014 to imple-ment the avionics system using IMA architecture. The Orion avionics system structure selects Time Triggered Ethernet (TTE) as the backbone network [8]. Each device of the system is connected to the network switch, including 18 time triggered Ethernet switches and 46 terminal nodes. The on-board com-puter (VMC) is used as the processing core of the spacecraft to complete the main functions of the whole device control, human-computer interaction, and system communication. In 2019, NASA proposed the avionics system architec-ture of the "Artemis" manned lunar exploration program. This architecture is based on the TTE network, which can provide three different types of data services in the same network, which are best effort, rate limited, and time trig-gered. Europe launched researches on its new generation of avionics architecture, SAVOIR, in 2010. The latest architecture is shown in Fig. 1. At the protocol level, the architecture integrates the standards of the Consultative Committee on Space Data Systems (CCSDS) and European Cooperation for Space Stan-dardization (ECSS). The operating system supports time-sharing and partition,

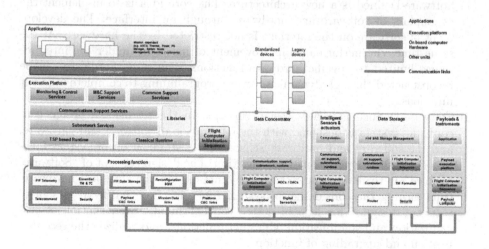

Fig. 1. The avionics architecture of SAVOIR

and the software development mode is to use software components to assemble and realize message communication between multiple application processes through software bus.

In 2015, Zhao Heping proposed that the spacecraft avionics system, as the center of spacecraft intelligence, should have the communication capability of unified information network services, support distributed parallel computing, modular expansion and upgrading, and the computing and storage capabilities of system reconfiguration [9].

It can be seen that the software-hardware decoupling, hierarchical design, fault tolerance and system reconfiguration design, hardware modularization, software reconstruction, time-sharing and partition operating system are the consensus of the next generation avionics systems to supporting the development trend of software-defined spacecraft.

3   Avionics System for Software-Defined Spacecraft

3.1   Features of Software-Defined

The core idea of "Software-Defined" is to decouple software and hardware through a unified interface. Under the premise of sufficient hardware performance, software developers are responsible for meeting different needs of different users. And hardware developers can focus on improving hardware performance under a unified standard architecture. This software-defined method can minimize the development cycle and cost, and give the flexibility of system function update and upgrade.

The core connotation of Software-Defined technology is summarized as follows:

(1) Software-Defined is a new architecture. The core idea is to implement the decoupling of software and hardware through an interface. The development of software on the interface is not restricted by the hardware. At the same time, the performance improvement of hardware under the interface is not limited to specific hardware functions. The same hardware can be reconstructed through dynamic software programming to complete different functions.
(2) Software-Defined is a new design concept. In the traditional design concept, the system is designed with the integration of software and hardware, and the software and hardware achieve the customization of system functions with the cooperation of solidification. The design concept of "Software-Defined" is to realize the software of functions on the standard hardware, thus turning the core design of system functions from hardware design to software design. This leap in design concept breaks the situation of customization and solidification of system functions, and realizes the reconfiguration and upgrading of functions.

(3) Software-Defined is a new design method. Regarding to the hardware design, we can pursue a simplified structure, adopt an open and scalable general platform design, "decouple" from the system functions, and pay more attention to the performance of the hardware platform itself. Regarding to the software design, the component-based design idea is adopted, and the design is carried out according to the requirements of modularization, reconfiguration and upgradability, so as to configure and reconstruct as many functions as possible through software [10].

To summarize the concept, connotation and application of "Software-Defined" technology, we can summarize the development requirements of "Software-Defined" technology as follows: Hierarchical design, architecture standardization, hardware generalization, software-implemented functions and resources virtualization.

(1) Hierarchical design: Hierarchical design of software and hardware is the premise to achieve functional decoupling of software and hardware. Through an interface (such as an operating system), software definition technology separates software and hardware relatively, breaks the traditional structure and design of software and hardware integration, and realizes the independent development of both. Software can be customized, while hardware is more standardized.
(2) Architecture standardization: Generally, the operating system is used as the interface, and standardized or open application programming interfaces (APIs) are open to the upper layers and the hardware platform is used through the hardware abstraction layer to the lower layer. At present, several mainstream software-defined architecture specifications have been formed, including the Software Communication Architecture (SCA) specification, the Space Telecommunication Radio System (STRS) architecture specification developed by NASA, and the OpenDaylight software definition network architecture specification.
(3) Hardware generalization: the hardware here refers to the hardware of the computing and processing platform, not the hardware of physical resources such as antennas. The generalization of hardware lays the foundation for realizing the "decoupling" between system functions and hardware. Therefore, the hardware design should focus on the underlying general computing and processing as much as possible, and try to unbind with the specific functions of the system. Hardware designers focus on the improvement of hardware performance to improve the real-time processing capability of software.
(4) Software-implemented functions: Software-Defined technology changes the system functions from traditional software and hardware customization to software implementation, which is the most characteristic of software definition technology. Functional software consists of software "components", which are configured or reconstructed according to different functional requirements and application scenarios.

(5) Resource virtualization: Virtualization is to provide an abstraction layer between software and hardware by using various technologies, so as to convert physical resources into logical or virtual resources, and enable users, applications or management software running on the abstraction layer to manage and use these resources without having to master the physical details of underlying resources. Therefore, resource virtualization is also a major feature of software definition technology.

3.2 Requirements of Software-Definition Spacecraft

In various spacecraft application fields, the corresponding application requirements put forward some specific requirements for the development of software-defined spacecraft:

(1) Communication Satellites: the new generation of communication satellites will enter a new era of massive, high-speed, flexible and diversified integration. Under such a development trend, satellites are required to provide a unified on-board software radio universal platform to achieve flexible switching of communication, electronic reconnaissance and electronic countermeasure functions through uploading software or reconstruction. In particular, in the construction of the space-ground integrated network, the communication satellite platform will play an important role as a cloud computing node, provide a unified space based computing and storage platform, and define the network based on software to achieve flexible loading and dynamic access of on orbit functions and provide services for other satellites.
(2) Navigation satellites: At present, the development trend of various satellite navigation systems in the world is characterized by continuous upgrading of the system, continuous enhancement of autonomous operation capability, multi-task integration, parallel development of multiple enhancement systems, and spiral development of new technologies. BeiDou-3 Navigation Constellation is the largest space-based network on-orbit in China at present. Its network routing update strategy still relies on ground injection, and ground operators are heavily burdened. The subsequent highly efficient and intelligent navigation constellation network requires spacecraft to provide a unified space-based software definition switch platform, support software definition network, and realize network topology construction and network routing customization on demand.
(3) Remote sensing satellites: With the continuous development of remote sensing payload technology, the mission of remote sensing satellites has begun to change from data acquisition to information acquisition, and has shown a trend of networking and collaborative work. Therefore, subsequent development requires spacecraft technology to provide a unified and universal hardware platform for on-board real-time information processing, and support on-demand loading and upgrading of data compression, target detection, target recognition, cloud judgment and other functions.

(4) Deep space probes: Long mission cycle and uncertainty of mission environment are the prominent features of deep space missions. For future deep space missions, spacecraft are required to provide a unified on-board avionics hardware platform to support on-orbit loading of intelligent autonomous management related APPs, and to support on-orbit upgrading of autonomous command management, autonomous health management, autonomous communication management as well as autonomous payloads management [11–13].

(5) Manned spacecraft: With the subsequent construction of space stations and the development of manned lunar exploration projects, from a single manned spacecraft, cargo spacecraft to multi-purpose spacecraft, and even to a multi-purpose platform, and gradually move towards commercial operation, the requirements for the intelligence, flexible scalability, reasonable cost and sustainable development of manned spacecraft are becoming higher and higher, requiring spacecraft to provide a universal on-board computer platform, in order to support flexible migration and reconstruction of multiple functions.

These requirements from the above application fields all focus on the avionics systems of software-defined spacecraft. In addition to the telemetry, remote control, housekeeping, time management, thermal control management, energy management and other functions of the traditional avionics system, the requirements focus on supporting mass production, function definition, spatial networking and autonomous intelligence. The specific requirements are summarized as follows:

(1) Mass production: In order to adapt to the increasingly fierce market competition, mass production can effectively reduce the design and production cycle of spacecraft, thus reducing costs and increasing profits. For spacecraft, the separation of software and hardware is an effective technical approach to achieve batch quantization. The standardization and modularization of avionics system hardware platform can effectively alleviate the problems of high cost, long development cycle and unstable quality. Compared with hardware, software is inherently characterized by short development, debugging, test cycle and low cost. It is easy to reuse and can quickly meet user requirements.

(2) Function definition: under the premise of ensuring the safety of spacecraft, the internal resources of avionics systems are fully open and accessible, and the potential of spacecraft hardware can be utilized through software reconstruction. Through virtualization technology, the software modules can be reused to the greatest extent, the development process can be shortened, so that functions can not only be defined, but also be rapidly reconstructed, and users can pay attention to the expanded function APP as needed, so as to adapt to the flexible needs of users, achieve one satellite multi-purpose, and maximize the application of spacecraft.

(3) Space networking: The avionics systems provide the core components, protocols and software for the integration and interconnection of space and

spacecraft, realizes the flexible networking of spacecraft, the interconnection and interworking of satellites in communication, navigation, tele-control and other fields, and forms the space-ground integrated network (SGIN), which supports the improvement of application efficiency through information fusion and collaboration. With "software-defined" development, the avionics system can quickly complete system resource allocation and response by software according to user requirements (delay, bandwidth, packet loss rate, etc.), and realize the agile reconfiguration of the network (topology change, function deployment, etc.).

(4) Autonomous intelligence: the avionics system provides mission level autonomous capability and constellation level autonomous capability. Among them, the mission level autonomous capability needs to achieve health monitoring and fault reconstruction, inter-device and intra-device data management, on-orbit resource scheduling, multi-source information fusion through high-performance task management units to reduce the dependence on the ground. Constellation level autonomy is mainly aimed at communication satellites, navigation satellites and remote sensing satellites for formation detection. Through intelligent routing, intelligent forwarding and processing, it can reduce the ground operation and maintenance pressure brought by the increase in the number of spacecraft.

3.3   Avionics Architectures for Software-Defined Spacecraft

Regarding to the requirements mentioned above, the avionics architectures for Software-Defined Spacecraft consists of three parts, which are protocol architecture, hardware architecture and software architecture.

The protocol architecture of avionics architectures for Software-Defined Spacecraft as shown in Fig. 2.

The protocol architecture consists of application layer, transfer layer and subnet layer. Standard protocols of the CCSDS [13] and the ECSS are adopted. With this architecture, different spacecraft can be interconnected, and different equipment inside the spacecraft can also be interconnected, providing a basis for software-defined, task migration on demand and APP dynamic loading.

The main features of the proposed protocol architecture include:

(1) Space and internal network integration design: The space and internal network integration of low-speed links (measurement and control links and low-speed buses) is realized through the space package protocol of the transfer layer, and the space and internal network integration of high-speed links (data transmission/inter satellite links and high-speed buses) is implemented through the IP protocol of the transfer layer.

(2) Layered protocols: Protocols at different levels can be flexibly extended, replaced and upgraded.

(3) Separation of the common-used services and the customized services in the application layer: A large number of common-used services are provided through the application support layer, while functions in the application

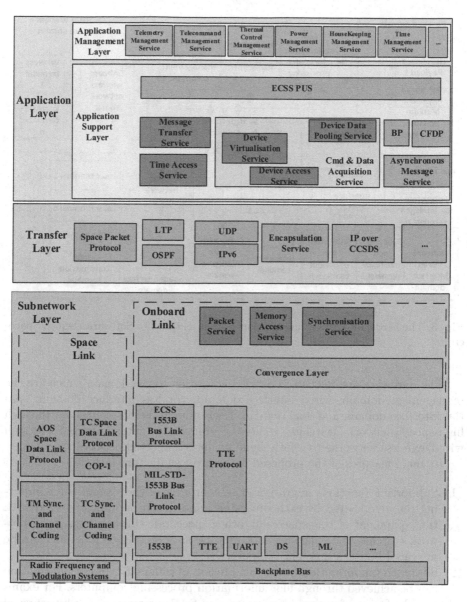

Fig. 2. The protocol architecture of avionics architectures for Software-Defined Spacecraft

management layer and extended applications can be implemented through the service combinations in the application support layer.

The hardware architecture is shown in Fig. 3.

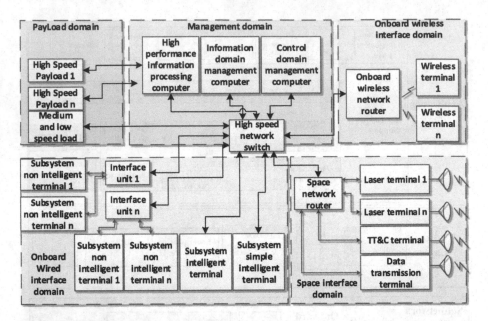

Fig. 3. The hardware architecture of avionics architectures for Software-Defined Spacecraft

The hardware architecture is divided according to the domain which are the management domain, wired interface domain, wireless interface domain, spatial interface domain and load domain. Each domain is interconnected through high-speed network switches, while the domain is interconnected through wired/wireless networks to jointly build an interconnected network.

Its main features of the proposed hardware architecture include:

(1) Supporting functions migration: The computer of the system is a computing resource shared by each subsystem, and it can be interconnected with the equipment of this spacecraft/other spacecraft through high-speed network switches and space network routers, so that various functions can be migrated between different computers.

(2) Supporting information fusion: The fusion of different types of information can be achieved through high information processing computers. For example, the fusion of optical information and SAR information can be achieved by remote sensing satellites to generate comprehensive intelligence.

(3) Network definability: The internal network and the inter-device network can be defined by software. The network parameters, such as network topology, bandwidth and routing policy, can be configured as required.

(4) Hardware reconfiguration: the reconfiguration in case of hardware failure can be achieved through the combination of modules, and the algorithm reconfiguration and upgrading of on-orbit hardware FPGA can also be completed through on-orbit loading.

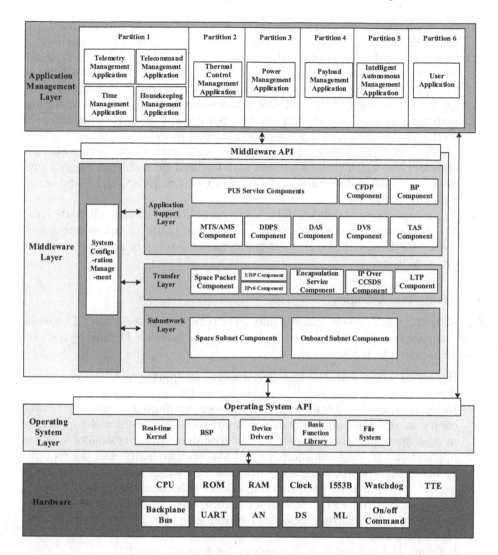

Fig. 4. The software architecture of avionics architectures for Software-Defined Spacecraft

(5) Software loading-ability: the time-sharing and partition operating system is adopted to support the on-orbit loading of various software and to implement the expansion and upgrade of functions.

The software running in each computer/interface unit/intelligent terminal/space network router adopts a unified architecture, which is configured and tailored according to requirements. The corresponding software architecture is shown in Fig. 4. The above software architecture is mainly divided into the following parts:

(1) Hardware layer: Hardware layer plays as the basis of software architecture, which includes components of various on-board computers such as CPU.

(2) Operating system layer: Operating system layer is the underlying supportive layer of the software architecture, which encapsulates the interface of the operating system, provides a unified application programming interface for the operating system, and uses a time-sharing and partition operating system to support the safe and reliable operation of applications of different levels developed by different users on a unified processor.

(3) Middleware layer: Middleware layer is the basic service layer of the software architecture, which realizes various standardized protocols and algorithms in the protocol architecture, and supports CCSDS, ECSS, IETF and other standard protocols.

(4) Application layer: Application layer is a combination of multiple partitions. These partitions can not only realize the normal platform and load management functions, but also support the dynamic loading of applications from different users.

3.4 Key Technologies

Based on the requirements analysis and architecture proposed above. The main key technologies relevant to the avionics systems for Software-Defined Spacecraft are summarized as follows.

(1) Heterogeneous distributed high performance computing technology on satellite.

Heterogeneous distributed high performance computing technology is necessary to develop high-performance multi-core computers and supporting management and scheduling algorithms to support the operation of multiple applications on the same computer. At the same time, to meet the requirements of high-performance computing such as image processing and information fusion, it is necessary to support the efficient collaboration between CPU, GPU, DSP, FPGA and other heterogeneous processing modules, as well as the collaborative processing requirements of computers between multiple spacecraft.

(2) Software Defined Network Technology for Space Network

In order to meet the requirements of different spacecraft to reconstruct the network topology, customize or reconstruct the network routing, it is necessary to develop software definition network technology suitable for space networks, support the interconnection between heterogeneous spacecraft, support the on-demand change and expansion and upgrading of space network protocols, etc.

(3) Dynamic loading and migration technology of space APP

In order to meet user-specific demand to load applications in on-board computers, it is necessary to break through the space APP dynamic loading technology, support lightweight online dynamic links, support the security isolation of different APPs, and support the dynamic migration of APPs between different computers.

(4) Space Software Middleware Technology

It is necessary to developing software middleware suitable for space, and provide unified interfaces such as device access, file access, plug-and-play, message sharing, reliable transmission, network management, time synchronization and operation synchronization for various APPs, making the development of APP regardless the underlying protocols and hardware.

4 Conclusion

In view of the requirements from multiple space application fields, this paper proposed architectures of avionics systems for Software-Defined Spacecraft and sorts out the key technologies. The proposed architectures consists of protocol architecture, hardware architecture and software architecture. The adoption of avionics systems for Software-Defined Spacecraft will bring innovations to spacecraft design concept and design method, which can be conducive to the realization of mass production, function on-orbit definition, spatial networking, and autonomous intelligence of the next generation of spacecraft. The key technologies proposed in this paper still need further research and breakthrough.

References

1. Zhou, Y., Zhang, X., Zhi, M.Y.: Research on software defined satellite payload technology. J. Northwestern Polytechn. Univ. **38**(S1), 96–101 (2020)
2. Walker, J.L., Mckinnon, D.: Future digital flexible and software defined payload systems for commercial space. In: AIAA International Communications Satellite Systems Conference and Exhibition, pp. 2–13. Queensland, Australia (2015). https://doi.org/10.2514/6.2015-4325
3. Li, W., Chen, J.: Latest progress of European and American software defined satellite project. Int. Space. **1**, 53–55 (2020)
4. Yang, X.: Concept research on "Software satellite". Electron. Warfare. **1**, 1–5 (2002)
5. Zhao, J., Wu, F., Liu, G., et al.: Systematic idea and technical practice of developing software defined satellite. Sat. Netw. **4**, 44–49 (2018)
6. He, X., Li, N., Xu, Y., et al.: Requirements analysis of intelligent spacecraft avionics system and discussion of its architecture. Spacecr. Eng. **27**(4), 82–89 (2018)
7. Baggerman, C., Mccabe, M., Verma, D.: Avionics system architecture for the NASA orion vehicle. In: SAE AeroTech Congress and Exhibition, pp. 1–10, Seattle, the United States (2009). https://doi.org/10.4271/2009-01-3276
8. Black R., Fletcher M.: Next generation space avionics: layered system implementation. IEEE Aerosp. Electron. Syst. Mag. **20**(12), 9–14 (2005)
9. Cheng, B., Liu, W., He, X., et al.: Research on Orion electronic system. Spacecr. Eng. **25**(4), 102–107 (2016)
10. He, X., Guo, J., Li, Y.: Autonomous health management requirements and software architecture for deep space probe. Control Theory Appl. **36**(12), 2065–2073 (2019)
11. Feng, X., Li, Y., Yang, C., et al.: Structural design and autonomous mission planning method of deep space exploration spacecraft for autonomous operation. Control Theory Appl. **36**(12), 2035–2041 (2019)

12. Xu, Y., Li, J., Lin, X., et al.: An optimal bit-rate allocation algorithm to improve transmission efficiency of images in deep space exploration. China Commun. **17**(07), 94–100 (2020)
13. CCSDS 850.0-G-2. Spacecraft onboard interface services. CCSDS, Washington D.C. (2013)

Research and Application of Energy Efficiency Optimization Algorithm for Spacecraft Simulation Platform

Zhou An[✉], Yi Yuan, Xun Zhou, Wenlong Song, Qi Miao, and Huifang Pan

Beijing Institute of Spacecraft System Engineering, Beijing 100094, China
anzhou163@163.com

Abstract. High performance computing plays an increasingly important role in the simulation and verification of the aerospace. The high-performance simulation and computing platform for spacecraft provides effective support for various professional fields such as spacecraft orbit design, mechanical structure analysis, electromagnetic simulation, etc. With the increasing scale and quantity of spacecraft, all kinds of simulation tasks tend to be complex and require high solving time, which puts forward higher requirements for the computing capability of the platform. While improving the computing power of the platform, its performance and scale are growing year by year, and its energy consumption is also growing synchronously. This paper combines the characteristics of various professional computing tasks in spacecraft simulation, experimental verifies with the actual operation data, analyzes the platform energy consumption model, and compares the optimized scheduling algorithm with the conventional scheduling algorithm. On the premise of not affecting the platform throughput and operation time, the overall energy consumption of the platform is reduced by an average of 25%, effectively improving the energy efficiency of the platform and saving the operation cost.

Keywords: Spacecraft Design · Simulation Calculation · Energy Efficiency Optimization · Job Scheduling

1 Introduction

High performance computing technology has been widely used in meteorology, energy, medical, industrial simulation and other fields. It is an important symbol of a country's scientific-technical development level and comprehensive national strength. Among them, high-performance computing plays an increasingly important role in the simulation and verification of the aerospace field. The high-performance simulation and computing platform for spacecraft (hereinafter referred to as the platform) provides effective support for various professional fields, such as spacecraft orbit design, mechanical structure analysis, electromagnetic simulation, etc. In the aerodynamic prediction and verification of Tianwen-1, the specific experiments of aerodynamics and aerothermodynamics were carried out in the Martian atmosphere during the Mars Entry, Descent and Landing (EDL) mission [1]. In the Chang'e-5 mission, an expanded mission orbit scheme was designed for the orbiter, and the trajectory design dynamics model simulation was carried out to maximize the use of mission resources [2]. The landing simulation of the return capsule of a new generation manned spacecraft, the airbag finite element model is established to simulate the landing buffer process of the return capsule, effectively reducing the possibility of hard landing [3].

With the increasing scale and quantity of spacecraft, all kinds of simulation tasks tend to be complex and require high solving time, which puts forward higher requirements for the computing capability of the platform. While improving the computing power of the platform, its performance and scale are growing year by year, and its energy consumption is also growing synchronously. The power consumption of China's data centers has increased at a rate of more than 12% for eight consecutive years. In 2018, the total power consumption of China's data centers accounted for 2.35% of the total social power consumption [4]. IBM and the US Energy Administration have identified the top ten challenges in building exascale supercomputer system as energy efficiency [5, 6]. In May 2022, the Frontier Supercomputer located in the Oak Ridge National Laboratory (ORNL) of the United States achieved 1.102Exaflop/s of actual test computing capacity in the Top 500 ranking, becoming the world's first exascale supercomputer. At the same time, the Frontier Supercomputer ranked first in the Green 500 with an extremely high energy efficiency ratio of 52.23 gigaflops per watt [7].

To improve the energy efficiency ratio of the data center is to balance the energy consumption and performance of the platform. The biggest challenge is to reduce the energy consumption of the platform on the premise of ensuring the overall throughput and quality of service of the platform. In the high-performance computing data center, the energy consumption of information technology (IT) equipment mainly comes from the operation of jobs on computing nodes. Different scheduling strategies make the distribution of jobs on computing nodes different. For servers without computing tasks in idle state, a large amount of energy consumption is wasted. A large part of the platform's energy consumption comes from the vacancy rate of computing nodes. How to optimize the job scheduling strategy on the premise of ensuring the platform throughput and computing efficiency is of great significance to improve the energy efficiency of the platform. In this paper, by analyzing the computing characteristics of spacecraft simulation tasks, modeling the platform operation distribution, resource utilization and energy consumption, then proposing a scheduling algorithm based on energy efficiency optimization, which effectively reduces the platform energy consumption and carbon emissions.

2   Related Work

With the rapid growth of energy consumption in data centers, the problem of high energy consumption has aroused widespread concern. The data center energy efficiency standard commonly used in the industry is mainly Power Usage Effectiveness (PUE) [8]. The ratio of the total energy consumption of the data center to the total energy consumption of IT equipment, it is used to measure the effective energy consumption of the data center.

Technologies for energy consumption optimization of IT equipment include dynamic voltage and frequency scaling (DVFS) and dynamic power management (DPM) [9]. DVFS reduces the power consumption and performance of the processor by reducing the frequency and voltage of the processor. DPM technology dynamically configures components according to the running status of processors, memory and other components, and provides the minimum number of moving components to reduce energy consumption.

Etinski et al. [10] based on the integer linear equation of power configuration, proposed a scheduling strategy using DVFS to dynamically adjust the power consumption of computing nodes to control the power consumption of the entire platform. Although the overall power consumption is effectively reduced, the job execution time is also increased.

Yang et al. [11] proposed a cloud infrastructure that monitors the status of the OpenStack platform and the real-time status of the virtual machine on it. The monitoring indicators include CPU utilization, memory load, energy consumption, and so on. Energy consumption can be saved through online migration of virtual machines. The cloud service of the data center strengthens the centralized management of resources, it through the integrated management of various resources and the distributed self-organization mechanism based on game theory, making decisions on dynamic resource calls with less delay, so as to reduce the operation power consumption [12].

The energy consumption of the data center mainly comes from the operating load of IT equipment and the operating consumption of refrigeration equipment [13]. Among them, 15% - 30% of servers in IT equipment are idle, and the energy consumption in idle state accounts for 50% - 60% of the full load energy consumption [14]. The server runs with the highest energy efficiency under full load and the energy efficiency drops sharply when the load decreases. For the common server utilization rate of 20% - 30%, its energy efficiency is less than 50%.

3   Energy Consumption Model Analysis

In the spacecraft simulation computing platform, computing nodes account for more than 90% of IT equipment. This paper mainly focuses on how to improve the energy efficiency ratio of computing nodes, thereby reducing the overall energy consumption of the platform.

In the process of spacecraft design simulation, due to the large scale of calculation model, the large number of calculation conditions and iterations, and the frequent parallel of multiple models, it is necessary to quickly respond to simulation tasks and modify design parameters. A satellite finite element model can reach the scale of 250000 nodes and 200000 units. The satellite static analysis condition and dynamic analysis condition need to carry out multiple iterative calculations. Deep space exploration, manned spaceflight, communication and navigation satellites and research projects are need to be analyzed and designed in parallel. The computing capacity of the platform is required to be high. At the same time, the model task has certain periodicity, which leads to the platform resources cannot be fully utilized in real time. When the platform resources cannot be used 100%, some computing nodes are idle, resulting in waste of energy consumption.

Assume that the number of platform nodes is N, the number of CPU cores per node is K, and the platform CPU resource is N × K. To simplify the model, set the node status as: idle, busy. The idle means that the node has no computing job running. The busy means that there is more than one calculation job running on this node. The system resources are divided by time dimension. The total time of platform resources is:

$$T = \sum_{i=1}^{N} t_i^{idle} + t_i^{busy} \tag{1}$$

The t_i^{idle} represents the time when the node i is idle and the t_i^{busy} represents the time when the node i is busy.

The platform resource utilization rate (UR) is the ratio of the sum of nodes running calculation jobs to all resources of the platform.

$$UR = \frac{\sum_{i=1}^{N} t_i^{busy}}{\sum_{i=1}^{N} t_i^{idle} + t_i^{busy}} \tag{2}$$

If no energy saving measures are taken, all nodes in idle status are in running status. The platform power consumption is:

$$E_{IT} = \sum_{i=1}^{N} t_i^{idle} \times e_i^{idle} + t_i^{busy} \times e_i^{busy} \tag{3}$$

The e_i^{idle} represents the power consumption when the node i is idle, and the e_i^{busy} represents the power consumption when the node i is busy. For node power consumption in idle state, it is assumed that the power consumption is the same when the node types are the same.

For a computing node in idle state, it maintains the same level of power consumption as the normal operation state. That result a waste of energy. How to reduce the use of computing nodes and improve the utilization of a single computing node, without job scheduling and running time be affected. It is a breakthrough to improve the overall energy efficiency of the platform.

4 Algorithm Design and Implementation

Resource management and scheduling are the core components of high-performance computing platforms. A scheduling algorithm based on energy efficiency optimization is designed. Through reasonable resource scheduling and allocation, the power consumption of computing nodes is reduced while avoiding frequent node state transitions, ensuring platform throughput and efficient operation of jobs. If the node sleeps and wakes up frequently, it may lead to hardware failure, which will affect the stability of the platform. And it is not conducive to improving the energy efficiency of the platform.

The computing nodes $Node = \{N_1, N_2, \ldots, N_i\}$. The logical partitions $Partition = \{P_1, P_2, \ldots, P_j\}$, it is used to logically isolate computing nodes. The partition also provides targeted computing services such as node limit, CPU memory resource limit, and job number limit. When submitting a calculation job, it needs to be specified a partition. The job can be submitted to the partition according to the scheduling strategy. First, the platform match resources required by the job to available resources of the partition, and then select node to run the job (see Fig. 1).

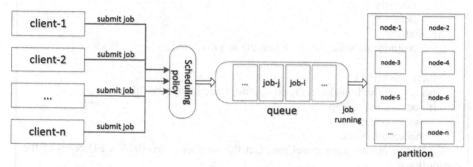

Fig. 1. Operation process of job submission

The scheduling algorithm based on energy efficiency optimization mainly focuses on the resource scheduling level of partition computing nodes. First, the computing nodes in the partition are numbered. In the process of job scheduling, the computing nodes with the highest number are preferred. Then initialize the computing nodes in the partition. All nodes are set to the running state and can receive jobs.

```
Algorithm 1: Job scheduling algorithm
queue=list(job-1,job-2,...job-n);
partition=list(node-1,node-2,...node-n)
allocateNode=list();
isSatisfy=false;
i=1;
while i<n
  job=queueList(i);Get the current task
  nodeNum=job.getNode();Get the number of nodes required for the job
  cpuNum=job.getCpu();Get the number of CPU cores required by the job
  for(j=1;j<n;j++)
    node=partitionList(j);Get the computing node j in the partition
    if node.status == busy || node.status == idle
      spareCpu=node.getSpareCpu();Get the number of available CPU cores of the
computing node j
      if cpuNum<spareCpu
        allocateNode.add(job,node);
      if allocateNode.getJobNode>nodeNum
        isSatisfy=true;
        break;
    if isSatisfy
    job.run(allocateNode);Run job i on the acquired node
    else
    for(j=1;j<n;j++)
    node=partitionList(j);Get the computing node j in the partition
    if node.status==sleep
      node.start();
      node.status=idle;
      spareCpu=node.getSpareCpu();Get the number of available CPU cores of the
computing node j
      if cpuNum<spareCpu
        allocateNode.add(job,node);
```

The strategy can be used combination with traditional scheduling strategies. First, the platform can receive submitted jobs in real time. Second according to certain strategies, it selects the first node in the partition that meets resource requirements to the selected job. This can effectively improve the utilization of computing nodes and optimize the energy efficiency of every single computing node.

```
Algorithm 2: Partition node energy consumption optimization algorithm
partition=list(node-1,node-2,...node-n);
i=1;
while i<n
  node=partitionlist(i);Get partition computing node
  if node.status==busy
    continue;
  if now-node.jobendtime>24
    node.status=sleep;
  node.sleep();
```

In the process of resource scheduling, it is necessary to uniformly manage resource state switching, dynamically configure switching opportunities and conditions. It combines maintenance with scheduling strategies and energy consumption management requirements (see Fig. 2).

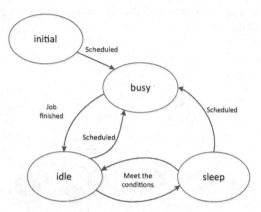

Fig. 2. Computing node resource state switch

1) When the partition computing node is idle for more than a certain period of time (such as 24 h), switch the node to the sleep state. That reduce the overall power consumption of the platform and improve the energy efficiency ratio.
2) When the node switches to the sleep state, configure the number of simultaneous switching nodes. That can avoid a large number of computing node simultaneous be sleep.
3) When the number of queued jobs in the partition exceeds a certain number (such as 5), the dormant node will be switched to the running state, and the number of switched nodes will be controlled to avoid the impact of energy consumption caused by a large number of node state switching.

In the process of simulation job scheduling on the platform, it is necessary to ensure that the job can obtain enough computing resources. Through saving the running time of a job, it can reduce energy consumption required by the job; On the other hand, by sleeping the idle nodes to reduce the number of running computing nodes, and then it will reduce the overall energy consumption of the platform.

When scheduling computing node resources, the running computing nodes should have high priority. So that the least recently used computing nodes are finally allocated, while reducing the frequent sleep and wake-up of resources. It also can improve the reliability of the platform.

Input. Job resource requirements (number of nodes, number of CPU cores), node sets.

Output: assigning node sets.

1) The initialization allocation node set is empty;

2) Select the running nodes from the node set in order;
3) Judge whether the number of available CPU cores of the selected node is greater than the number of CPU cores required by the job. If it is greater than the number, it will be placed in the allocation node set;
4) Judge whether the number of nodes in the allocation node set is greater than the number of job demand nodes, and return to the allocation node set if greater; Otherwise, repeat steps 3) and 4).

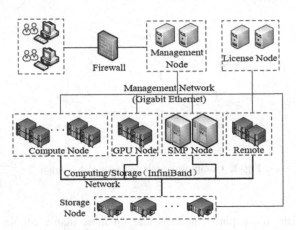

Fig. 3. The platform architecture

5   Simulation Experiment and Analysis

On the spacecraft simulation computing platform, we submit job for experiment verification. The platform architecture is shown in the Fig. 3.

5.1   Running Environment

The platform uses Slurm as a resource management and scheduling tool. Scheduling strategy uses first-come-first-service (FCFS). Computing nodes are composed of 20 blade servers. Computing networks are connected by IB switches. Key indicators of nodes are shown in the Table 1.

Table 1. Key indicators of nodes.

Name	Indicators
Type	Blade server
OS	CentOS7.6
CPU	2*24 Intel Xeon Gold 6240R 2.4GHz
Memory	12*16GB DDR4 2933MHz
IB Network	1*2 EDR 100Gb/s InfiniBand HCA Card

5.2 Data Acquisition

Data collection uses out-of-band monitoring and in-band monitoring. The out-of-band monitoring uses Intelligent Platform Management Interface (IMPI), and the in-band monitoring is based on an open source monitoring tool Nagios.

The real-time power of each computing node is obtained based on the IMPITOOL tool, and the power consumption data are summarized to the management node. Key services of Nagios monitoring tools include icinga and nrpe. The nrpe services deployed on the computing nodes is to monitor the usage of CPU and memory resources. It also can monitor the operation of job process services. The nrpe services transfer monitoring indicator data to the icinga services deployed on management nodes. The management node configures the relational database MariaDB and the sequential database InfluxDB, which annotates the collection time for all collected data and facilitates the association analysis.

Set collection frequency to 1m for the monitoring data. The collection index and data style are shown in the Table 2.

Table 2. Sample of Energy Consumption Data.

Name	IP	Power(W)	CPU(%)	Memory(%)	Time
node1	30.10.10.1	405	68.2	32	2022–03-20 12:28:10
node2	30.10.10.2	468	93.3	23.2	2022–03-20 12:28:10
node3	30.10.10.3	474	88.7	19.7	2022–03-20 12:28:10
node4	30.10.10.4	436	82.7	15.3	2022–03-20 12:28:10
...	...	...	...	...	...
node20	30.10.10.20	243	1	4.8	2022–03-20 12:28:10

5.3 Experimental Settings

Job selection: From the structure, fluid, heat, electromagnetic simulation calculation, select typical application examples to build a real simulation job sequence.

Platform Load Settings: In order to comprehensively analyze the energy consumption comparison of the optimization algorithm in the platform simulation environment, different platform loads are controlled by the number of jobs. On this basis, the CPU usage and power consumption of nodes are counted according to the time distribution, and the CPU usage and energy consumption distribution under different load conditions are analyzed.

Job Scheduling Strategy: A comparative test of FCFS scheduling strategy and scheduling strategy based on energy efficiency optimization.

5.4 Result Analysis

In the actual simulation calculation job, three jobs are selected from the specialties of structure, fluid, heat and electromagnetism to form 12 different size and professional operation sequences, which cover the routine calculation tasks. During the testing process, control the number of running jobs and the parallel core of each job to obtain different CPU utilization of nodes.

Statistical analysis is conducted for the empty load and the load of 30%, 60% and 90% respectively, lasting for 13 h. The CPU utilization changes with time are shown in the figure. Under the corresponding load, the power consumption of the computing node is monitored in real time for 13 h. The power consumption changes with time as shown in the figure. Through comparative analysis of CPU utilization and power consumption over time, it is found that CPU utilization is positively related to power consumption, and power consumption increases with the increase of CPU utilization. When the computing node is empty, the power consumption is about 240W. When the computing node is 90% loaded, the power consumption is about 470W. The empty load power consumption of computing nodes is half of the full load power consumption. When the overall load of the platform is low, the proportion of idle node power consumption will be greatly increased. It is very important to reduce the empty load ratio of computing nodes to improve the energy efficiency ratio of the platform (Fig. 4).

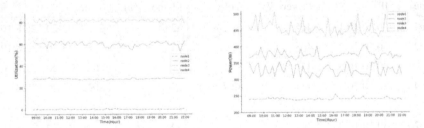

Fig. 4. Changes in CPU and memory utilization of computing nodes under different loads

Under the condition that the running jobs are consistent, the scheduling algorithm based on energy efficiency optimization is compared with the FCFS scheduling algorithm. The total power consumption is counted under different platform loads. The load and power consumption changes of computing nodes are shown in the Fig. 5.

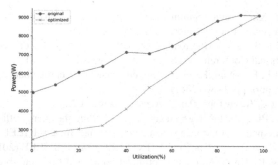

Fig. 5. The load and power consumption changes of computing nodes under different platform loads.

The scheduling algorithm based on energy efficiency optimization is compared with the FCFS algorithm, and the power consumption is reduced by 25% on average. When the overall load of the platform is low, the power consumption is reduced by 50%, and the energy-saving effect is obvious. As the overall load of the platform increases, the rate of power reduction continues to decline. Under full load, the power consumption of the two algorithms tends to be the same.

At the same time, in order to avoid the impact of the scheduling algorithm based on energy efficiency optimization on the platform throughput and job running time, the idle state computing node is reserved in the scheduling algorithm to ensure that the job response time is equal to the conventional scheduling algorithm.

6 Conclusion

This paper analysis the characteristics of spacecraft simulation based on the space-craft simulation computing platform. Collecting the actual operation data and analyze the platform energy consumption model. On the premise of not affecting the platform throughput and operation time, compare the optimized scheduling algorithm with the conventional scheduling algorithm, the overall energy consumption of the platform is reduced by an average of 25%. The algorithm effective improving the energy efficiency and reducing the cost. Later, we can further analyze simulation computing tasks based on historical job operation data, develop timing analysis and prediction based on machine learning algorithms, to make it more energy efficiency.

References

1. Li, Q., Rao, W., Cheng, X., Wei, H., Wang, C., Dong, J.: Aerodynamic design, analysis, and validation techniques for the Tianwen-1 entry module. Astrodynamics **6**(1), 39–52 (2022). https://doi.org/10.1007/s42064-021-0123-z
2. Liu, L., Liu, Y., Chen, M., et al.: Trajectory schemes of chang'e-5 extended missions to liberation points. J. Astronaut. Astronaut. **43**(3), 293–300 (2022)
3. Li, J., Zhang, C., Xing, W.: Numerical simulation studies of the cushion process for the new generation of manned spacecraft re-entry capsule. Aerosp. Return Remote Sens. **42**(2), 12–19 (2021)

4. Lin, H., Peng, Y., Xia, Y., et al.: Summary of energy consumption evaluation method standard for China's data center. Energy China. **42**(8), 36–39 (2020)
5. Agerwala, T.: Challenges on the road to exascale computing. In: Proceedings of the 22nd Annual International Conference on Supercomputing, vol. 2, (2008)
6. Lucas, R., Ang, J., Bergman, K., et al.: Top ten exascale research challenges. DOE ASCAC subcommittee report, pp. 1–86 (2014)
7. TOP 500 list. https://www.top500.org/. Accessed June 2022
8. Jaureguialzo, E.: PUE: the green grid metric for evaluating the energy efficiency in DC (Data Center). Measurement method using the power demand. In: 2011 IEEE 33rd International Telecommunications Energy Conference (INTELEC), pp. 1–8. IEEE (2011)
9. Chen, G., Huang, K., Knoll, A.: Energy optimization for real-time multiprocessor system-on-chip with optimal DVFS and DPM combination. ACM Trans. Embed. Comput. Syst. (TECS) **13**(3s), 1–21 (2014)
10. Etinski, M., Corbalan, J., Labarta, J., et al.: Parallel job scheduling for power constrained HPC systems. Parallel Comput. **38**(12), 615–630 (2012)
11. Yang, C.-T., Wan, T.-Y.: Implementation of an energy saving cloud infrastructure with virtual machine power usage monitoring and live migration on OpenStack. Computing **102**(6), 1547–1566 (2020). https://doi.org/10.1007/s00607-020-00808-7
12. Khani, H., Yazdani, N., Mohammadi, S.: Power-aware game for cloud computing: a distributed mechanism based on game theory for minmizing power consumption in cloud scale datacenter. In: 6th International Symposium on Telecommunications (IST), pp. 598–601. IEEE (2012)
13. Samadiani, E., Joshi, Y.: Energy efficient thermal management of data centers via open multi-scale design: a review of research questions and approaches. J. Enhanc. Heat Transf. **18**(1), 15–30 (2011). https://doi.org/10.1615/JEnhHeatTransf.v18.i1.20
14. Barroso, L.A., Hölzle, U.: The case for energy-proportional computing. Computer **40**(12), 33–37 (2007)

SADA: SDN Architecture Based Secure Dynamic Access Scheme for Satellite Network

Dong Yan[✉], Ming Gu, Luyuan Wang, and Xiongwen He

Institute of Spacecraft System Engineering CAST, Beijing 100094, People's Republic of China
yandong200@163.com

Abstract. In view of the characteristics of limited resources and insufficient security guarantee capability of satellite network nodes, this paper proposes a secure dynamic access scheme for satellite network based on SDN architecture. By adopting SDN architecture, the operation efficiency of the network system can be effectively improved. The access process is divided into two stages. In the first stage, node reputation is confirmed to ensure the network security. In the second stage, resource aware dynamic access is performed to improve the network QoS guarantee capability. Finally, the performance of the algorithm is verified by simulation experiments, which proves the advantages of the algorithm in data transmission success rate.

Keywords: Satellite Network · SDN Architecture · Node Reputation · Dynamic Access

1 Introduction

Satellite network has the characteristics of wide coverage, no influence of natural conditions on the ground, simple and flexible access. It can be efficiently applied to rescue, weather prediction, resource detection, environment and disaster monitoring. It is considered to be an important part of the next generation Internet by many researchers and also a space infrastructure to be actively developed and constructed.

Satellite networks can be divided into backbone nodes and access nodes according to node different functions. Among them, backbone nodes are usually composed of GEO/MEO satellites in high and medium orbits, and their responsibilities are mainly to process information exchange and transmission, while access nodes are usually composed of LEO satellites in low orbit to realize real-time information transmission and other functions. With the development of satellite network, the types and application types of access nodes are becoming more abundant, and the requirements for network service quality are becoming higher. Currently, the common network access and application mode, which relies on the ground system to plan in advance and reserves access bandwidth and processing resources, is relatively simple, but its fixed and inflexible manner makes it difficult to provide more efficient access methods and better service

© ICST Institute for Computer Sciences, Social Informatics and Telecommunications Engineering 2023
Published by Springer Nature Switzerland AG 2023. All Rights Reserved
R. Li et al. (Eds.): MOBILWARE 2022, LNICST 507, pp. 177–185, 2023.
https://doi.org/10.1007/978-3-031-34497-8_15

quality assurance. Meanwhile, with the continuous increase of access users, it will also greatly increase the complexity of ground planning.

At present, researchers have conducted some research on the access methods of satellite networks and propose a variety of schemes [1–3]. Most of these schemes still give advance connection planning. Although the bandwidth utilization efficiency and processing delay of the link slot are improved to a certain extent, the current state of the backbone node and the security performance of the access node are not considered. When the current load of the newly established backbone node is heavy, the connection state may be unstable, the processing and switching capacity may be reduced, and even the service may not be provided. When the security of the access node is not confirmed, it may lead to malicious behavior in the network, affect the performance of the whole network, and in some serious cases, cause network interruption. In view of these problems, this paper proposes SDN architecture based secure dynamic access scheme for satellite network, called SADA, which can authenticate the security of network access nodes and avoid the impact of network performance due to the overload of management nodes in the network.

The rest of this paper is organized as follow: the second part introduces the related work, the third part introduces the dynamic access mechanism in detail, the fourth part evaluates the performance of the algorithm through simulation experiments, the fifth part is the conclusion.

2   Related Work

Chen et al. [4] studied the routing technology based on the double-layer satellite network structure and proposed satellite grouping and routing protocol (SGRP). By using the relative position relationship between high and low orbit satellites, the low orbit access satellites are divided into several groups, and high orbit satellites corresponds to an access group. They collect and exchange the link delay, and calculate the routing table according to the shortest path principle. When the relative position relationship between the high and low orbit satellites changes, the grouping relationship will also change. At this time, a new group will be generated. The satellite network topology within the time when each packet has not changed can be considered as unchanged. This method is mainly applied to the scenario where the network connection relationship is relatively stable, and does not pay attention to the state of the network node itself and the scenario of dynamic access.

The distributed QoS routing algorithm (DQA) proposed by Xu et al. [5] takes into account the status of satellite nodes and can avoid the overload of nodes to a certain extent. When calculating and planning the routing table, it optimizes the two performance parameters of network delay and link utilization, which can reduce the network congestion probability. However, the algorithm is only designed according to specific limited QoS parameters, which limits the applicability of the algorithm, and does not consider the security of nodes, which may lead to network security risks.

Zhu et al. [6, 7] designed a network control architecture combining master controller and slave controller according to the idea of SDN. In this method, the users on the earth surface are divided into fixed logical areas, and each area corresponds to a corresponding slave controller, which realizes the sub network division of the satellite communication network. The functions of the two controllers are different. The slave controller is responsible for collecting the network and node status information of the corresponding subnet and uploading it to the master controller. The master controller manages the satellite communication network topology according to the global network state and calculates the routing path between multiple subnets. The satellite only realizes the functions of information transmission, routing and forwarding to minimize the requirements on the on-board processing capacity.

The secure dynamic access mechanism of satellite network based on SDN architecture proposed in this paper uses SDN controller to master the global information of satellite network, which can obtain the real-time status of network nodes. The mechanism in this paper realizes adaptive dynamic access with intelligent selection method of network access with multiple QoS parameters. At the same time, the reputation model of satellite network nodes is designed to evaluate the security of access nodes, so as to avoid nodes with poor security from joining the network and affecting the network performance. Through this method, the newly added access nodes can be prevented from connecting to some high load backbone nodes, and the network security performance can be guaranteed, which can effectively solve the problems in the above research.

3 SDN Architecture Based Secure Dynamic Access Scheme for Satellite Network

3.1 SADA Network Model

SDN is a new network control architecture with decoupling advantage and forwarding function. In recent years, it has received more attention from researchers. By separating control and data and combining programmable control manner, it can realize flexible control and centralized management of the network. For the satellite network, the control plane node is responsible for collecting the node state information, authenticating the identity of the new access node, and completing the calculation, generation and distribution of the key. The data plane node no longer needs to have powerful computing and storage performance to complete complex tasks, but only needs to focus on basic tasks such as data forwarding. This remarkable feature of SDN technology is suitable for satellite network scenarios with severe resource constraints, which can effectively reduce node overhead and ensure more stable and efficient operation of satellite networks.

The control plane needs to complete the functions of node identity authentication, key calculation and distribution, node state collection, routing calculation, etc., and needs powerful basic performance. Therefore, most SDN researches are placing the control plane nodes on the ground. Although the ground node as the control plane can have more powerful basic capabilities, it may lead to insufficient timeliness of key control information due to the inability to realize global ground station construction. It is difficult to adapt to the higher real-time and dynamic requirements of the future satellite network. In this paper, a SDN satellite network model with master-slave controller structure is proposed, which is called SADA model. Taking the double-layer satellite network scenario composed of GEO-LEO as an example, a two-level structure control plane is designed. The master controller is located on the ground, and its main functions are key generation and distribution, node state storage and analysis, routing calculation and other complex tasks according to specific algorithms. The slave controller node is located at the high orbit satellite node, and more than three GEO nodes can basically achieve full coverage of the low earth orbit satellites operating in the middle and low latitudes. They also maintain relatively stable and continuous communication with the master controller. As the backbone node in the network, it mainly completes new node discovery, node status collection and sending to the master controller. The slave controller nodes obtain the network operation rules from the master controller and sent to the data plane node. Compared with the traditional satellite node, the slave controller node usually has higher basic performance, so it can also ensure higher work efficiency when realizing the controller function. As an access node, the data plane node completes the routine data collection, distribution and transmission tasks after network access request and obtaining the control plane access authentication. The Fig. 1 of SADA model is shown as follows.

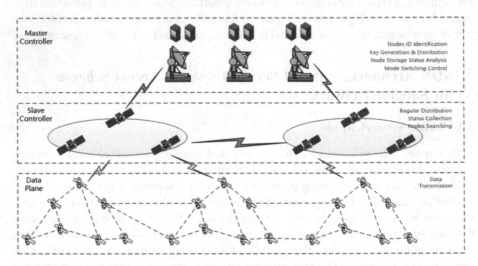

Fig. 1. SADA Model Figure

3.2 Dynamic Access Mechanism of Satellite Network

The current satellite network access methods mainly improve the bandwidth utilization efficiency and processing delay, but less consider the problems of limited resources and service capacity of satellite nodes and the security of access nodes, which makes it difficult to ensure the security of satellite network access and subsequent operation, data transmission efficiency and flexible management of the network.

Based on the dynamic access model of satellite network with two-level SDN control structure designed above, this paper intends to design from the following aspects: firstly, it proposes a node reputation evaluation strategy, analyzes the behavior of the access node by collecting the network data of the access node, and then dynamically adjusts its network access capability according to the obtained reputation evaluation value to provide support for ensuring network security. Then, a load aware dynamic access mechanism for backbone nodes is proposed to avoid network congestion and high packet loss rate during satellite network access.

A. Reputation Evaluation

Reputation is used to express the credibility of an individual in group interaction. The main objectives of the reputation evaluation method designed in this paper include three main points. It can provide reliable information to determine whether a node is trusted. It can give priority to ensuring access requests of nodes with good reputation. It can limit response or even no response to the access request of the bad node. Reputation [8] is described as: the reputation of an entity refers to the expectation of its future behavior based on the observation of other entities or the information of its historical behavior at a given time and context. This definition emphasizes the contextual relevance of reputation, and explains that reputation occurs in the interaction between different entities, and also explains the continuity of node reputation and the relevance of future behavior. In 2004, S. Ganeriwal and M.B. Srivastava designed a reputation evaluation model BRSN [9] for the application scenario of wireless sensor networks with limited resources. The model uses Bayes formula to fit the reputation distribution and beta distribution, and obtains the conclusion that the reputation of the node follows the beta distribution, which can calculate the expected value of the beta distribution to obtain the trust value of the node. BRSN model performs fitting analysis on reputation distribution and beta distribution, and it is known that beta distribution can conveniently describe reputation distribution.

$$R_{kn} = B(\alpha_{kn} + 1, \beta_{kn} + 1) \tag{1}$$

R_{kn} represents the reputation distribution of node k with respect to node n, α_{kn}, β_{kn} means the number of normal behaviors and the number of abnormal behaviors obtained by the node K with respect to the node n respectively.

SADA reputation model makes use of BRSN reputation method, and improves the specific application environment of satellite network. The reputation behavior of nodes is divided into data generation behavior, data transmission behavior and data response behavior. Data generation behavior mainly refers to the nodes, which are the source of data, actively initiates network attacks and other malicious behaviors, such as DDoS attacks and black hole attacks. Data transmission behavior attack mainly refers to whether there are malicious behaviors such as data discarding and content tampering in the process of routing exchange and data forwarding. The data response behavior mainly refers to the malicious behavior which causes no respond normally to the protocol requests of the control plane node or other nodes of the data plane, resulting in the interaction failure. When applying the SADA reputation model to calculate the reputation value of a node, it is necessary to combine the specific application scenarios and assign different weights according to the degree of influence of their behavior. The calculation method of the reputation value of node k to node n can be obtained:

$$C_{kn} = \begin{cases} W_s \times C_{kn-s} + W_t \times C_{kn-t} + W_r \times C_{kn-r} - m \times \Delta C & \text{(firstaccess or malicious actions before)} \\ W_s \times C_{kn-s} + W_t \times C_{kn-t} + W_r \times C_{kn-r} + \Delta C & \text{(no malicious actions before)} \end{cases}$$

$$\tag{2}$$

$$W_s + W_t + W_r = 1 \tag{3}$$

$$C_{kn-s/t/r} = E(R_{kn}) = E(B(\alpha_{kn} + 1, \beta_{kn} + 1)) = \frac{\alpha_{kn} + 1}{\alpha_{kn} + \beta_{kn} + 2} \tag{4}$$

C_{kn} represents the reputation value of node k for node n. W_S, W_t and W_r respectively represent the influence weight of data generation behavior, data transmission behavior and data response behavior in the application scenario, and C_{kn-s}, C_{kn-t} and C_{kn-r} respectively represent the reputation value of data generation behavior, data transmission behavior and data response behavior, ΔC represents the control change amount. $C_{kn-s/t/r}$ represents the special behavior reputation, which is the statistical expectation of the reputation distribution. It can be expressed by $E(R_{kn})$. Any kind of abnormal behavior will cause β_{kn} to add 1, and each normal behavior will cause α_{kn} to add 1.

The calculation of reputation value takes the historical behavior of the node as an important measurement element, and takes the time period of each access to the network as the calculation cycle. When calculating the reputation of this cycle, the reputation of the first two cycles needs to be considered. Therefore, when calculating the reputation value, there are two cases. The first case is that the access node accesses the network for the first time or has a malicious behavior before. When calculating the reputation value of this cycle, the control change amount is reduced to punish. M represents the number of cycles in which the malicious behavior occurred before, and can be taken as 0, 1, 2. In the second case, the access node has not had any malicious behavior before, and the control change amount can be additionally rewarded when calculating the reputation value of the current cycle. Set the minimum reputation threshold C_0 and the normal threshold C_1. When the reputation value of a node is less than C_0, the node is prohibited from joining the network. When the reputation value of a node is greater than C_1, the node is fully allowed to join the network. When the reputation value of a node is between C_0 and C_1, the node's access request is permitted with the ratio of p. p is set according to the application scenario.

B. Resource Aware Dynamic Access Mechanism

The traditional satellite access methods mainly consider coverage and connection time. However, with the continuous demand of space applications for QoS guarantee capability, the traditional methods have been difficult to meet the needs of user applications. Due to the limited resources of the satellite network nodes, when the nodes handle the high load state, large packet loss is likely to occur. This may affect the normal communication of the satellite network and even threatens the network security. In this paper, a node load aware dynamic access mechanism is designed, which focuses on the real-time load state of the satellite while improving the utilization efficiency of satellite resources. During the access process, the dynamic access selection is made by evaluating the current load state of the backbone nodes, so as to avoid the excessive load of the satellite network nodes and ensure the secure and stable operation of the satellite network.

SADA designs a multi metric parameters dynamic access mechanism, and selects the node CPU utilization rate, the signal-to-noise ratio and the connection service time as the access metric parameters for dynamic access processing, which can be replaced with the application scenario. When an access node wants to join the network, the backbone node makes dynamic access selection according to its current performance and connection status with the access node.

$$R_{kn} = A\frac{c_{max} - c}{c_{max} - c_{min}} + B\frac{10^{\frac{s}{10}}}{10^{\frac{s_{max}}{10}}} + C\frac{t_{remain}}{t_{max}}. \tag{5}$$

$$A + B + C = 1 \tag{6}$$

R_{kn} represents the probability value of the current access to the satellite network. c represents the current CPU utilization value. C_{max} and c_{min} are two thresholds, which can be called upper threshold and lower threshold. s represents the signal-to-noise ratio of the satellite, and s_{max} represents the maximum value of the signal-to-noise ratio. T_{remain} is the coverage time that the satellite to be accessed can provide, t_{max} is the maximum coverage time that a single satellite can provide. A, B and C are the weights of the three parameters. Set the minimum threshold R_{min} for dynamic access. If R_{kn} is less than R_{min}, it indicates that the current access resources are insufficient and the current access is rejected. Otherwise, dynamic probabilistic network access is performed according to the calculated R_{kn}.

C. Satellite Network Security Dynamic Access Mechanism
The satellite network secure dynamic access process is divided into two stages. In the first stage, the node reputation is confirmed. When the slave controller nodes receive the access request of the data plane node, it is necessary to confirm the reputation of the access node, besides conventional ID identification, key authentication etc. With the method proposed in the paper, the reputation value of the access node is obtained according to its reputation behavior. A threshold value is set for the reputation value of the node accessing the network. The process can start the second stage, only when the minimum value of the network access reputation is met. Otherwise, the control plane rejects the node accessing the network. In the second stage, resource aware dynamic access is performed. The control plane node judges the current access resource status of the backbone node according to the resource aware dynamic access mechanism in this paper, and calculates the access probability to perform network dynamic access. If the current access resource status is insufficient to meet the node's efficient access and subsequent high-quality network services, the access request is rejected.

4 Performance Evaluation

In order to verify the performance of SADA, this section selects one of the most representative QoS algorithms DQA to compare the performance of the end-to-end transmission success rate of satellite nodes. The end-to-end transmission success rate of satellite nodes is one of the most important network performance indicators, which can reflect the rationality of network architecture, access and transmission strategy, and QoS guarantee capability.

The experiment topology in this section is composed of 3 GEO satellites and 66 LEO satellites. The LEO satellites consist of 6 orbital planes, 11 satellites in each orbital plane. On the basis of this topology, 3–5 access nodes are set as malicious nodes, and the destination nodes are randomly selected. The paths between them can be called malicious paths. Set the packet loss rate of intermediate nodes passed by a single malicious path as 0.7, the packet loss rate of intermediate nodes passed by two malicious paths as 0.6, the packet loss rate of intermediate nodes passed by three or more malicious paths as 0.5, and the packet loss rate of intermediate nodes not passed by malicious paths as 0.9. Compare the data transmission capability that different algorithms can guarantee when facing different numbers of malicious nodes. In order to ensure the authenticity and effectiveness of the test, 100 tests are conducted for each test condition, and the average value is taken to finally obtain the data transmission success rate under this condition.

Figure 2 shows the impact on the DQA data transmission success rate in the face of different numbers of malicious nodes, and Fig. 3 shows the performance comparison of SADA and DQA in the transmission success rate.

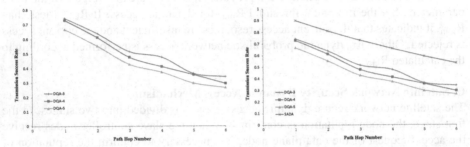

Fig. 2. Data transmission success rate of DQA under different conditions

Fig. 3. Transmission success rate of SADA and DQA

It can be seen from the experiment results in Fig. 2 that the transmission success rate will decrease with the increase of the number of malicious nodes. It is not difficult to see from the test results in Fig. 3 that the algorithm performance of SADA is better than that of DQA. The main reason is that SADA's reputation evaluation and resource aware dynamic access mechanism can effectively prevent malicious nodes from joining the network, avoid the overload of network nodes, and improve the network QoS guarantee capability.

5   Conclusion

SADA is a secure dynamic access mechanism of satellite network based on SDN architecture. The method mainly consists of the following parts: 1) SDN architecture is adopted to separate the data plane from the control plane. The control plane is divided into a master controller on the ground and a slave controller on the space part, effectively improving the operation efficiency of the network system. 2) Reputation evaluation comprehensively evaluates the current and historical network reputation behavior of a node, and responds to the network access request of a node, supplies limited response or no response according to the obtained reputation value of the node, so as to ensure the security of the network. 3) The mechanism of resource aware dynamic access selects typical performances that affect network access and operation, and conduct dynamic probabilistic network access, which can avoid overload of network nodes and improve network QoS guarantee capability. Finally, the simulation results show that SADA has a better performance in data transmission success rate.

References

1. Papapetrou, E., Karapantazis, S., Dimitriadis, G.: Satellite handover techniques for LEO networks. Int. J. Satell. Commun. Netw. **22**(2), 231–245 (2004)
2. Papapetrou, E., Pavlidou, F.: QoS handover management in LEO/MEO satellite systems. Wirel. Pers. Commun. **24**(2), 189–204 (2003)
3. Chowdhury, P.K., Atiquzzaman, M.: Handover schemes in satellite networks: state-of-the-art and future research directions. IEEE Commun. Surv. Tutor. **8**(4), 2–14 (2006)
4. Chen, C., Ekici, E.: A routing protocol for hierachical LEO/MEO satellite IP networks. ACM Wirel. Netw. J. **11**(4), 507–521 (2005)
5. Xu, H., Wu, S.: A distributed QoS routing based on ant algorithm for LEO satellite network. Chinese J. Comput. **30**(3), 361–367 (2007)
6. Fan, Z., Wu, H., Xu, J., et al.: An optimization algorithm for spatial information network self-healing based on software defined network. In: Proceedings of the 12th International Conference on Computer Science and Education (ICCSE), New York, pp. 369–374 (2017)
7. Li, Y., Teng, Q., Kong, Z., et al.: Design of spatial information network routing strategy based on SDN architecture. Spacecr. Eng. **28**(5), 54–61 (2019). (in Chinese)
8. Hu, N., Zou, P., Sun, P.-D.: Reputation-based collaborative management method for inter-domain routing security: reputation-based collaborative management method for inter-domain routing security. J. Softw. **21**(3), 505–515 (2010). https://doi.org/10.3724/SP.J.1001.2010.03479
9. Saurabh. G., Laura, K., Srivastava, B., et al.: Reputation-based framework for high integrity sensor networks. ACM Trans. Sensor Netw. **4**(3), 15 (2008)

Research on the Concept and Connotation of Space Proving Grounds (SPG)

Dan Wang[✉], Zhengji Song, and Chaoji Chen

Beijing Institute of Spacecraft System Engineering, Beijing, China
wangdan_ict_hit@163.com

Abstract. In view of the limited overall planning of experiments in various fields of space technology/Science/application, the unclear mechanism faced by some core space technologies and the insufficient driving force of space as a strategic commanding point for the national economy and the people's livelihood, academician Luan Enjie put forward the concept of Space Proving Grounds (SPG) for the first time, hoping to systematically plan and lead the follow-up space test tasks by building a series of space facilities. SPG focus on three aspects: S science, E (exploration) and T (Technology). Through extensive investigation of the status quo of space tests at home and abroad, this paper puts forward the development trend of space experiments, studies the concept of space proving grounds, studies the composition of SPG from the three aspects of space segment, ground segment and soft environment. It also puts forward the phased objectives and system service framework in the future, so as to provide suggestions for China's "systematic and phased" construction of space test infrastructure, and provide decision-making reference for China's space test management to achieve "demand and high efficiency".

Keywords: Space Proving Grounds · Space technical tests · Space science

1 Introduction

Spacecraft is a type of equipment with the most complex system and the most advanced technology. It has high cost and needs to face the extreme and complex environment of space. For developing aerospace technology and equipment, it is necessary to go through the ground test stage, the space test stage and the application stage, of which the space test stage is the most indispensable and important one, which can accumulate flight experience for the development of spacecraft systems, reduce Satellite cost and reduce operational risk [1]. It is usually the first step to carry out space experiments and launching technology test satellites, for a country to enter the aerospace field.

With the advancement of technology and the further deepening of space cognition, the existing technical test system has been unable to satisfy the development demands of China's space technology, thus the construction of a basic space test platform serving China's space activities has become very urgent [2].

R. Li et al. (Eds.): MOBILWARE 2022, LNICST 507, pp. 186–194, 2023.
https://doi.org/10.1007/978-3-031-34497-8_16

At present, the United States, Russia, Germany and other major space countries have coordinated space tests to some extent [3–6], and carried out some space programs to coordinate space tests locally, including the "Space Test Program" (STP) carried out by the U.S. Department of Defense. The program of "On-Orbit Verification" (OOV) has been carried out by the German Space Agency and the plan of "Space Environment Reliability Verification Integrated System" (SERVIS) has been carried out by the Japanese Ministry of Economy, etc. These plans achieve the purpose of reducing duplication and reducing costs by establishing a platform for overall management of space experiments, setting up projects for space experiments or providing flight opportunities.

The space technology of China has developed to a critical stage of becoming a aerospace power. The construction of a space power requires a comprehensive understanding of the elements of space, and must strengthen the construction of space proving grounds to promote space science, space exploration, space applications and other fields. The overall and orderly development and technological progress of space resources will improve the efficiency of space resource application. The construction of the space proving ground is a comprehensive planning and top-level design for space experiments in various fields. It is necessary to clarify the concept and connotation of the space proving ground, study the framework and composition of the space proving ground, and provide support for China's comprehensive utilization of space resources.

2 Related Works

2.1 Development Status Abroad

Space is a testing ground for technological transformation and scientific progress. The purpose of the "Space Proving Ground" is to coordinate test projects and flight opportunities, avoid duplication of construction, and speed up technological upgrading. The core lies in sharing and coordination. Developed countries such as the United States consider the space as a test base, test a variety of advanced technologies, and promote them into applications [6–8], such as the International and Day Coexistence Program, the James Webb Space Telescope Program, and the Mars Exploration Mission Program [8–10]. NASA has substantially increased success rates and benefits by establishing a series of specifications and guidelines for the test site. The core is to use resources rationally, invest in more economical projects, and provide guidelines to ensure the effectiveness of NASA's investment. In particular, space technology experimentation is a technical area of particular concern to countries, but the way of development differs.

The United States has formed a relatively complete satellite technology test system, mainly based on a series of dedicated technology test satellites, including manned spacecraft platform loading and technical test parts of various application satellite series. In recent decades, a number of technical test satellite development plans have been formulated successively [1–3], among which the more famous ones are Lincoln Test Satellite Program (LES), Applied Technology Test Satellite Program (ATS), Space Test Program (STP) and New Prosperity Project (NMP) [4], etc.

"On-Orbit Verification" (OOV) is a national space program in Germany, which aims to provide test opportunities for applying new technology solutions to space projects, especially high-tech on-orbit verification. The key element of the plan is the demonstration flight of regarding the microsatellite "Technology Experiment Carrier" (TET) as a platform [5].

Russia has comprehensively developed a series of spacecraft such as communication and broadcasting, navigation and positioning, civil remote sensing, military reconnaissance, data relay, missile early warning, manned spaceflight, and space exploration. The early development scale was large, and the technical level in some fields was in a leading position. In the 21st century, since the total number of satellites launched by Russia has dropped sharply to less than 20, the number of satellites launched by its technology test satellites is very few.

Japan has formed a special and stable series of technical test satellites, and mainly relies on the series of technical test satellites to carry out engineering technology tests of various application satellites including communication and remote sensing.

Japan has vigorously carried out technology development in the fields of microsatellite technology, space optical communication technology, large-scale communication platform, mobile communication and broadcasting technology, broadband multimedia technology, commercial off-the-shelf (COTS) products and other fields. Many aerospace countries have formed two series of comprehensive space technology test satellites—Engineering Test Satellites (ETS) and space planes, including Communication and Broadcasting Engineering Test Satellites (COMETS), Optical Inter-orbit Communication Technology Test Satellites (OICETS) and a series of communication test satellites, etc.

2.2 General Situation of China's Space Experiments

According to the support channels, space technology test satellites of China have categories such as military, civilian, and enterprise-independent. As shown in Fig. 1, Space technology test channels also include manned serial loading, application satellite loading and other forms [11]. Figure 1 shows current technology test system framework in the field of satellite development. Among them, the enterprise independent technology test satellite series and the national civil technology test satellite series have just begun. For the civil technology test satellite series, which aims at verifying the development achievements of each "five-year" plan of national aerospace, improving satellite system capabilities, and solving satellite common problems, long-term planning at the national level is also required. Strict test project selection criteria, sufficient ground and on-orbit verification and rational use of limited funds are also necessary to enhance aerospace technology capabilities.

In general, the development of international space experiments shows the following trends:

- The space test verification system has been continuously developed and improved
- The test satellites move towards the special application test and the synchronous development of common basic support
- Participation in the test becomes more extensive, and the opportunity to enter orbit becomes more convenient

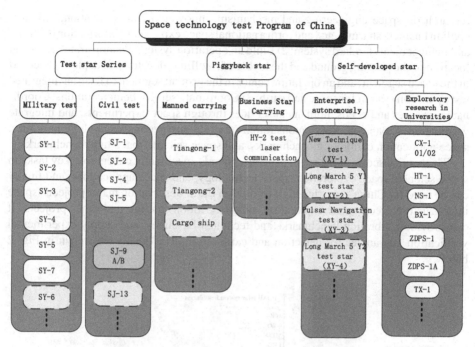

Fig. 1. Space technology test channel of China

3   The Concept and Connotation of Space Proving Grounds (SPG)

As an independent field of aerospace technology, space technology experiments of China focus on three aspects: S (science), E (exploration), and T (technology). Considering national conditions of China, relevant test tasks should include space science experiments tasks, technical verification test tasks, and application test tasks related to the national economy and people's livelihood.

The overall goal of the SPG is to build a basic space test facility for China, to implement space science, technological innovation, and application development "according to demand, into a system, and with high efficiency". Advanced layout to break through the international leading technologies such as near-earth space, in-situ arrival in the solar system, and extra-system remote sensing; build and improve the experimental engineering system for systematic access, cognition and control of space commanding heights and new frontiers; exploring major scientific discoveries and innovations, verifying key core technology products, smoothing the transformation mechanism of scientific and technological applications, and supporting the construction of major national projects related to the national economy and people's livelihood.

The SPG is to "promote the comprehensive development of space science, space technology, and space applications", guide the strategic direction of space power, and implement a set of system coordination, standardized operation, and autonomous and controllable national space test infrastructure, including: 1) Sound soft environment. Establish a space experiment information system, to strengthen basic and normative research on space engineering and mechanism, innovation and application, military-civilian business sharing, etc., and form a national space experiment information database and management standard system; 2) Build an operation system. Demonstrate the spatial location of the proving ground and the layout of satellites, develop and deploy spacecraft in the space segment, and an operation center in the ground segment to form an integrated test operation system for space and earth; 3) Coordinate service demonstrations. Coordinate resources and needs, implement services through space experiments, and integrate verification, expansion, and demonstration of space engineering technology baselines, space application calibration benchmarks, and space science space-time benchmarks.

The service scope of the space proving grounds specifically covers four key tasks in space science, space exploration, space technology, and space applications, and finally can be used for China's existing high-resolution Earth observation major projects, space infrastructure, deep space exploration, manned, moon landing and other projects. It can provide calibration benchmarks and technical baselines, and supply experimental verification guarantees for detection and exploration. The details are shown in Fig. 2 below.

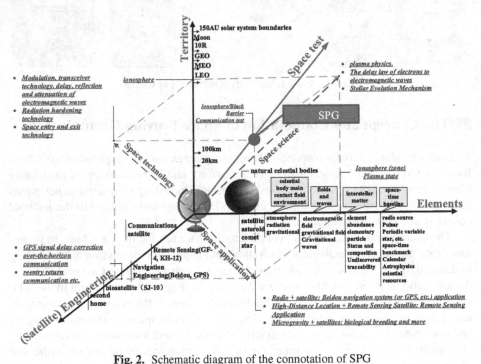

Fig. 2. Schematic diagram of the connotation of SPG

4   The Composition of the SPG

The SPG consists of three parts: the soft environment, the space segment, and the ground segment, which are shown in Fig. 3.

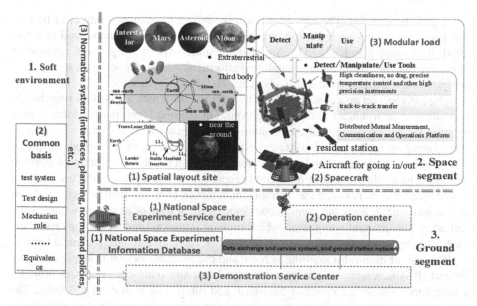

Fig. 3. Schematic diagram of the composition of SPG

4.1 Space Segment Design

The space proving grounds aims to be a national space test infrastructure that conforms to national conditions, develops in an orderly manner, and has a complete system. It coordinates the common needs of space science, technology, and engineering through tests, to form a functions-oriented space science platform architecture, which covers the six major capabilities of "entry, station, exit, exploration, control, and use".

The SPG is a materialized concept. It is based on the systematic perspective of space as a unified overall research. Oriented by application development, the SPG system will consist of a series of various technical test platforms and loads with multi-type orbital layouts. The orbits should be distributed, including large elliptical orbits and other tracks with special significance, etc.

Considering the space orbit design and the space physical characteristics, three categories of traditional low, medium and high orbits, space dynamic balance points and extraterrestrial objects are selected to design the space proving grounds structure. The space segment test platform is divided into types of locations, including low orbit test platform, medium orbital general test and transfer platform, high-orbit test platform, space dynamic balance point test platform, lunar test base and deep space exploration test base. Different users can choose different test platforms according to their needs.

4.2 Test Platform Design

For the LEO space experiments, the SPG continues to learn from the existing management plan, which adopts the space station as the long-term resident test platform, and uses various technology test satellites as the dynamic test platform to build the LEO space proving grounds. The low-orbit test mission can be launched into orbit by normal carrying or carrying into orbit, and can carry out technical tests related to active removal of space debris in LEO orbit, material space exposure flight test, application of new technology verification of satellite platform, new load technology test, sky Base comprehensive calibration and space benchmark technology test.

The SPG will set up a general test and transfer platform with a relatively fixed height in a suitable environment in the middle orbit. On the one hand, the platform is used to solve the common needs of the medium-orbit space test, and can also be used as a springboard for transferring to different orbit heights to solve the test needs at special orbit heights. On the other hand, as a transfer platform, it is necessary for the platform to have on-orbit refilling, charging or assembly capabilities. The medium-orbit test platform can be utilized to carry out space environment detection tests, on-orbit flight tests of new microelectronic devices and commercial devices, flight tests of new high-voltage solar cell arrays, on-orbit refueling tests, orbital transfer station related technology tests, and medium-orbit application satellite technology Tests and other related technical tests.

The cost of high-orbit satellites is high, and the available orbital resources are very limited. It is necessary to configure a general test site platform to stay in orbit for a long time to meet the needs of long-term and multi-type high-orbit test tasks. The high-orbit test platform can be used to carry out continuous real-time monitoring of the space environment detection such as the evolution process of active regions, the process of solar eruption, orbital radiation environment and radiation effects. It can also explored for flight tests such as new microelectronic devices and commercial devices, new high-voltage solar cell arrays, and spacecraft charge and discharge effects.

The dynamic balance point in space attracts many researchers. Various types of space exploration and technology application experiments can be carried out, and orbital position resources are extremely important. A general-purpose special test field is configured at the L1 point of the earth and the moon. This point can not only carry out test missions such as interstellar highways, but also serve as a transit platform for space exploration, providing for subsequent moon, Mars and interstellar exploration. It can support the development of deep space probe fueling, energy relay, communication relay, earth or orbiting satellite weapon delivery, communication navigation and earth observation (including electromagnetic spectrum).

The use of lunar test bases can realize the development and utilization of lunar resources, and carry out in-depth research and exploration of space science. It can also verify key lunar test base construction technologies such as lunar engineering construction, energy, lunar movement, thermal control, data communication, base structure configuration, life support and space protection.

4.3 Ground Segment Design

A dedicated data receiving and processing system for space experiments will be built on the ground, and a network of space experiment data receiving stations will be formed by establishing multiple data receiving stations to uniformly receive and manage the data of various space experiment platforms in the space segment. The SPG will develop a comprehensive information system platform for the reception and processing of space test data, and form a comprehensive database of space technology test projects, resources, on-orbit test databases, ground test databases, parallel management information systems, and assessment and evaluation result databases. The ground part of SPG will have the capabilities of data processing and distribution.

4.4 Soft Environment Design

First, the SPG makes it easy for users to design relevant application interfaces by clarifying the specifications of different sequence platforms, operation services and carrier interface services. At the same time, according to the national space test and evaluation standards, SPG will evaluate the feasibility of different test requirements, and reasonably select test projects.

Secondly, the on-orbit test operation management system, as a guarantee system for the test and verification of new space technologies, supports the unified planning of multiple space test platforms and tasks in the space segment, and completes the overall planning of various space technology test work. Effective operational management of life processes.

Finally, by improving the ground evaluation mechanism and facilities for space technology experiments, the informatization management and service capabilities of space technology experiments will be realized. An experiment mission planning and assessment evaluation platform will be built to support multi-satellite and multi-mission planning. The SPG also can effectively store and manage on-orbit test data information, and promote the rapid popularization and application of the results of major test projects.

5 Conclusion

This paper discusses the concept, connotation and development route of the space proving grounds. The SPG of China will build an engineering technology system for systematic entry and exit, cognition and control of space, avoid duplication of space resources construction, realize high-efficiency space experiments, and can be used as the next-generation space test infrastructure. The service platform system of the SPG has a variety of platform types, covering the six major capabilities of "entry, station, exit, exploration, control, and use", which will provide platform means for space science; will formulate national space test and evaluation standards and specifications, space technology capability baselines, and provide exploration for space technology.

References

1. National Aeronautics and Space Administration (NASA): International Space Station Facilities-Research in Space 2017 and Beyond (2017)
2. https://www.nasa.gov/sites/default/files/atoms/files/np-2017 04 014-a-jsc_iss_utilization_brochure_2017_web_6-5-17.pdf
3. Marlow, M., Walden, H.: The DoD space test program-standard interface vehicle (STP-SIV) evolved expendable launch vehicle (EELV) standard payload adapter (ESPA) class program. In: Proceedings of the AIAA/USU Conference on Small Satellites (SSC6-III-5), pp. 1–8 (2006)

4. German Aerospace Center (DLR): OOV TET-1 (2012). http://www.dlr.de/sc/en/desktopde fault.aspx/tabid-139/8653_read-11878/

5. China National Defense Science and Technology Information Center: 2015 NASA Technology Roadmap—Technical Field II: Space Propulsion Technology, pp. 44–57. National Defense Industry Press (2015)

6. Guo, S.: Overview of 2015 Foreign Space Science and Application Development, pp. 130–176. National Defense Industry Press, Beijing (2016)

7. China Manned Space Engineering Office: 2019 World Manned Space Development Report, pp. 35–67. China Aerospace Press, Beijing (2020)

8. Smith, M.: DoD Space Test Program (STP) (1996). https://ntrs.nasa.gov/api/citations/199600 5416/downloads/19960054106.pdf

9. Sharon, K.R., Joyce, A.D.: Materials international space station experiment 5 polymer film thermal control experiment. J. Spacecraft Rockets **48**, 15–23 (2011)

10. Zhang, R.: Study on U.S. technology development and verification application on international space station. Space Int. (10), 58–63 (2017)

11. Su, H., Zhao, Z., Sun, Y., Wang, F.: Research on space science application in manned space station. Chin. J. Astronaut. **35**(9), 985–991 (2014)

A Multi-agent Based Satellite Health Management System Architecture and Implementation Scheme

Bo Pang[1,2](✉), Wenquan Feng[1], Baoling Fu[3], Wei Wu[2], and Zhenhui Dong[2]

[1] Beihang University, Beijing 100191, China
Spartan_email@sina.com
[2] Beijing Institute of Spacecraft System Engineering, Beijing 100094, China
[3] Beijing SunWise Space Technology Ltd., Beijing 100190, China

Abstract. Health management is one of the important contents of satellite intelligent and autonomous management. Its goal is to ensure the normal operation of satellite system on orbit, improve system reliability and safety, and reduce the dependence on ground and human resources. In this paper, we analyze the task requirements faced by satellite intelligent health management, and propose a satellite distributed health management system architecture based on Multi-Agent System. Combined with the layered model and system characteristics of the satellite on-board integrated electronics system, the scheme design of the health management system is completed, and a health management system architecture conforming to the integrated electronic standard is established, which provides a feasible scheme for future engineering design.

Keywords: Health management · Multi-agent system · Intelligent

1 Introduction

The Modern satellite system is a complex system integrated by machinery, electricity, and heat. Because of its harsh space operation environment, its work is prone to failure [1]. Moreover, due to the high difficulty of satellite in orbit maintenance, redundancy designs are generally taken to improve the reliability of long-term operation. Therefore, fault diagnosis, processing and recovery methods have always been one of the focuses of satellite system research. Satellite fault diagnosis focuses on how to timely and accurately diagnose the faults that have occurred or predict the faults that will occur, so as to take measures to avoid the spread of faults and reduce losses. In recent years, with the rapid development of on-board electronics system technology and the growing maturity of artificial intelligence technology, the level of satellite intelligence has also been greatly improved. The onboard autonomous processing capacity of traditional satellites is very limited, and health management mainly depends on the monitoring and judgment of ground systems, which can no longer meet the needs of long-term on orbit operation of complex systems in the future.

R. Li et al. (Eds.): MOBILWARE 2022, LNICST 507, pp. 195–205, 2023.
https://doi.org/10.1007/978-3-031-34497-8_17

In this paper, according to the characteristics of the future intelligent satellite system, a satellite health management system architecture based on Multi-Agent System (MAS) is proposed. Combined with the engineering constraints of the satellite integrated electronics system, the health management system scheme design was completed, and solutions were provided for communication mechanism, system expansion and other problems, forming a system architecture that conforms to the integrated electronics standard, providing reference for future engineering design.

2   Requirements and Challenges of Satellite Intelligent Fault Diagnosis

With the deep application of computer technology and artificial intelligence technology, future space missions will require more and more intelligent and autonomous satellites. For example, due to the limitation of measurement and control conditions in deep space exploration, the traditional method of dealing with faults by making plans and sending orders from the ground is far from meeting the task requirements. Generally, satellites are required to be able to independently complete system status monitoring, judge health status and formulate appropriate commands to deal with various faults and complete various established tasks.

On the other hand, with the increasing number of satellites in orbit, the pressure on the ground operation management system is increasing. With the existing management mode, the diagnosis and handling of failures are heavily dependent on manual work, which may easily lead to a long time of satellite anomaly processing, cause the spread of failures, and even bring disastrous consequences. Therefore, through intelligent and autonomous health management, satellites can quickly locate known faults themselves, make corresponding disposal and timely complete fault recovery; For unknown faults or complex faults, it can also provide more reference information for satellite ground managers.

Based on various requirements of satellite system engineering development and in orbit operation, the design objectives of satellite intelligent fault diagnosis mainly include the following aspects.

a. Fault detection and diagnosis: it can timely detect the faults occurring on the satellite, and quickly diagnose and locate the faults.
b. Self-disposal of real-time faults: according to the specific faults detected and diagnosed, evaluate their severity and development trend, timely provide fault countermeasures, and independently complete system reconfiguration, fault recovery or degraded operation according to available resources and task requirements to ensure the safety of satellite operation.
c. Fault and life prediction: find the fault trend in advance, deploy corresponding prevention and reconstruction strategies, and take measures in time to minimize the occurrence of serious faults and ensure the reliable and stable operation of the satellite.
d. Health status assessment: regularly conduct comprehensive analysis on the status of satellites, master the health of systems, subsystems, and equipment of satellites

in orbit, provide reference for operation management, and achieve the purpose of improving the overall availability of satellite systems.

The satellite system is generally composed of multiple subsystems with different functions to complete the system tasks together. The functions and implementation methods of different subsystems vary greatly. The stand-alone machines, components and software running in some subsystems are also different. With the increasingly powerful function of modern satellites, the complexity of the system is further improved, and the heterogeneity of the system is more significant. Therefore, the failure modes, detection methods and diagnosis methods of the objects faced by the satellite system health management are greatly different from each other. If they are all managed in the satellite data tube or the satellite affairs system, the software structure and functions will be too complex. Moreover, due to the limitation of on-board computing capacity and resources, it is difficult to centralize the implementation of complex diagnostic algorithms, comprehensive evaluation and intelligent decision-making in engineering.

On the contrary, if all subsystems independently manage their own health, it is difficult to achieve overall coordination, and the effectiveness of fault diagnosis and the completeness of disposal strategies are insufficient. In particular, for the failure modes with related relationships, different subsystems may have conflicts in operation, which may bring potential system security risks.

The health management system based on MAS can effectively solve the above problems. The function of health management is decomposed and abstracted through MSA to build a health management system that is organically integrated with the integrated electronics system and can be flexibly expanded.

Because different agents in the same system can be heterogeneous, the MAS technology has a very strong expression ability for complex systems. It provides a unified model for various actual systems, thus providing a unified framework for the research of various systems. Its application field is very broad [2].

3   Development and Application of Multi-agent System Theory

The application research of multi-agent technology originated in the 1980s and was widely recognized in the mid-1990s. It has become a hot spot in the field of distributed artificial intelligence since its development [3]. In the field of artificial intelligence, agent usually refers to an active entity with knowledge objectives and capabilities, and can make reasoning decisions independently or under a little guidance of people. It is a computer system in a specific environment. Agent generally has such attributes as autonomy, social ability, reaction ability, spontaneous behavior, mobility, reasoning ability, planning ability, learning and adaptability [4]. A MAS is a collection of multiple agents, whose multiple agent members coordinate and serve each other to jointly complete global or local tasks [5]. The main goal of MAS is to solve large-scale complex problems beyond the ability of a single agent through an interactive community composed of multiple agents, and to decompose large and complex systems into small, mutually communicating and coordinated systems that are easy to manage. On the one hand, the activities of each agent member in the MAS system are autonomous and independent, and their own goals and behaviors are not limited by other agent members. On the other hand, agent members resolve their conflicts and contradictions through competition and negotiation mechanisms, and jointly complete the overall task goal. Multi agent system provides a new method to control large-scale distributed and adaptive complex systems, such as process control, intelligent human-computer interaction, and distributed computing [6].

The advantages of MAS in solving practical problems are mainly shown in the following aspects:

a. The independence and autonomy of different agents in MAS can enable them to have the ability of autonomous reasoning and planning, and can be used to solve different sub problems by selecting appropriate strategies;
b. MAS has good modularity and scalability, supports distributed applications, helps solve the management and expansion problems of large and complex systems, and reduces the total system cost;
c. MAS reduces the complexity of the system and single agent problem solving by constructing multi-level and diversified agents to solve the complex system after decomposition;
d. Agents in MAS communicate with each other, coordinate with each other, and solve problems in parallel, which can effectively improve the ability to solve problems, and solve large-scale complex problems through mutual coordination;
e. Multi agent technology breaks the limitation of using only one expert system in the field of artificial intelligence. In the MAS environment, different experts in various fields may cooperate to solve problems that one expert cannot solve or cannot solve well, improving the ability of the system to solve problems;
f. Different agents can be different individuals or organizations, developed with different design methods and computer languages, so they may be completely heterogeneous and distributed.

As a whole, the MAS needs different agents to cooperate with each other to achieve the overall task of the system. Interoperability between agents is one of the core issues of MAS. Agents within the same MAS or between different MASs must rely on communication mechanisms to share knowledge and information, interact and negotiate, and then cooperate to solve complex heterogeneous problems. Building MAS must have a set of communication language and data model standards to realize the interoperability between agents, and a set of perfect top-level mechanisms to realize the management and coordination of all agents.

The Fig. 1 shows the MAS's model recommended by FIPA (Foundation for Intelligent Physical Agents) [7].

According to the above model, a MAS consists of the following parts.

Message Transport System (MTS) provides communication services between different agents.

Agent Management Service (AMS) is responsible for managing and coordinating the work of all agents in the MAS.

Directory Facilitator (DF) provides directory retrieval services for various agents.

Function Agents (Agent1~N) corresponding to different tasks.

The Non-Agent connected to the system interacts with other agents through a specific functional agent.

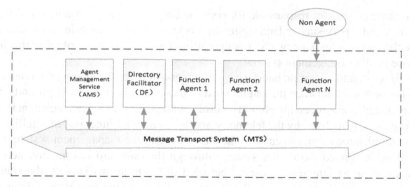

Fig. 1. Reference Model of Multi Agent System

4   Design of MAS Based Satellite Health Management System Framework and Layered Architecture

Referring to the structure of the agent platform shown in Fig. 1 above, and according to the composition of the satellite system structure, the general principles for building the health management MAS are as follows: the health management system adopts a hierarchical architecture, and the corresponding health management agents are configured at different levels of the system to handle health management transactions within this level. Each agent can include monitoring, diagnosis, fault recovery, prediction, and other functions. According to the system composition of the satellite, the regional health management agent is configured according to the different functions of each subsystem to complete local fault diagnosis, disposal, and other functions. Each regional agent synthesizes the results of multiple diagnostic modules from the system level through message transmission, information fusion, joint diagnosis and other technical means within the system agent to form system level fault diagnosis conclusions, and the top level proposes system level disposal measures.

The composition framework of the MAS based satellite health management system built according to the above principles is shown in Fig. 2.

The health management system based on MAS includes the following types of agents:

a. Regional Agent (including subsystem level agent and equipment/component level agent): According to the functional characteristics of the region, independent regional agents are configured for different subsystems and equipments in the satellite, focusing on the internal health management of the subsystem or equipment.
b. System level Agent: Configures system level agent for the whole satellite, responsible for completing system level health management transactions. The system level agent can carry out fault diagnosis, prediction and other health management transactions at the system level according to the status information or diagnosis report send by the regional agent of each subsystem, recheck and evaluate abnormal reports, diagnosis results, disposal strategies, etc. and make decisions. At the same time, relevant system constraints and other inputs should be provided for each regional agent.

c. Coordination Agent: responsible for coordinating the work consistency of different agents, and supervising and managing the working status of subordinate agents. Manage the entrance, exit, parameter configuration, fault tolerance etc. of all agents in the entire health management system.

d. Satellite-ground operation interface agent: responsible for completing the interaction and cooperation between the satellite health management system and ground operation management, receiving ground control, and reporting health management results. It is generally realized by the telemetry and telecommand functions of satellite.

e. Communication service agent: it is the basis of the health management system. In the satellite integrated electronics system, through the on-board information network, the information interaction channel between different agents is built, the standard communication protocol and mechanism are defined, and the data format of the agent is standardized to ensure that all the information and output results required by the agent work can be correctly and timely transferred.

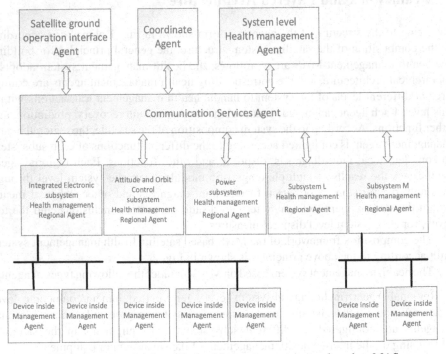

Fig. 2. Framework of satellite health management system based on MAS

The advantage of the above framework scheme is that each regional agent has a certain degree of autonomy, and can choose the most reasonable scheme, algorithm or processing process to achieve regional health management according to the function or design characteristics of its subsystem and stand-alone. The internal composition of the agent is shown in Fig. 3. Its internal algorithm, knowledge base, diagnostic processing and other functional units are designed according to different tasks. For example, a subsystem does not need to predict its life, but only needs fault diagnosis; Some subsystems adopt diagnosis and disposal decisions based on simple rule knowledge, while some systems are difficult to abstract rules, so model-based diagnosis methods may be required. In a word, in the MAS based system, under the constraint of the same external interface and communication specification, the regional agent adopts a similar structure to carry out independent design.

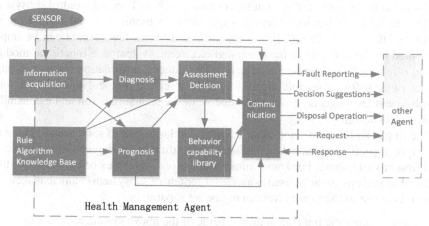

Fig. 3. Internal structure reference of health management agent

5   Implementation Scheme and Key Problem Analysis

5.1   Implementation Scheme

In the satellite engineering design, agents at different levels in the MAS-based satellite health management system architecture are implemented using the following scheme.

a. The integrated electronics subsystem gathers all subsystems and single machine telemetry, commands, etc. The system level agent is implemented in the integrated electronic system to complete the health management of the entire satellite/spacecraft. Since the integrated electronics system of the satellite is responsible for collecting and processing the telemetry signals of the whole satellite, such as temperature, analog quantity, switching value, etc., the status telemetry required by the subsystem level agents to complete fault diagnosis needs to be obtained from the integrated electronics system. At the same time, the monitoring abnormal event reports, diagnostic results, evaluation conclusions, decision-making suggestions, fault handling requests and other information sent by the subsystem level agents also need to be reported to the integrated electronics system in a timely manner.

b. The subsystem level agent is implemented by the intelligent units in each subsystem, such as the Attitude and Orbit Control Subsystem (AOCS), whose control computer can be responsible for the health management of the AOCS itself and the management of the single machine and components (various sensors, actuators, etc.) in the system. For subsystems with telemetry acquisition capability, the state parameters required for health management are obtained through internal interfaces; Other parameters collected through integrated electronics can be obtained from the integrated electronics system through the satellite internal network. Abnormalities and fault diagnosis results found in the subsystem can be handled by itself or submitted to system level management according to the severity and scope of influence of the fault.

c. For some subsystems without intelligent units, such as Thermal Control subsystem, the integrated electronics system is responsible for monitoring and controlling the state of the heating circuit. In this case, the subsystem level Agent can be implemented by the software of the integrated electronic system as a functional module, and is relatively independent in structure. The external information interaction interface of the software module should follow the interface protocol equivalent to other subsystem level agents, which is conducive to the standardization and extensibility of system design.

d. The implementation of stand-alone agent is similar to that of subsystems. There are also two specific implementation schemes according to the degree of intelligence of different stand-alone. For some simple stand-alone machines or components, their health management can be used as a specific content of subsystem health management, and the agent of their own level can not be set separately.

Figure 4 shows the implementation scheme of the above system architecture.

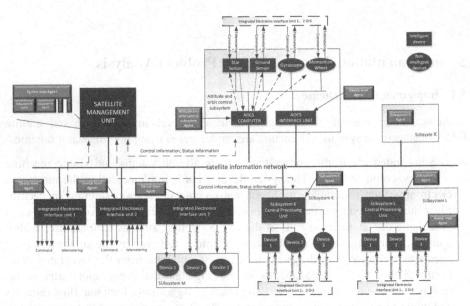

Fig. 4. Implementation Scheme of Satellite Health Management System Architecture

5.2   Analysis of System Characteristics and Key Problems

MAS not only describes the basic capabilities of each agent, but also expresses the structure, function and behavior characteristics of the whole system through agent's communication, cooperation, coordination, management and control. In MAS, the inter-operability of agents, the negotiation and cooperation among agents are the key problems to be solved in system design. Compared with the general distributed system, the establishment of intelligent health management system based on MAS in satellite has certain particularity. Although the information system of the intelligent satellite system has certain characteristics of networking, it adopts the integrated electronics system as the center, and realizes the interconnection architecture among different subsystems through the communication network, but it is essentially a hybrid system combining centralized and distributed mainly in the following aspects.

a. For safety and other reasons, most commands of the satellite, especially the power on/off commands of various equipment, are sent by the integrated electronics system, and the control of on-board equipment is often subordinate to the whole satellite system level. The commands issued by each subsystem can only operate some equipment in its area. Therefore, in the design of function agents in each region, because local control cannot cover all functional units in the subsystem, the control commands of some functional units need to be sent to the superior system.

b. Like the command, in order to save hardware overhead, the telemetry status of each device, especially the analog telemetry of voltage, current, temperature, etc., is usually collected by the integrated electronics system, organized and transmitted in the integrated electronics system's software. Therefore, part of the condition monitoring information of the equipment is first collected into the software for processing and downloading. During the operation of health management by the regional agent, the agent cannot obtain all the required observations through local sensor collection, and needs to obtain them from the integrated electronics system.

c. Some subsystems do not have intelligent equipment with management function in the subsystem, and the control and monitoring of the equipment are completed by the integrated electronics system. In this case, the regional agent has no implementation carrier and needs to rely on the integrated electronics system to complete.

d. In order to obtain high reliability, satellite systems usually take a lot of fault tolerance and redundancy design measures. As a result, the satellite system model is complex, and there are many logical branches and cross links. The agent in the health management system will have dynamic access, exit, replacement and other situations, which requires the system to have strong scalability.

e. Compared with the electronic information system on the ground, the network communication bandwidth, computing power, storage capacity and other resources of the on-board electronic information system are very limited. The implementation of related agents needs to be more concise and efficient.

Based on the above characteristics, to construct a satellite health management system based on MAS, the following key problems need to be solved and the corresponding design and implementation strategies are as follows.

a. The regional division and implementation strategy of agent should be organically combined with the system architecture based on integrated electronics system.
b. The communication system design should realize the information interaction between different agents in the existing system communication architecture to meet the needs of distributed management.
c. The allocation of system control rights can realize the reliable transmission of control information between the lower layer and the upper layer, legitimacy inspection, authority confirmation, etc.
d. Realize the dynamic management of multi-agent, and dynamically realize the access, exit, online, offline and other functions of agent according to the system configuration.
e. Agent implementation and optimization under the condition of limited resources, including optimization of diagnosis and prediction algorithms, sampling or compression of monitoring measurement data, optimization of agent implementation overhead, etc.

6 Conclusion

Intelligentization is an important direction of the development of space technology in the future, and improving the level of intelligent fault diagnosis is one of the important goals. By improving the intelligent autonomous ability of fault management during in-orbit operation and reducing the dependence of satellite operation management on ground and manual, the availability of the system can be greatly improved. In order to meet the requirements of satellite tasks, we conducts research on the architecture and system scheme of the health management system in view of the characteristics of intelligent and networked integrated electronics system in the future. Under the framework of the on-board information system with integrated electronics system as the core, a distributed health management system based on MAS is proposed, and a multi-agent health management system model is given, a feasible solution is proposed for the design of future satellite autonomous health management system. By analyzing the design characteristics of the satellite system, the key problems and implementation strategies of the above health management system are given, which can provide effective reference for the actual satellite engineering design.

References

1. Yang, T.: On-Orbit Satellite State Detection and Health Management Technology. National Defense Industry Press (2019)
2. Li, J.: A remote distributed fault detection model based on multi-agent system. Comput. Digit. Eng. **39**(06), 58–60+78 (2011)

3. Liu, J., Er, L.: Overview of application of multiagent technology. Control Decis. (02), 133–140+180 (2001)
4. Wooldridge, M.: Intelligent agents: theory and practice. Knowl. Eng. Rev. **10**(2), 115–152 (1995)
5. Kohu, W., Nerode, A.: Multiple agent autonomous hybrid control systems. In: Proceedings of the IEEE Conference on Decision and Control, Tucson, pp. 16–18 (1992)
6. Li, Y., Xu, F., Xie, G., et al.: Survey of development and application of multi-agent technology. Comput. Eng. Appl. **54**(9), 13–21 (2018)
7. Technical Committee of FIPA: FIPA Agent Management Specification. SC00023J (2002)

Integrated Satellite-Terrestrial Intelligent Information Processing, Decision and Planning (2)

Avionic System Architecture Design of the Manned Deep Space Exploration Spacecraft

Yan Liu(✉), Yuchen Jia, Songtao Fan, and Ruixun Chen

Beijing Institute of Spacecraft System Engineering, Beijing 100094, China
410989732@qq.com

Abstract. The avionic system is an important part of spacecraft, which controls and manages many functions such as telemetry and remote control, energy management, thermal control management, health management, etc. The development trend of spacecraft avionic system at home and abroad is summarized and combed. Considering the development requirements and technical characteristics of manned deep space exploration mission, an avionic system architecture of manned deep space exploration spacecraft is proposed from the aspects of network integration, computing generalization, implementation integration, software APP, etc., which provides a reference for the subsequent avionic system design.

Keywords: Manned Deep Space Exploration Spacecraft · Avionic system · Network Integration · Computing Generalization · Implementation Integration · Software APP

1 Introduction

With the continuous development of computer and chip technology, the function and performance of integrated avionic systems are continuously improved, and the application of the integrated electronic concept in spacecraft systems is more and more extensive. The spacecraft integrated avionic system covers the function of the control and management of telemetry and remote sensing, energy management, thermal control management, health management and other functions, which plays an important role in information sharing and comprehensive utilization, function integration, resource reorganization and optimization, as well as information processing and transmission [1].

The manned deep space exploration mission is complex and large in scale, with the characteristics of multiple data types, large data volume, and far data distribution. At the same time, as a manned spacecraft, it requires high reliability and security of data communication, which puts forward higher requirements for real-time performance, synchronization, interface uniformity and autonomy of avionic system response, as well as the standardization, integration, modularization, and miniaturization of electronic equipment.

R. Li et al. (Eds.): MOBILWARE 2022, LNICST 507, pp. 209–221, 2023.
https://doi.org/10.1007/978-3-031-34497-8_18

The traditional avionic system design generally adopts the "bottom-up" development mode. It is carried out according to the process of "device scheme design - subsystem selection - system integration". Each subsystem is equipped with an independent controller and takes its own responsibility, resulting in a great waste of weight, volume and computing resources, which can no longer meet the requirements of manned deep space exploration mission. In order to optimize the resource allocation, realize the system integration and improve the system redundancy, it is urgent to establish a new development mode with unified sorting of requirements, unified allocation of resources, unified integration of functions and unified design of modules, which is called "unified avionic system".

This paper takes network integration, computing generalization, execution integration, and software APP as the design goals, and proposes a new integrated avionic system according to the functional requirements of general computing, data exchange, acquisition drive, and astronaut support for manned deep space exploration spacecraft. This design has the advantage to optimize system configuration effectively, achieve the resource integration, and improve the system reliability.

2   Development Status of Spacecraft Avionic system

2.1   Orion Spacecraft of USA

Orion spacecraft utilizes the Time Triggered Ethernet (TTE) technology to achieve the transmission of data with different transmission reliability requirements and different data bandwidth in the spacecraft using a unified network form. High performance and high reliability general-purpose computer technology is adopted to realize the integration of the whole spacecraft control, human-computer interaction and system communication. The standard power data unit is adopted and configured nearby according to the demand to realize the distributed management of the whole spacecraft power distribution and data. The time-sharing and partition operating system is adopted to support the integration of a large number of complex software in the system and avoid the problem of system reliability reduction caused by different software operations. The independent modification and update of the software of each subsystem is supported without affecting other subsystems, which is helpful to improve the testability of the system, reduce the development and maintenance costs, and facilitate future upgrades. The avionic system architecture of Orion spacecraft is shown in Fig. 1 [2].

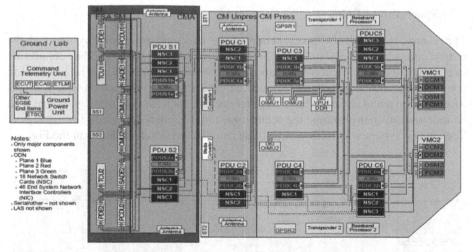

Fig. 1. The structure of avionic system in Orion spacecraft.

2.2 Ariane 6 Launch Vehicle of Europe

Ariane 6 launch vehicle adopts dual redundancy architecture, and utilizes TTE real-time bus as the backbone network communication data bus of the whole vehicle. Each level adopts modular integrated electronic equipment with the same architecture, and the equipment adopts a general backplane composed of different modular boards. The avionic system architecture of Ariane 6 launch vehicle is shown in the Fig. 2 [3].

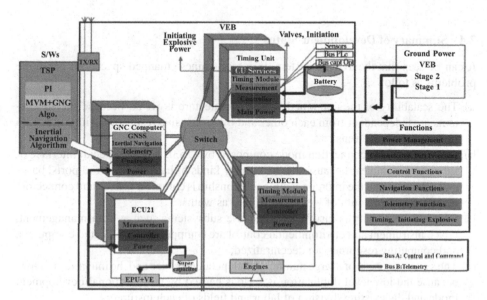

Fig. 2. The structure of avionic system in Ariane 6 launch vehicle.

2.3 Spacecraft of China

The manned spacecraft of China generally adopts the combined avionic system with the central computer as the BC of the 1553B bus, which supports the 1553B bus connection to complete the platform communication and control. The special interface is used to complete the transmission of image, voice and load data. The information system adopts a three-tier pyramid architecture. In this architecture, each subsystem is configured with an independent controller, and the acquisition and execution equipment is customized. The avionic system architecture of Chinese manned spacecraft is shown in the Fig. 3.

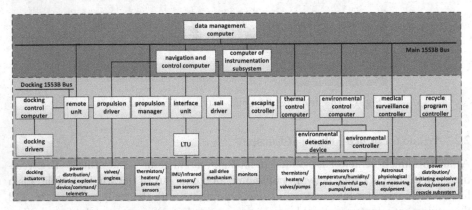

Fig. 3. The structure of avionic system in Chinese manned spacecraft.

2.4 Summary of Development Status

It can be seen that the avionic system design of Chinese manned spacecraft has some problems as follows.

a) The scalability of the combined system architecture is weak, because the subsystems are independent from each other and own exclusive resources, with little or no integration of functions;

b) The network interconnection mode composed by 1553B bus and special interface or Ethernet is complex, because there are many kinds of hard wires, serial ports, buses and networks, and the interconnection relationship is complex. Cables and connectors occupy a large amount of weight and space as well;

c) Computing capacity is insufficient, because subsystems such as data management, GNC, instrument and environmental control are equipped with dedicated computers, and computing resources are decentralized;

d) The system consists of a large number of independent device and the integration is low, because the low-level duplication is serious caused by the traditional development mode and the existing division of labor and fields of each institute;

e) Software and hardware are tightly coupled, and the development is difficult, because the scale and number of software have increased dramatically, but applications developed by different software developers cannot be seamlessly transplanted. Therefore, the further unified interfaces are needed.

In order to solve the above problems, referring to the development of the avionic system of foreign manned spacecraft, the design scheme of the avionic system of manned deep space exploration spacecraft is inspired as follows.

a) More open system architecture: adopt the top-down integrated system design to achieve a distributed, integrated, and modular system architecture;
b) More simplified and efficient network interconnection: a unified network is used to realize the integrated transmission of command and telemetry data (with high reliability and real-time requirements) and high-speed data such as image data, voice data, and payload data;
c) Faster on-board computing speed: constantly improve computer performance to meet the needs of different functions and tasks, and promote the development of spacecraft towards high intelligence and high autonomy;
d) Electronic equipment with higher integration: achieve top-level optimization and integration of electronic equipment by utilizing modular board cards to make up independent device and developing the board cards as chips.
e) Better and easy-to-use software development ecosystem: a universal software framework with hierarchical structure and time-sharing and zoning operating system are adopted to build a spacecraft software development ecosystem that supports multi-party joint and parallel development.

3   Requirements Analysis

3.1   Requirements for Higher Capacity of Independent Health Management and Task Planning

At present, China has the autonomous orbit control capability based on the target orbit and the health management capability based on the telemetry threshold. It has been successfully implemented in several tasks. The on orbit operation is normal, reducing the burden of ground personnel, improving the reliability of the whole mission, and achieving the desired results. The manned deep space exploration mission has the characteristics of greater space ground communication delay, smaller measurement and control coverage, and lower ground personnel intervention. Therefore, higher requirements are put forward for the autonomous health management and task planning capabilities of the electrical system. Common processor chips can no longer meet the task requirements, because the electrical systems need higher processing performance and computing capabilities [4].

3.2   Requirements for Higher Functional Density

According to preliminary calculation, the carrying capacity of the earth-moon transfer orbit is about 1/3 of that of the low earth orbit. Therefore, in order to complete the same function of low earth orbit spacecraft, the requirements for launch vehicles are up to three times. This requires that the manned deep space exploration spacecraft should have a higher functional density, which means that the equipment should have more functions under the condition of unit resource consumption. The key to achieve this goal is the optimal network topology and the software and hardware implementation technology of generalization, integration and modularization.

3.3 Requirements for Higher Reliability

Manned space flight is a matter of human life and can't be lost. Compared with unmanned lunar exploration missions such as Chang'e, the requirements for the reliability of the spacecraft are higher and the requirements for the redundancy design capability are stronger. In addition, because the coverage of the earth moon transfer orbit and the lunar orbit measurement and control is less, it cannot meet 100% coverage during the mission task. Once the failure occurs, there is a possibility that it cannot be handled in time, which requires the spacecraft to have higher reliability.

3.4 Requirements for Higher Capability of Attended Closed-Loop Control

Compared with machines, human intelligence has obvious advantages in target recognition, danger perception, task decision-making, etc. From the perspective of ensuring manned safety, manned deep space exploration tasks must include astronauts in the closed loop of the control system, and develop human-computer interaction technology to enable spacecraft to have higher manned closed-loop control capability.

4   Avionic System Architecture

Taking into account the technological development gap at home and abroad and the development needs of manned deep space exploration spacecraft, the avionic system design of manned deep space exploration spacecraft is mainly aimed at integration, lightweight, intelligence and convenience. The equipment integration and performance have to be greatly improved. The number, weight and volume of onboard electronic equipment should be significantly reduced, the interface has to be extremely simplified, and the cables have to be significantly reduced. Through adaptive control, autonomous fault diagnosis and fault-tolerant nursing, the autonomy, intelligence and fault adaptability of manned spacecraft during flight can be greatly improved, and the goal of upgrading and leapfrog development of avionic systems of manned spacecraft and leading the international technology direction can finally been achieved.

According to the requirements analysis, the avionic system architecture of manned deep space exploration spacecraft is proposed, as shown in Fig. 4. The avionic system of manned deep space exploration spacecraft can be divided into five functional subsystems, including general computing subsystem, data exchange subsystem, data acquisition and device drive subsystem, astronaut support subsystem and TT&C communication subsystem. The subsystems cooperates with each other to realize the functions of the integrated avionic system. The general calculation subsystem completes the numerical calculation and logic control according to the input parameters and established strategies, and outputs the calculation function of the execution results. The data exchange subsystem completes the transmission of control and measurement information between equipment in the same subsystem or different subsystems. The data acquisition and device drive subsystem completes the acquisition and drive functions of analog telemetering acquisition, temperature telemetering acquisition, sensor data acquisition, pulse command drive, power distribution control, initiating control of initiating explosive devices, heating circuit control, motor drive, valve drive, etc. The astronaut support subsystem completes voice, image, display, alarm and manual control support. The TT&C communication subsystem supports the data communication between space and ground, between different spacecraft, and supports the tracking and orbit measurement as well.

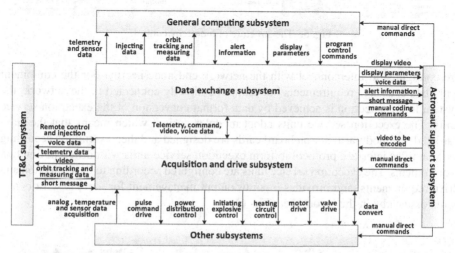

Fig. 4. The structure of avionic system in manned deep space exploration spacecraft.

The information network adopts the design idea of unified switching network. Multiple TTE network switches complete the platform control task through the connection of several general-purpose, standardized high-performance computers and modular execution service units (ESU). The three-layer hierarchical control structure of traditional manned spacecraft, which is system management - subsystem control - regional execution, is simplified into a two-layer hierarchical control structure, which is unified management - regional execution. The control hierarchy is compressed, and the probability of errors is reduced in the process of control information transmission and processing, and the system reliability is improved (Fig. 5).

High-performance computers are implemented to receive the status telemetry and sensor data transmitted by the equipment of each subsystem through the TTE network. The computers implement numerical calculation and logic control through the application strategy, and transmit the calculation results to the execution, control and display terminals through the TTE network to achieve unified closed-loop management on system level. According to the network access requirements, the TTE network switches

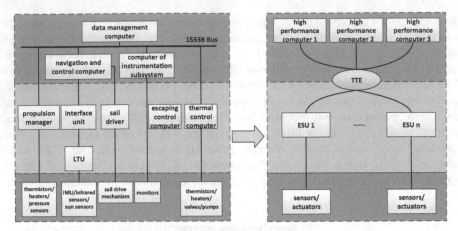

Fig. 5. The structure of hierarchy control.

are configured to interconnect with the network end node nearby. For the equipment with data exchange requirements but cannot be directly connected to the network, the system interconnection is achieved by data format conversion of the execution service units. The execution service units adopt modular design, which means that the standardized and modular function board cards are designed and then assembled according to the unified interface protocol to form execution service units with different function requirements. The execution service units are configured according to the collection and drive requirements, and provides input or output management for various sensors and actuators nearby in the layout area (Fig. 6).

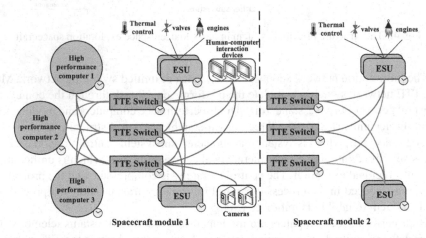

Fig. 6. The information network structure of manned deep space exploration spacecraft.

5   Key Technology Development Ideas

Aiming at the development requirements of integrated, lightweight, intelligent and convenient avionic systems, the following key technical directions will be studied.

a) Calculation generalization: high performance computers are used to upgrade the calculation ability, realize the calculation and closed-loop control functions of each subsystem, and improve the intelligence;
b) Network integration: data transmission with different real-time requirements and different service bandwidths is realized based on TTE, and integrated transmission is realized using standard protocols;
c) Implementation integration: the implement service units are modular and integrated, and different modules are configured to manage equipment nearby to achieve distributed control;
d) Software APP: the time-sharing and partition operating system is adopted to provide API and external environment interface, and to support independent compilation and dynamic loading of software APP.

5.1   Generalized Computing Technology

In order to meet the numerical calculation and logic control requirements of each subsystem and achieve the general calculation of the spacecraft, high-performance computers need to be configured. As the computing center of the spacecraft, the high-performance computer realizes computing functions of the subsystems such as data management, GNC, instrument, environmental control, thermal control, propulsion and recovery. The multi-mode redundant backup and standard modular design scheme based on high-performance processor is adopted. Internal modules are interconnected through the multi redundant high safety standard backplane bus [5], which supports the increase or decrease of module number and performance upgrade, and provides technical support for realizing system intelligence (Fig. 7).

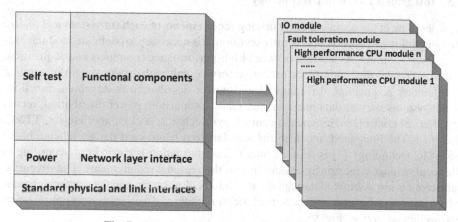

Fig. 7. The structure of high performance computer.

5.2 Integrated Network Technology

The main task of implementing data exchange through TTE is to use a unified form network to complete the reliable exchange of command, telemetry, time, sensor data, control information, image, voice, load and other data, and to support the integration of ground-spacecraft audio, video and file communication. Tasks to be completed include data management, command management, operation mode management, autonomous management, image and voice services, astronaut information services, manual operation support, etc. (Fig. 8).

Layers	Communication protocol		
Application system	ET data		TT data
Application layer	Network programming interfaces		
Transport layer	UDP		
Network layer	IP		
Data link layer	802.3 MAC protocal		TT Synchronization and service-control protocol
Physical layer	802.3 PHY		

Fig. 8. The system structure of TTE protocol.

5.3 Integrated Execution Technology

In order to meet the acquisition and driving requirements of each subsystem and realize the integration of the whole spacecraft execution, it is necessary to configure modular execution service units. As a bridge between high-performance computers and acquisition, drive and power distribution, the executive service unit realizes the system integration of telemetry acquisition, drive control and power distribution management functions of subsystems such as data management, GNC, propulsion, power distribution, recovery, thermal control, environmental control, pyrotechnics, docking mechanism, TT&C, and load. The integrated, modular and standardized board card design scheme based on ASIC technology [7] is adopted, and the configuration is carried out according to the local management principle according to the regional requirements. The execution service units are assembled through the standard backplane bus and the standard chassis, which improves the functional density of the equipment and realizes system optimization and weight reduction (Fig. 9).

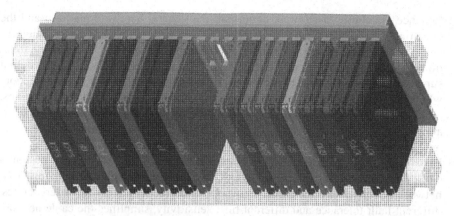

Fig. 9. The schematic diagram of ESU.

5.4 APP Based Software Technology

In order to meet the application function requirements of multiple subsystems for safe, reliable and non-interference operation on a unified computer, a time-sharing partition operating system is configured in the computer [8]. The time-sharing partition operating system enables multiple virtual partitions to run in a central processor at the same time. The running time of the partition and the storage space used are set in advance, thus the running partitions do not interfere with each other. The time-sharing partition isolation protection scheme enables software of different subsystems and different security levels to run in the same central processor, even if one partition fails, it will not affect other partitions.

The application of time-sharing and partition operating system supports the integration of a large number of complex software in the system, as well as avoiding the problem of system reliability reduction caused by the operation of different software. It also support the independent modification and update of the software for each subsystem without affecting other subsystems, which is helpful to improve the testability of the system, reduce the development and maintenance costs, and facilitate future upgrades.

6   Analysis of Technical Advantages

The avionic system of manned deep space exploration spacecraft proposed in this paper can meet the requirements of the model task, and has certain advantages in capabilities such as system fault tolerance, software definition, network transmission, system computing, acquisition and driving. These advantages are analyzed in detail as follows.

a) Enhance system fault tolerance: the configuration of multi-mode high redundancy high-performance computers, standardized distributed execution service units, and TTE networks enables the electronic devices of the whole spacecraft to have consistent functions and interfaces, providing basic technical support for the migration and reconfiguration of system tasks. With the help of the standard backplane bus with high redundancy and fault tolerance, the fault tolerance granularity of the system is reduced from a independent device to a hardware module.

b) Enhance the ability of software definition: the general hardware platform and the operating system with good compatibility and security establish the foundation for software functions definition. Load the application software APP with specific functions in the high-performance computer, and realize the software input and output support through the TTE network business planning and scheduling reconstruction, which can endow the high-performance computer with new application functions. Although the execution service unit does not use the time-sharing and partition operating system, it also has computing capacity and can use the TTE network to execute new application functions through on orbit maintenance and update of software.

c) Enhance the network integrated transmission capability: avionic system design is carried out based on the high bandwidth, high reliability and high certainty TTE network, which realizes the unified network transmission of data with different rates, different fault tolerance and different time sensitivity, simplifies the cable network of the spacecraft, reduces the number of equipment interface status, reduces the complexity of system test, and improves the spacecraft development efficiency.

d) Enhance the system computing integration capability: the computer business has been reintegrated, and hierarchical and standardized business planning has been adopted. All high-speed computing, parallel computing and closed-loop control functions are implemented in high-performance computers. The subsystems do not configure separate computers and only develop application software for independent tasks and load into independent partitions of high-performance computer operating systems to achieve system computing integration.

e) Enhance the integration capability of acquisition and drive: the concept of equipment integration is adopted to integrate the similar acquisition and drive functions of different subsystems in addition to the integrated design of the whole spacecraft's computing function. Similar functions are realized by using the same type of board cards, reducing the types of avionic device and hardware boards, and realizing the integration of acquisition and drive

7 Conclusion

Based on the analysis of development status of foreign spacecraft avionic systems, the disadvantages in China's spacecraft design, and the needs of manned deep space exploration spacecraft, this paper proposes an avionic system architecture of manned deep space exploration spacecraft. The development direction of related key technologies is put forward from the aspects of general computing, integrated network, integrated execution and software APP. Finally, the technical advantages are summarized. This architecture provides a reference for the avionic system design of manned deep space exploration spacecraft in the future.

References

1. Jianning, G., Youcheng, F., Li, S., et al.: Design of integrated electronic subsystem of YH-1 Mars probe. Aerosp. Shanghai 30(4), 139–146 (2013)
2. Bowen, C., Weiwei, L., Xiongwen, H., et al.: Research on Orion electronic system. Spacecraft Eng. 25(4), 102–107 (2016)

3. Yue, P., Yu, M., Jingqun, S.: Research on the development of avionic and electrical system in Chinese next generation launch vehicle. Astronaut. Syst. Eng. Technol. **4**(2), 13–24 (2020)

4. Xiaotao, L., Chongfeng, Z., Zhenyu, H., et al.: Requirement analysis of the first manned lunar rover in China. Manned Spaceflight **25**(5), 693–698 (2019)

5. Weiwei, L., Bowen, C., Luyuan, W., et al.: Design if distributed spacecraft avionics system. Spacecraft Eng. **25**(6), 86–93 (2016)

6. Wandong, C.: Industrial Ethernet Technology - AFDX/TTE Network Principle, Interface, Interconnection and Security. Electronics Industry Press, Beijing (2020)

7. Li, Z., Junshe, A., Qingwen, F., et al.: Design of an ASIC chip spacecraft integrated avionics. Chin. J. Space Sci. **34**(4), 497–504 (2014)

8. Haifeng, S., Junyang, L., Sheng, C., et al.: Integration technology of avionic for next-generation launch vehicle. J. Astronaut. **40**(3), 334–344 (2019)

Research on Tianwen-1 Mars Probe Relay Communication Technology

Fan Bai[✉], Yu Han, Ting Zhang, Huiping Qiang, Ji Xue, and Jionghui Li

Beijing Institute of Spacecraft System Engineering, Chinese Academy of Space
Technology, Beijing 100094, China
baifan_waseda@163.com

Abstract. As an important part of China's first Mars exploration mission, Tianwen-1 Mars probe relay communication system is responsible for supporting the capability of whole process communication self-management between the rover and orbiter, such as autonomous relay communication link establishment and communication parameters self-adaptive change mechanism. In the view of the limited resources and communication capacity of the rover and relay link, the X-band relay communication scheme is proposed for the first time in the world, which forms a backup with the UHF-band link to realize the relay communication at multi-node of the Mars relay orbit. In this paper, the UHF/X dual band relay communication system of Tianwen-1 Mars probe is firstly introduced, including the method of system design, relay communication protocol and operating mode are given. Finally, the results of on-orbit flight data are analyzed. The flight results show that the relay communication system of Tianwen-1 Mars probe successfully achieves the exploration mission objectives. Meanwhile, the system design, implementation and application can provide a technical reference for the China's deep space relay communication system in the future.

Keywords: Tianwen-1 Mars probe · deep space exploration · relay communication

1 Introduction

Mars is one of the important targets of human deep space exploration in the future. The establishment of efficient and stable communication links between earth and Mars is an important prerequisite and basic guarantee for the successful completion of Mars exploration missions. The deep space relay communication technology with high communication capability and low communication cost is regarded as the preferred solution to provide EDL (Entry, Descent and Landing) and Mars surface relay communication service to the Mars probe.

The NASA has proposed the idea of Mars relay communication network, which plans to launch multiple Mars orbiters carrying UHF-band relay communication equipment to realize the data communication between the Mars lander

R. Li et al. (Eds.): MOBILWARE 2022, LNICST 507, pp. 222–233, 2023.
https://doi.org/10.1007/978-3-031-34497-8_19

and the orbiter. Nowadays, the Mars relay network consists of the Mars Odyssey, the Mars Reconnaissance Orbiter (MRO), and Mars Express. The establishment of the Mars relay communication network enhances the deep space probe all-weather communication capability, obtains the efficient data return capability, and reduces the Mars lander's mass and power limitations [1].

At the same time, the space data system advisory committee (CCSDS) formulated the Proximity-1 space link protocol according to the characteristics of the inter-satellite relay communication mission scenario. The UHF-band relay communication system of Tianwen-1 adopts the Proximity-1 protocol, and uses the automatic repeat queuing (ARQ) mechanism of the protocol to ensure the accuracy and efficiency of information transmission. In the future, with the development of the unified space data link protocol (USLP), it is expected to unify the all link protocols, and guide the inter-satellite relay communication in various frequency bands.

As China's first spacecraft to explore Mars, Tianwen-1 Mars probe has completed the Mars exploration mission of "orbiting, landing and roving" all in one journey. The Tianwen-1 Mars probe consists of an orbiter and a lander-rover combination. After launch, the probe will undergo the flight phase of earth-Mars orbit transfer, Mars braking and capture, orbiting Mars, and EDL.

After landing, the rover will conduct scientific exploration, and establish a relay communication link with the orbiter to transmit the exploration data. The areocentric orbit period is about 8.27 h, and the communication distance varies from 265 km to 15000 km.

Due to the large elliptical relay communication orbit of the Tianwen-1 Mars probe, the communication distance varies widely and is limited by the attitude of orbiter, the relay communication control cannot be completed in the real time. The probe relay communication system has high requirements on link autonomy and reliability. In view of the above characteristics, Tianwen-1Mars probe proposed a multi-node and multi-system relay communication system scheme, which alternates the far-Mars arc and near-Mars arc to build a communication link, and the transmission link of X-band and UHF-band operates selectively, so as to realize the relay communication of deep space exploration data with high speed, efficiency and large capacity. In this paper, the design of the Tianwen-1 Mars probe relay communication system is introduced, and the key technologies are analyzed, and the communication link design is presented. Finally, the in-orbit flight test results are analyzed.

2 Design of Tianwen-1 Mars Relay Communication System

2.1 System Configuration

The orbiter and the lander-rover are integrated in the launch phase, earth-Mars transfer phase and Mars capture phase. The ground TT&C systems realizes the control and state monitoring of the lander-rover by the wired communication through the orbiter, and the lander-rover has no requirement of RF measurement and control data transmission link. After the landing on the surface of Mars, the ground TT&C systems can control the lander-rover, monitor its status and transmit service data through the orbiter UHF-band relay communication link, or through the X-band Mars-earth communication downlink. In addition, lander-rover provides the bidirectional coherent carrier Doppler tracking beacon, and the Doppler information extracted by the orbiter is used for mutual positioning for mutual positioning between the rover and orbiter during the relay data communication.

The relay communication system of the Tianwen-1 Mars probe is composed of the orbiter relay communication subsystem and lander-rover TT&C system. Among them, the lander-rover TT&C system is composed of X-band communication equipment and UHF-band relay communication equipment. The orbiter relay communication subsystem is composed of X-band communication unit and UHF-band communication unit. The composition of Tianwen-1 probe relay communication system is shown in Fig. 1.

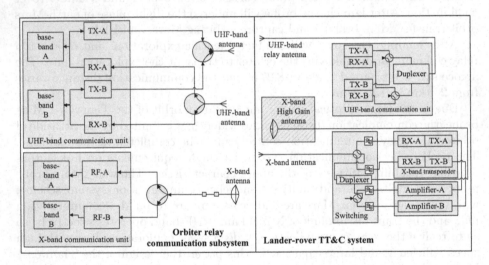

Fig. 1. Configuration of Tianwen-1 Mars probe relay communication system.

2.2   Design of Operation Mode

In the phase of Mars surface exploration, the Tianwen-1 Mars probe relay communication system is in a regular operation mode, and the rover establishes a bidirection relay communication link with the orbiter through the UHF-band transceiver and UHF-band antenna. In addition, as a complement to the relay communication in the UHF-band, the rover establishes a unidirection (rover-to-orbiter) X-band communication link with the X-band deep space transponder and X-band high gain antenna. See Table 1 for the Tianwen-1 Mars probe relay communication system operation mode.

Table 1. Tianwen-1 Mars Probe relay communication system Operation Mode.

Operation Mode	Data Rate (encoded)	Carrier Frequency
UHF-band	forward: 1 kbps–64 kbps return: 1 kbps 2 kbps 2 kbps 4 kbps 8 kbps 16 kbps 32 kbps 64 kbps 128 kbps 256 kbps 512 kbps 1024 kbps 2048 kbps	forward: 435.6 MHz 437.1 MHz 439.2 MHz 444.6 MHz return: 404.4 MHz 401.585625 MHz 397.5 MHz 393.3 MHz
X-band	2048 bps 4096 bps 32 kbps 64 kbps 128 kbps 256 kbps 512 kbps 1024 kbps 2048 kbps	8400.062 MHz

2.3 Signal Modulation and Demodulation Scheme Design

The X-band relay communication link uses suppressed carrier modulation. The UHF-band relay link is implemented by Manchester coding assisted residual carrier BPSK modulation. Through the adoption of less than of $\pi/2$ (rad) modulation index, makes the signal spectrum in discrete component (residue) carrier, at the same time, the Manchester coding power spectral density at zero frequency is zero, residual modulation signal and carrier component can be effectively separated, through the filter and narrow bandwidth loop tracking, realize to the extraction of carrier tracking.

According to the characteristics of residual carrier modulation, the carrier is locked in I-branch and the information is locked in Q-branch by using Costas phase detection and tracking method, which avoids solving the problem of phase inversion of I and Q, and reduces the processing complexity. Through the multi-stage filter extraction module, the taps of each rate range are extracted, and all other information except the carrier is filtered out to realize the tracking of very low SNR.

Based on the characteristics of Manchester coding, the Q-branch signals on each rate tap are matched with correlation and energy integration, and the current transmission data rate can be judged without prior information through the cumulative judgment of positive and negative energy, so as to realize the adaptive estimation and demodulation of communication data rate.

2.4 Design of Trajectory Measurement

In the Mars surface exploration phase, the orbiter provides X-band DOR for VLBI observation from the ground station to complete angle measurement, and combines tone ranging to complete orbit measurement of the orbiter. The ground station uses SBI (Same Beam Interferometry) observation to place the orbiter and rover signals in the same antenna beam for relative positioning.

On this basis, the position of the rover can be determined by combining the communication Doppler changes between the UHF-band link providers of the two probes. The rover's UHF-band transceiver provides the coherent forward channel to support orbiter extractor Doppler change data.

2.5   Channel Coding

The channel coding methods suitable for deep space communication mainly include convolution coding, R-S coding, turbo coding and LDPC. The Tianwen-1 Mars probe relay communication system adopts convolution coding as the channel coding method of UHF-band relay channel. The convolution coding (7, 1/2) recommended by CCSDS is adopted, and the channel coding gain of about 4.5 dB can be achieved at the BER of 1×10^{-6}.

X-band relay communication channel coding adopts R-S+ convolution coding, with (7, 1/2) convolution code as the inner coding and (255,223) R-S coding as the outer coding. At a bit error rate of 1×10^{-6}, the channel coding gain of about 7 dB can be achieved.

The Tianwen-1 Mars probe relay communication system includes UHF-band bidirectional communication and X-band unidirectional communication. For bidirectional communication in UHF-band, CCSDS Proximity-1 is used. This protocol is suitable for bidirectional short distance wireless communication between fixed or mobile nodes.

Considering the large delay characteristics of the communication between the rover and the earth, the ground station cannot inform it to send the wrong data transmitted by the communication system again in time. In order to ensure the timing and correctness of the command, telemetry and other data, it is necessary for the rover to automatically select the data that has not been correctly received for re-transmission.

Common ARQ systems can be divided into three categories: equal-stop ARQ, back-off N-frame ARQ, and selective re-transmission ARQ. As for the communication link, its transmission distance is short, signal transmission delay is small and signal attenuation is relatively small. At the same time, considering the resource limitation and storage space overhead of the Mars rover platform, the back-off N-frame ARQ scheme of error control processing is adopted to ensure the correctness of data transmission [2].

The ARQ protocol mainly includes the functions of error detection, receiver feedback, data re-transmission, and transmission timeout control. The sender automatically re-transmits the incorrect data according to the feedback from the receiver.

Specifically, after the transmitter sends a data frame, the receiver needs to reply a proximity link code-word (PLCW) if it successfully receives the data frame. PLCW contains the serial number information of the valid frame received by the receiver. The maximum sending interval of two PLCW is defined as 20 s. The sender checks whether the data frame is successfully sent according to the PLCW feedback from the receiver. If the data frame is not successfully sent, the sender needs to resend the data frame. In order to improve efficiency, the sender does not need to send the next frame after sending a certain frame and waiting for receiving PLCW of this frame.

The unidirectional communication link in X-band multiplexes the downlink resources of the rover, and its data format and communication protocol are consistent with the Mar-earth downlink, which belong to a non-ARQ system.

When a data error occurs in the X band relay link, the Earth station on-demand re-transmission mechanism is used.

2.6   Design of Link Data Rate

In view of the dynamic characteristics of the trajectory, the forward link design of the probe UHF-band supports 7 levels of data rates: 1 kbps, 2 kbps, 4 kbps, 8 kbps, 16 kbps, 32 kbps and 64 kbps, and the return link supports 12 levels of data rates: 1 kbps, 2 kbps, 4 kbps, 8 kbps, 16 kbps, 32 kbps, 64 kbps, 128 kbps, 256 kbps, 512 kbps, 1024 kbps and 2048 kbps.

In the periareon, the orbiter realizes bidirectional communication to the rover through UHF-band narrow beam ($\pm 30°$), and adaptively switches the communication data rate according to the change of relay communication orbit. The implementation of the adaptive date rate scheme mainly includes the following technical approaches:

1) Signal averaging, SNR estimation and data rate switching mechanism automatic gain control (AGC) telemetry in the receiving channel can reflect the input signal size to a certain extent. However, when the signal power is below -105 dbm, thermal noise occupies the main proportion of the input power detected by the AGC module, and the change of the input signal power is difficult to cause significant changes in the telemetry level of the AGC. The signal power threshold is directly related to the power detection bandwidth of the AGC.
2) Design and implementation of SNR threshold for data rate switching communication systems with adaptive transmission capability usually take the SNR as the standard to measure the channel conditions. The receiver estimates the SNR in real time and compares the SNR with the threshold required by technical indicators to select the appropriate transmission data rate. Then, the appropriate data rate is fed back to the transmitter in the form of control messages. When the transmitter detects the relevant control message, it issues the control command at the correct time to switch the transmission data rate.

Therefore, in order to better react the level fluctuation of the weak signal and accurately evaluate the quality of the received signal, the design detects the SNR or carrier-to-noise ratio (C/N_0) of the input signal by means of digital signal processing.

In view of the characteristics of Manchester coding, the relay communication system is put forward a way based on Manchester coding minimalist SNR estimation algorithm, through the algorithm can achieve a very reliable solution to Manchester code fuzzy and auxiliary input frequency error, reduce the carrier tracking loop to reduce the loop into the lock time, At the same time, it only occupies very little hardware processing resources, and the working mechanism is as follows:

1) By using the characteristics of Manchester coding, the signal branch and noise branch are separated, and the SNR is estimated by the two branches, and the fitting method is adopted to obtain a more simplified estimation method.
2) The estimated SNR can be directly used as an important criterion for carrier synchronization assistance, which can complete the fast acquisition function of initial frequency offset and speed up the locking process when the tracking capability of carrier tracking loop is limited.

The design of X-band unidirectional communication link supports 9 levels of data rates: 2048 bps, 4096 bps, 32 kbps, 64 kbps, 128 kbps, 256 kbps, 512 kbps, 1024 kbps, and 2048 kbps.

3   Analysis of Relay Communication Link

3.1   Analysis of UHF-Band Relay Communication Link

In the periareon of exploration, there are at most two relay communication arcs in each Martian day, which are called type I arc and type II arc. Among them, the type I arc is that the periareon appears near the zenith direction of the rover during relay communication, and the type II arc is that the apoareon appears near the zenith direction of the Mars rover during relay communication. Among them, the type I arc appears in the local daytime of Mars, and the longest communication window is about 10 min. Due to the close distance between the two probes, the peak data rate of the return link can reach 2048 kbps (encoding), which can be used for transmission of engineering telemetry and large load data. Type II arcs occur at night on Mars, with a relatively long communication window of several hours. The range of relay communication distance in type I arc is 265 km to 3500 km, and that in type II arc is 5000 km to 15000 km.

In the communication window a of periareon, the UHF-band communication link is adopted by default. In the communication window of apoareon, X-band communication channel is adopted. During the Mars surface exploration phase, the communication mode between orbiter and rover is shown in Fig. 2.

UHF-band relay communication link uses two UHF-band devices for bidirectional communication. The forward link data rate of the channel is 2 kbps (encoding), and the return link data rate is 1 kbps to 2048 kbps (encoding). The maximum communication distance between the orbiter and rover can reach 15000 km. Due to the different antenna gains in different beam ranges of the UHF band relay antennas of the two devices, the maximum 15000 km communication can only be achieved within the (±30°) beam of the UHF-band relay antennas of the two devices. Therefore, the relay communication in the UHF-band cannot cover all the arc segment of type II. Figure 3 shows the UHF-band communication performance with different received power and data rate.

1) In type I arc segment (communication distance varies from 265 km to 3500 km), it can ensure that both the surround device and rover relay antenna in UHF band can relay normally within the range of (±80°), and the channel code is convolution coding (7, 1/2). The specific code rate is as follows:

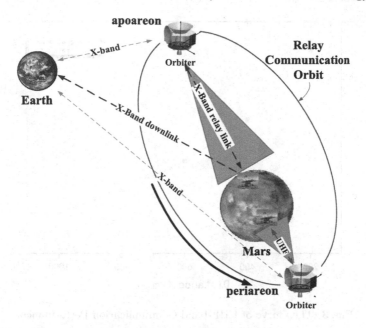

Fig. 2. Diagram of Tianwen-1 Mars probe relay communication link.

①When the communication distance is 265 km to 3500 km, the antenna beam angle of the two devices is within the range of (±80°). According to the distance, the forward code rate is 2 kbps (encoding), and the data rate is 2 kbps to 256 kbps (encoding).

②When the communication distance is 265 km to 3500 km, the antenna beam angle of the two devices is within the range of (±30°). According to the distance, the forward data rate is 2 kbps (encoding), and the return data rate is 16 kbps to 2048 kbps (encoding).

2) When the communication distance is 5000 km to 15000 km, the angle range of (±30°) cone angle of the surround UHF-band antenna can ensure the orientation of the rover in any arc. The forward and return channels are coded as convolution (7, 1/2). The data rate is as follows:

3) When the communication distance is 5000 km to 9000 km, the antenna beam angle of the rover is within the range of (±80°). According to the distance, the forward data rate is 2 kbps (encoding), and the return data rate is 1 kbps to 2 kbps (encoding). Forward data rate 2 kbps (encoding) up to 12500 km;

4) When the communication distance is 5000 km to 15000 km, the antenna beam Angle of the rover is within the range of (±30°). According to the distance, the forward data rate is 2 kbps (encoding), and the return data rate is 1 kbps to 8 kbps (encoding).

3.2 Analysis of X-band Relay Communication Link

X-band relay communication is multiplexed with X-band Mars-earth downlink, and X-band directional antenna is used to transmit return data, corresponding to

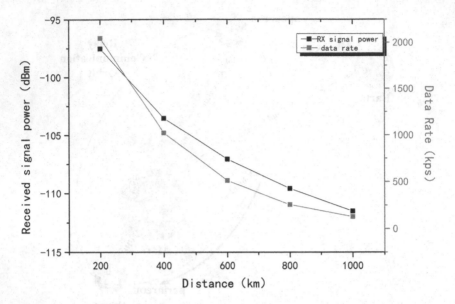

Fig. 3. The Curve of UHF-band Communication Performance.

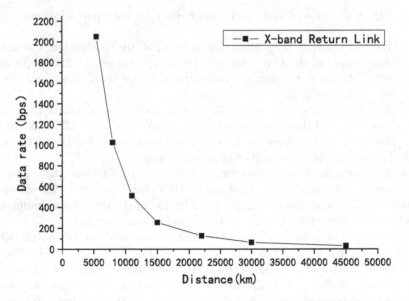

Fig. 4. The Curve of X-band Communication Performance.

orbiter relay receiving antenna, and BPSK modulation is used. The date rate of 32 kbps to 2048 kbps (encoding) is used for the X-band communication during the relay track operation of the orbiter. 15000 km is the maximum communication distance during the relay track operation of the orbiter, and 2048 kbps (encoding) can support the communication of up to 5500 km. Figure 4 shows the relationship between the communication data rate and the communication distance of X-band relay communication.

4   Analysis of Flight Test Results

At 7:17:58 on May 15, 2021, the lander-rover successfully landed at the pre-selected landing zone in the southern Utopian Plain on Mars. Figure 5 shows the Tianwen-1 Mars probe relay communication system received power during the EDL phase.

At 10:40 on May 22, 2021, the rover safely left the landing platform and reached the Martian surface. By August 16, 2021, the rover had completed 85 apoareon UHF-band relay communication missions, 85 periareon UHF-band relay communication missions, 6 forward UHF-band communication missions, and X-band return communication missions, and transmitted delay telemetry, sensing, exploration data and EDL process data with a total data amount of 16.5 Gb.

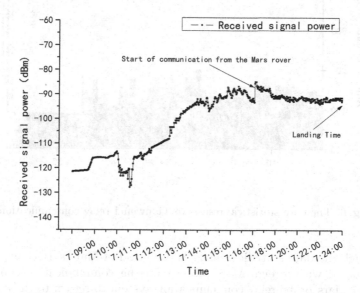

Fig. 5. The curve of received power during EDL phase.

According to the actual operating planning of the rover and orbiter, considering the characteristics of UHF-band antenna and X-band antenna, the relay communication in the periareon arc is carried out at around 14:00 local time of each Martian day in the early and middle exploration phase of the Mars surface, and the communication window duration is about 8 min. In the apoareon arc, one hour of relay communication is selected according to the task arrangement during the Mars night.

In the later phase of the Mars surface exploration, considering the data transmission requirements of large-capacity load data and the path planning strategy of the rover, 6 relay communication missions of forward UHF-band and return X-band were carried out in orbit, with the maximum data amount up to 550 Mb.

From June to July 2021, 60 Mars day periareon relay communication data volumes were selected for statistics. Among them, from July 16 to July 28, due to the adjustment of the communication window time of the orbiter, the transmission of relay data was limited, and the amount of data received by the ground station was about 90 Mb/Sol. The data statistical results are shown in Fig. 6.

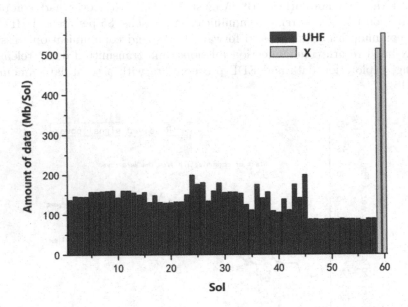

Fig. 6. The data statistical results of Tianwen-1 relay communication.

Through the data statistical analysis of period of Mars surface exploration, and compared with foreign Mars probe trunking communication capabilities, Tianwen-1 Mars probe relay communication system to return to the amount of data transmission in unit time is equal to MRO, and higher than the capacity of Odyssey and Mars Express relay communication link [3]. At the same time, if X-band relay communication link is adopted, the amount of data by the relay communication system of Tianwen-1 Mars probe is about 2.87 times than MRO in unit time. The comparison results of the relay communication systems on Mars at home and abroad are shown in Table 2.

Table 2. Comparison of Relay Communication Capability of Mars Probe at Home and Abroad [4].

Probe Name	Altitude	Average Data Volume (Mb/Sol)	Average Communication Duration (Min/Sol)
Tianwen-1 (UHF)	$265 \times 15000\,km$	150	8
Tianwen-1 (X)	$265 \times 15000\,km$	500	8
Odyssey	$400\,km$	111	23.4
Mars Express	$250 \times 10142\,km$	83	124
MRO	$255 \times 320\,km$	327	15

5   Conclusion

The relay communication system of the Tianwen-1 Mars probe is working normally in orbit, successfully completing the engineering objectives of China's first Mars exploration mission. Mars is verified by in-orbit flight test nodes and relay communication system of the correctness of the scheme design, verify the distances and long time delay under the condition of deep space exploration, the automatic relay communication technology, for our future deep space mission relay communication system for celestial bodies surface probe design and key technology provides the valuable experience of development, it lays a technical foundation for realizing high efficiency and large capacity deep space relay communication.

References

1. Edwards, C.D.: Relay communications for Mars exploration. Int. J. Satell. Commun. Network. **25**, 111–145 (2007)
2. Tian, J., Han, Y., Wang, W., Shi, P.: The high efficient CCSDS proximity-1 bidirectional ARQ communication method for MARS exploration. In: 72nd International Astronautical Congress (2021)
3. Lewis, J.A.: Mars Odyssey relay operations development. In: IEEE Aerospace Conference (2005)
4. Sun, Z., et al.: Design and verification of the multinode and multisystem relay communication system for the Tianwen-1 Mars probe **11**, 226–236 (2022)

Design and Practice of Communication System During EDL for Mars Probe

Ting Zhang$^{(\boxtimes)}$ and Huiping Qiang

Beijing Institute of Space System Engineering, Beijing 100094, China
Zhangting_cast@126.com

Abstract. Tianwen-1 Mars exploration mission is a mission for China to "Orbit, Fall and Patrol" Mars though a launch. Entry, descent and landing (EDL) of Mars exploration mission is one of the most important links in the whole mission process. Based on the characteristics of relay communication task in this process, this paper introduces the relay communication system scheme and key technology of Tianwen-1 Mars probe to adapt to the characteristics of complex timing, high autonomy, black barrier phenomenon and high dynamics of EDL segment communication task. At the same time, combined with the landing mission of Tianwen-1, the in orbit verification of relay communication in EDL is summarized and analyzed. The relay communication scheme proposed in this paper successfully supports the relay communication mission of the EDL section of the Mars Exploration of Tianwen-1.

Keywords: Tianwen-1 Mars probe · Entry descent and landing (EDL) · relay communication system

1 Introduction

As the first Mars probe in China, Tianwen-1 has realized the exploration mission of "circling, landing and patrolling" Mars through one launch. The Tianwen-1 Mars probe consists of an orbiter and a landing rover, which consists of an entry module and a Mars rover.

The entry, descent and landing (EDL) phase of the Mars exploration mission is one of the most important links in the whole mission process. In this stage, the detector completed complex high dynamic maneuvers such as high-speed aerodynamic deceleration, parachute deployment, and back cover removal in a short time, which is the most difficult and risky stage of Mars exploration mission. The EDL communication is the only approach to understand the working status and health of the lander during the important process from separation of the two vehicles to landing on the surface of Mars. The relative distance between the lander and the earth in the EDL segment is generally 109 km, and the communication signal to the earth is very weak, with a one-way delay of about 20 min. The experience of previous Mars landing missions abroad shows that, Reliable communication links play a vital role in monitoring the flight status of the ground probe,

R. Li et al. (Eds.): MOBILWARE 2022, LNICST 507, pp. 234–246, 2023.
https://doi.org/10.1007/978-3-031-34497-8_20

the process of aerodynamic deceleration, the key information of parachute deployment and lander landing on the Martian surface, and providing flight decisions.

To ensure the implementation of the communication scheme, Geometric visibility between two detectors, Opportunity to enter the Martian atmosphere, Entry method, And the orbit and attitude of the Orbiter in the EDL process. All conditions constrain the scheme design. Therefore. EDL phase communication scheme and technical approach design are closely combined with the actual implementation of Mars exploration mission, The communication link is designed around the timing of the task; Meanwhile, The function, performance and equipment configuration of the communication system are all carried out for the purpose of uninterrupted communication throughout the whole process and to ensure the reliability and stability of the communication link.

This paper introduces the scheme design and in orbit verification of the EDL relay communication system of the Tianwen-1 Mars probe.

2 Task Characteristics

2.1 Task Difficulty

1) Complex time series

The landing phase of the Probe mainly includes the pre-atmospheric entry phase and the EDL process. After seprating from the Obiter, the lander arrives at the entry point of the Mars atmosphere after going through a descent orbit of about three hours, enters the EDL segment of about 7-9 minutes, and then lands on the Mars surface. In a few minutes of EDL, many complex tasks, such as atmospheric entry, ejection parachute, backshell separation, base separation, landing platform and Mars vehicle landing have been carried out, which require the stability, reliability, continuity and autonomy of the communication link.

The flight key events sequence of the EDL is shown in Fig. 1.

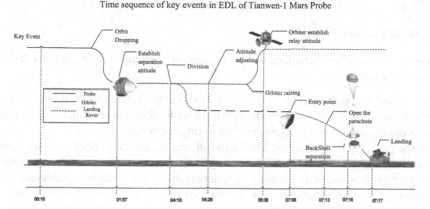

Time sequence of key events in EDL of Tianwen-1 Mars Probe

Fig. 1. Timing chart of key events in the EDL stage of Tianwen-1 Mars probe

2) Weak signal and large delay

The weight and power consumption of the Lander are constrained by a single launch task. It is not possible to configure large aperture high gain antenna and high power amplifier. Direct communication to the ground is facing huge space loss, and the received signal on the ground is very weak. During the EDL mission, the lander was approximately 300 million kilometers from the ground with a delay of more than 30 min. Large latencies cause EDL critical task segments to be in a fully autonomous "uncontrolled" phase.

3) High Doppler Dynamics

Actions in the EDL process result in a very high Doppler dynamic overlay on the communication signal, and the Doppler range and Doppler rate of change are very large. High Doppler dynamics in the EDL process can easily cause the receiver loop to be unlocked, resulting in data loss. It is difficult to achieve high dynamic tracking and high sensitivity receiving demodulation for transceiver at the same time, which puts forward higher requirements for electronic instrument design and system design.

4) Black Barrier Phenomenon

The Landing Rover enter the Mars atmosphere at hypersonic speeds, High temperatures around the Probe caused by a sharp deceleration in a short period of time ionize atmospheric molecules and some ablative materials, Form plasma sheath, The plasma sheath absorbs and diffuses electromagnetic waves seriously, thereby creating communication blackout. The blackout phenomenon is related to the shape of the probe, speed, flight angle of attack, heat-proof material and atmospheric density.

In 1997, the Mars Pathfinder encountered a 30-s signal interruption during its landing [1], Mars Curiosity encountered a similar situation when it landed in 2012 [3], Curiosity had a signal drop of 30–40 dB during EDL.

The disruption of communication signals during the EDL is a fatal threat to the safety of landing task. Therefore, it is necessary to rationally design the flight trajectory and speed, and take necessary measures to mitigate or avoid the impact of the blackout on the communication link.

2.2 Brief Summary

Considering the above challenges, the design of communication systems has the following requirements:

1) The Lander is separated from orbiter in Mars orbits. During EDL, it need to communicate through relay communication links with orbiter, to sending Earth-to-lander commands and receiving telemetry data during the process.
2) In the process of Entering the Mars atmosphere, parachuting, Backshell separation, and landing, The Lander will have a large angle posture change, According to the motion process and attitude change, it is necessary to design the lander antenna installation position, antenna beam, communication link channel parameters, so that the two antennas can point to each other, and the communication link remains uninterrupted during the process.

3) After the parachute and the backshell are separated, There is a relay and switching process between the lander's entry module and the Mars vehicle's communication equipment and antenna, We need to schedule the device switches and radio frequency signal transmission and reception, to ensure reliable switching and continuous communication.

3 EDL Communication System Design

3.1 Communication Process

Before separation, Lander and Orbiter begin to provide UHF band communication link. After separation, The Orbiter enters relay track, The Lander establish UHF band relay communication link with the Orbiter to maintain contact with the Earth from entry point to landing, The whole process takes about 3 h, EDL process takes about 7–9 min, Communication distance in the range of 600–1000 km.

The communication link of the Tianwen-1 task is in Fig. 2, The relay communication in EDL shows in Fig. 3.

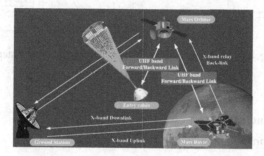

Fig. 2. Tianwen-1 Probe communication Links

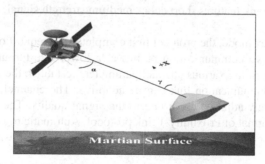

Fig. 3. Relay communication in EDL.

3.2 Design of Relay Communication System

3.2.1 System Configuration

Tianwen-1 relay communication system consists of the following equipment: UHF transceiver of entry module and Mars rover, Backshell antenna and UHF relay antenna for Mars rover, UHF relay communicator, UHF band relay receiving/transmitting antenna of the Orbiter, etc.

Figure 4 is the design schematic diagram of the Probe relay communication system.

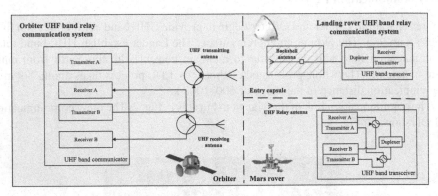

Fig. 4. Schematic diagram of relay communication system

3.2.2 Technical Indicators

1) System and communication protocol

According to the characteristics of the task, the relay communication protocol of Tianwen-1 Probe selects CCSDS Proximity-1. The physical layer of the protocol is UHF band. The protocol link features short delay, medium strength signal, short independent dialogue [4].

In the full duplex mode, the protocol first completes the request or negotiation process between the two communication parties at a lower rate through the handshake channel, After confirming various channel parameters, establish the service communication channel. Communication link can be adaptive, The channel, coding and code rate can be adaptively adjusted according to the signal quality. The data transmission uses the standard format of Proximity-1 link protocol, Automatic repeat request mechanism and sequence control service, Use 32 bit CRC check to establish two-way reliable connection.

The protocol uses ARQ automatic retransmission mode for data transmission, to ensure the reliability of data transmission. Use signal to noise ratio (Eb/N0) estimation method to achieve adaptive code rate switching, to improve bit error performance. It can support 8 forward rates (1–64 kbps) and 12 backward rates (1–2048 kbit/s) of circular adaptive switching. Figure 5 is the schematic diagram of the communication parameter switching process through the signal to noise ratio estimation method.

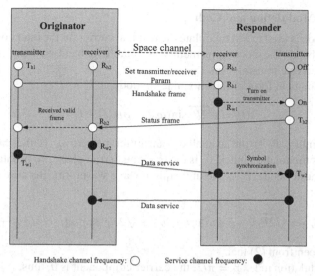

Fig. 5. Autonomous switching process of communication parameters

3.2.3 Working Status

With different communication capabilities and mission requirements, the working status of relay communication system can be full duplex, half duplex and simplex [5]. Table 1 shows carrier frequencies of forward and backward signals of relay communication.

Table 1. Carrier frequency of relay communication link

Channel number	Forward frequency(MHz)	Return frequency (MHz)
Handshake channel	435.6	404.4
Service channel 1	437.1	401.585625
Service channel 2	439.2	397.5
Service channel 3	444.6	393.9

In the full duplex working state of the relay communication system, the call process uses the handshake channel, and the communication process uses the service channel; In the simplex working state, the working channel is used.

To ensure link stability and timeliness, The relay link in the EDL section of Tianwen-1 adopts the simplex state in the above protocol. After landing on Mars, the communication between the rover and the orbiter is in full duplex working state.

3.2.4 Signal Modulation and Coding

Manchester code is used to PM modulate the residual carrier for the inter communication signal in UHF band, The modulation method is suitable for bandwidth unrestricted, short distance, low bit rate transmission.

The mathematical form of this modulation mode is:

$$s(t) = \sqrt{2P_t} \sin(\omega_c t + \beta m(t) + \theta_c) \tag{1}$$

In the formula, P_t is the available transmitter power; ω_c is the carrier angular frequency, β is modulation index, θ_c is the tracking carrier phase, m_t is data modulation.

For Manchester code, P_t is the unit square wave waveform, Because of the digital property of m_t:

$$s(t, \theta_c) = \sqrt{2P_t} \cos\beta \sin(\omega_c t + \theta_c) + \sqrt{2P_t} \sin\beta m(t) \cos(\omega_c t + \theta_c) \tag{2}$$

It can be seen from (2) that,

When modulation index $\beta = \pi/2$, the carrier component is 0, thus,

$$s(t) = \sqrt{2P_t} m(t) \cos(\omega_c t + \theta_c) \tag{3}$$

That is, ordinary BPSK modulated signal.

When modulation index $\beta < \pi/2$, the carrier component is not 0.

Therefore, less than $\pi/2$ is used in relay communication (β = Modulation index of 1.05), It makes effective separation of modulated signal and residual carrier, It is convenient to extract and track carrier signals with low SNR; Meanwhile, according to the characteristics of Manchester code (Map a symbol to a pair of [1, −1] or [−1, 1] sequences), Get the energy integration of modulated signal, Integrating obtains two phases of information, which is coherently accumulated with the local frame synchronization header, Obtain SNR estimation results, and decide if the threshold is exceeded. Then discriminate current data transmission energy and code rate, to achieve adaptive estimation and demodulation.

Relay communications use (7, 1/2) convolution codes as channel encoding, about 4.5 dB channel coding gain can be obtained at error rate of 10^6.

3.3 Communication Link Design

3.3.1 Pointing and Visibility Analysis

EDL relay link uses UHF band antennas and instruments for both-way communication. UHF band relay antenna has two beam ranges of $\pm 30°$ and $\pm 80°$, antenna gain varies greatly in different beam ranges, Therefore, the coverage of inter- communication link needs to be analyzed in combination with the attitude and orbit characteristics of the two devices during the task.

The angular relationship between the two probes after the separation and the separation of backshell is illustrated in Fig. 6. In the diagram, the angle α is the angle between two geometric centers and the mechanical axis of the Orbiter. The γ Angle between the geometric center line of the two vehicles and the mechanical axis of the lander. As the flight progresses, from the two probes are separated on orbit until the lander enters the atmosphere, γ Angle remains within antenna coverage, From entering the atmosphere to landing, A series of actions result in an unstable entry posture, γ appears irregular changes. The simulation curve is shown in Fig. 6.

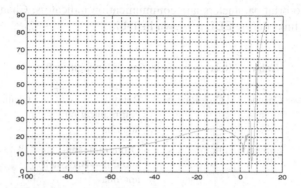

Fig. 6. Simulation analysis of antenna pointing in EDL

3.3.2 Channel Design

In EDL, Both UHF-band transceivers are working in a single mode, Forward and back-ward link code rates are 1 kbps and 2 kbps, The channel key indicators are analyzed below.

1) **Capture and demodulation threshold**

The carrier-to-noise ratio of the communication link is analyzed as follows:

$$C/N_0 = [P_C] - [N_0] = [P_C] + 174 - [N_F] \qquad (4)$$

Where, N_F is the noise factor, P_C is carrier power。When the noise figure is 3.5dB and the carrier capture threshold reaches -140 dBm, the C/N0 is 30.5dB/Hz, which makes the system possible.

For data demodulation, When the code rate is 1 kbps, the demodulation threshold is −126 dBm, Signal power can be calculated according to the formulas (2) and (4), According to the carrier-to-noise ratio andE_b/N_0,the result as follows (Noise Figure is 3.5):

$$C/N_0 = P_t \sin^2 \beta + 174 - 3.5 = 43.26 \text{ dB/Hz} \qquad (5)$$

$$E_b/N_0 = [C/N_0] - [R_b] = 13.26 \text{ dB} \qquad (6)$$

Therefore, when the channel error rate $P_e = 1 \times 10^{-6}$, there is still a 2.66 dB margin relative to the theoretical signal-to-noise ratio of 10.6 dB, and the system can be implemented.

2) **Channel Margin**

According to orbit parameters and communication indicators, Channel budget for communication links during EDL is shown in Table 2.

Table 2. Relay communication link margin in EDL

Sequence number	Channel	CodeRate(bps)	Relay communication antenna	Channel Margin(dB)
1	Forward	1k	Orbiter transmit antenna→Backshell antenna	8.43
2	Backward	2k	Backshell antenna→Orbiter Receiving Antenna	4.78
3	Forward	1k	Orbiter transmit antenna→Rover Relay Antenna	20.43
4	Backward	2k	Rover relay Antenna→Orbiter receiving Antenna	16.78

From Table 2, in order to keep a certain signal-to-noise ratio margin, to cope with large fluctuations and jumps in signals caused by complex flight conditions in the EDL phase, considering large channel margins when designing communication links is necessary.

4   On-Orbit Practice

On May 15, 2021, the Mars Explorer Tianwen-1 separated its two spacecraft in orbit. Lander experienced nearly 3 h of off-track landing, and EDL segment "Black 9 min", Successfully landed on the Utopian Plain of Mars. During the whole EDL task, the relay communication system works stably and reliably, and the communication link is uninterrupted throughout the whole process.

4.1   Received Signal Power and Doppler Dynamics

During separation from the Orbiter to landing on Mars, The change of signal power received by the UHF transceiver for the lander (Entry module + Mars Vehicle) is shown in the red curve in Fig. 7. Before entering the Mars atmosphere, communication link remains stable, The signal power steadyly change between −95 dBm and −122 dBm. Large fluctuations in signal strength occur when entering the Mars atmosphere, Combined with the analysis of working sequence, the changes of distance between two vehicles after entering, the effect of blackout caused by plasma sheath on signal, the changes of large angle attitude of lander caused by parachute, separation of backshell, and the channel changes caused by antenna index after Mars vehicle relay can be corresponded to.

Comparison of signal power received from on-Orbit relay link with design results, the performance index under different antenna beam angles is analyzed, and the actual pointing and coverage of two relay antennas during EDL can be obtained. The actual signal strength results are good to verify the correctness of the simulation results of antenna pointing.

The blue curve in Fig. 7 shows the change of doppler frequency offset in orbit in EDL. Before entering the Mars atmosphere, due to the lander's stable speed direction and attitude, the Doppler frequency offset is relatively small, varying from 0.1 to 0.6 kHz. From the point of atmospheric entry, with the change of velocity and posture, the Doppler dynamic changes sharply, and the frequency offset increases from 0.1 kHz to ±6 kHz. During this process, the forward-backward link of relay communication remains continuous, and the UHF transceiver receives stable loop tracking without losing lock, which enables the organic combination of high dynamic tracking and high sensitivity demodulation.

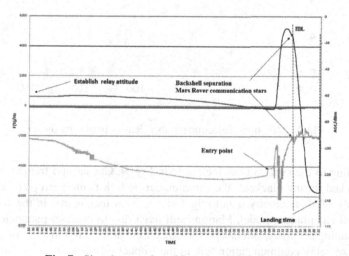

Fig. 7. Signal strength and Doppler shift during EDL

4.2 Black Barrier Impact

After entering the Mars atmosphere, electromagnetic waves around the lander are affected by plasma sheaths, creating a "black barrier phenomenon". Figure 10 shows the signal level of the relay link before and after the lander enters the Mars atmospheric point. As can be seen from Fig. 7, the signal received fluctuates significantly about 100 s after entering the atmosphere of Mars, Maximum signal jitter causes a sharp decrease in signal strength from −98 dBm to −139 dBm, which is about 40 dB.

In the design process, combining the aerodynamic profile of the landing patrol, flight trajectory, and atmospheric density after entering the Mars atmosphere, the simulation of electron number density in plasma sheath is carried out. The results are shown in Fig. 8. Simulation results show that,during the entry process, the electron number density increases and then decreases, and reach the maximum at around 95 s, about $16 \times 10^{13}/m^3$. The time when the maximum electron number density occurs corresponds to the time when the power of the communication signal between the orbiters fluctuates sharply. In the actual EDL process, the distribution of plasma sheaths is not static, it changes in both spatial and temporal dimensions. For this complex time-varying communication environment, In the simulation system, the influence of PSK signal with Manchester code is analyzed by establishing the dynamic model of electron density.

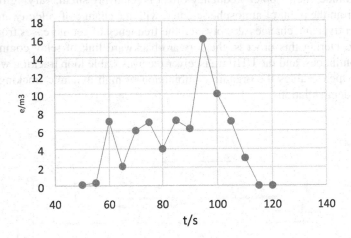

Fig. 8. Variation of electron number density in plasma sheath

According to the synchronous lock state in Fig. 9, Carrier and frame synchronization are locked during blackout, the communication link is uninterrupted, The Lander continuously sends telemetry data to the Orbiter. This means that in the communication channel calculation model, Margins still exist due to channel parameters such as antenna pointing accuracy, antenna performance indicators and transmission power, etc. Real datas of relay communication link in the impact of blackout can be used in subsequent Mars or other atmospheric planet missions, and correction of communication simulation model in Plasma Sheath of Blackout Process.

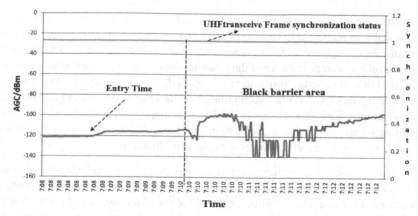

Fig. 9. Communication link affected by black barrier in EDL

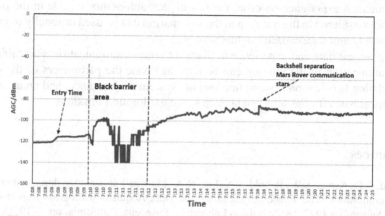

Fig. 10. Communication relay before and after back shell separation in EDL

4.3 Communication Link Switching

In the EDL, two minutes after entry, the parachute unfolds, and the backshell antenna separates with the backshell. At this time, the reley communication link is switched from the cabin to the Mars vehicle in real time, so as to achieve the relay link communication of the cabin. The change of signal strength during switching is shown in Fig. 10. We can see that, the signal strength received by Mars Vehicle is about 9 dB higher than that of the entry compartment, this matches the design status of both antennas and electronic instruments.

5 Summary and Revelation

As the engineering practice of the relay communication task of China's first Mars exploration mission, from the perspective of system optimization, the relay communication system has been designed and validated, from the overall design level to the electronic instruments technological approach according to the task characteristics of EDL. The system is stable and reliable to support the relay communication during the whole entry, descent and landing process. At the same time, in the following work on Mars surface, ensures the relay communication and data transmission tasks with the Orbier effectively.

The design and on-orbit verification of the EDL relay communication system for the Tianwen-1 Mars Explorer has accumulated valuable research and engineering experience, which provides useful reference value and support for the subsequent Chinese interplanetary and deeper space exploration missions. At the same time, through this successful experience, we can also get the following inspiration:

1) In order to achieve the communication process in EDL, considering the characteristics of the mission, and considering the factors such as orbit, probe attitude and communication system capabilities, various technical measures and paths should be reasonably selected to meet the requirements of the tasks for communication system.
2) EDL relay communication uses single-work communication mode in tasks. Based on the practical experience on-orbit, the full-duplex autonomous mode in the protocol can be considered in the future, and the link margin can be used rationally to improve the quality and data capacity in this process.
3) The practical data and experience of blackout zone communication, and cabin relay communication in the mission can be used to revise the parameters of the current simulation verification system, improve the system performance, and create a better technical basis for the subsequent deep space exploration missions.

References

1. Wood, G.E., Asmar, S.W., Rebold, T.A., Lee, R.A.: Mars pathfinder entry, descent, and landing communications, The Telecommunications and Data Acquisition Progress Report 42–131, July–September 1997, Jet Propulsion Laboratory, Pasadena, California, pp. 1–19, November 15, 1997
2. Desai, P.N., Knocke, P.C.: Mars exploration rovers entry, descent, and landing trajectory analysis. J. Astronaut. Sci. **55**(3), 311–323 (2007)
3. Chen, A., Vasavada, A., Cianciolo, A., et al.: Atmospheric risk assessment for the mars science laboratory entry, descent, and landing system. In: Aerospace Conference, IEEE, USA (2010)
4. Morabito, D.D., Schratz, B., Bruvold, K., Ilott, P., Edquist, K., Cianciolo, A.D.: The mars science laboratory EDL communications brownout and blackout at UHF. The Interplanetary Network Progress Report, vol. 42–179, Jet Propulsion Laboratory, Pasadena, California, pp.1–22, May 2014
5. Consultative Committee for Space Data Standards (CCSDS), Proximity-1 Space Link Protocol, Recommendation for Space Data System Standards, CCSDS 211
6. Tian, J., Wang, W., Shi, P.Y., et al.: A method for realizing the integration of full duplex/half duplex and simplex under CCSDS Proximity-1 Protocol. Microelectron. Comput. **37**(6), 66–69 (2020)

Study on EMC Influence of Zhu Rong Rover UHF Band Communication System

Yu Han[1], ChangFu Sun[2], ChangSheng Li[2], Qi Li[2], Ting Zhang[1], Huiping Qiang[1], and Fan Bai[1(✉)]

[1] Beijing Institute of Spacecraft System Engineering, Beijing 100094, China
fpgaise@126.com
[2] Shanghai Aerospace Electronics Co., Ltd., Shanghai 201821, China

Abstract. As a complex communication system, the rover has multi-band communication, and very low signal-to-noise ratio (SNR) communication puts forward high requirements on electromagnetic compatibility (EMC).In this paper, the influence of the wireless radiation in the UHF band transceiver on the receiving link is analyzed theoretically, including interference source research, interference path analysis and anti-interference ability improvement research. At the same time, a feasible engineering solution is proposed, and the experimental verification is completed, which provides a solution to the electromagnetic compatibility (EMC) problem of high-sensitivity complex communication in the future.

Keywords: Electromagnetic compatibility (EMC) · Wireless radiation · High sensitivity · Anti-interference improvement

1 Introduction

As a complex communication system, the rover has multi-band communication, including UHF band relay communication, X-band relay communication and X-band ground communication, etc. At the same time, it also has different frequency band detection radar and complex power conversion. As a result, the electromagnetic compatibility of multi-system communication is highly required by the rover. In the aspect of T&C subsystem, in order to be applied in the field of deep space exploration, both UHF relay communication and X-band communication are in a very low signal-to-noise ratio (SNR) communication state. Unnecessary radiation interference will seriously affect the communication ability of each band system and reduce the communication margin.

The UHF transceiver is one of the components of the core communication link of Mars exploration. The main function of the transceiver is to provide the radio frequency channel between the surround and the landing rover, establish the relay communication link, and complete the autonomous link construction between the two devices-2. The UHF link adopts PCM (Bi-Phase-L)-PM modulation and demodulation mode. There is a strong carrier component in the PM signal spectrum, and the carrier synchronization and tracking of the receiver can be realized by extracting the carrier component. This

R. Li et al. (Eds.): MOBILWARE 2022, LNICST 507, pp. 247–255, 2023.
https://doi.org/10.1007/978-3-031-34497-8_21

modulation method has low anti-interference ability. When the interference signal enters the carrier locking frequency range, the carrier false lock will be generated, which affects the normal acquisition and tracking, and deteriorates the demodulation sensitivity of the UHF link. The following Table 1 gives the parameters and characteristics of UHF transceiver.

Table 1. The parameters and characteristics of UHF transceiver

Parameter	Value
Protocol	CCSDS Proximity-1
Architecture	Software radio
Mode	Full-duplex operations modes
Mass	4.0 kg
Noise Figure	3.5 dB (Full-duplex)
DC Power	58 W (Full-duplex)
Frequency Bands	390–405 MHz; 435–450 MHz
Symbol Rates	1, 2, 4, 8, 16, 32, 64, 128, 256, 512, 1024, 2048 ksps
Coding	K = 7, 1/2 convolutional
Interfaces	1553B for Monitor & Control; LVDS for High-Speed Data

Through the whole device wireless test, the presence of wireless electromagnetic radiation in the UHF transceiver leads to carrier mislocking in a certain channel, resulting in interference and affecting the normal function implementation. In this paper, the influence of wireless leakage in UHF band transceivers on the receiving link is analyzed theoretically and effective solutions are proposed.

2 Mechanism of Electromagnetic Radiation Interference

Radiation interference is the radiation signal produced by two equivalent antennas inside electronic products:

1) the first is a equivalent antenna signal loop, the loop is equivalent antenna radiation, the radiation source is flowing in the loop of the current signal (the current signals is usually normal work, it is a sign of a differentia mode), as shown in Fig. 1, if the loop flow in the area of S loop current strength is I, the frequency signal for F, is in free space, In free space, the radiation intensity at the distance D from the loop is:

$$E = 1.3\,SIF^2/D \tag{1}$$

where: E is the electric field intensity (unit: $\mu v/m$);S is the area of the loop in cm^2;I is the current intensity in A;F is the signal frequency in MHz; D is the distance in m.

If the signal is alternating, the loop where the signal is located will generate radiation. When the current size and frequency of the product signal are determined, the

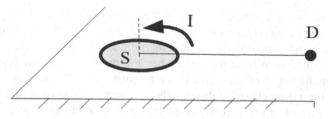

Fig. 1. Loop equivalent radiation antenna

radiation intensity generated by the signal loop is related to the area of the loop. There-fore, controlling the area of the signal loop can effectively control the EMC radiation interference.

2) Another equivalent antenna model or dipole antenna is a monopole antenna (as shown in Fig. 2), the equivalent of the antenna of cable conductor is usually a product or other long conductor size, the source of radiation is the long conductor size cable or other equivalent antenna in the flow of common-mode current signal, it is usually not cable or work long size conductor of the useful signal, Rather, it is a parasitic "useless" signal. Controlling the size of the common-mode current that produces common-mode radiation is the key to suppress radiation emission.

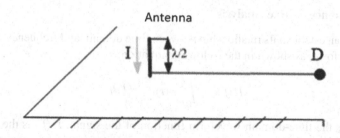

Fig. 2. Conductor equivalent radiating antenna

If a signal with current I and frequency F flows through the antenna, then the radiation intensity generated at distance D from the antenna is:

When F ≥ 30 MHz, D ≥ 1 m and L < λ/2: E≈0.63ILF/D

When L ≥ λ/2: E≈60*I/D

Where: E is the electric field intensity (unit: μV/m); I is the current intensity (unit: A); F is the signal frequency in MHz; D is distance, in m;L is the length of the cable in m.

In electronic products, in addition to product features the information expressed by the circuit principle diagram, there are more unknown information, such as the signal lines and parasitic capacitance and parasitic inductance between signal lines, signal lines, with reference to the parasitic capacitance, between the signal wire lead inductance and so on, these parameters are frequency-dependent parameters, and the value is smaller, in the case of dc or low frequency, Usually negligible, but in the high frequency range considered by radiation emission, these parameters will have an increasingly important impact.Is the reason makes these parasitic in the equivalent antenna in the product with A kind of common-mode current expectations, its current strength is very small or below level (usually in mA mu A level), but it is the product of the main causes of radiated interference, can be seen from the type, when the product in the equivalent antenna is greater than the length of the signal in the frequency of 1/2, The radiation intensity generated by the antenna is only related to the common mode current on the antenna.

Through a lot of practice, it is proved that the radiation interference problem in most products is caused by the equivalent monopole antenna or dipole antenna in the product. Especially with the application of multilayer PCB technology, the signal loop area is controlled to be smaller and smaller, and the radiation generated by the normal working signal loop is more and more limited. On the contrary, the radiation interference generated by the equivalent monopole antenna becomes more and more important for EMC interference as the product becomes more and more complicated.

3   Analysis of EMC Impact Measures

EMC interference radiation control measures mainly involve three aspects: reduce the interference intensity generated by the interference source, cut off the interference signal propagation path, and improve the interference ability of the interfered object.

3.1   Interference Source Analysis

Any signal can establish its relationship between time domain and frequency domain by Fourier transform, as shown in the following equation:

$$H(f) = \int_0^T x(t)e^{-j2\pi ft}dt \tag{2}$$

where $x(t)$ is the time-domain waveform function of the signal, $H(f)$ is the frequency function of the signal, $2\pi ft = \omega$, ω is the angular frequency, f and is the frequency. Digital signals in products are mostly trapezoidal impulse functions (rising along time t)$_r$, pulse width is t), and its spectrum analysis diagram is shown in Fig. 3, which contains two turning points, one is $1/\pi t$, the other is $1/\pi t_r$. The low end of the spectrum is constant, decreasing at -20 dB/10 octave after the first turning point and -40 dB/10 octave after the second turning point. Therefore, in circuit design, under the condition of ensuring the normal function of logic, increase the rise time and fall time as much as possible, which is helpful to reduce the high-frequency noise. However, because of the existence of the first turning point, those periodic signals with very steep rise edge and low frequency will not have high harmonic noise of higher level.

Because the spectrum of each sampling segment is the same, the spectrum of periodic signal is discrete, but it is characterized by high intensity at each frequency point, which is usually called narrowband interference. And aperiodic signal, because the spectrum of each sampling segment is not the same, so its spectrum is very wide, and the emphasis is weak, usually called broadband noise. In the general system, the clock signal is a periodic signal, and the data line and address line are usually aperiodic signals, so the cause of the system radiation emission exceeds the standard is usually the clock signal.

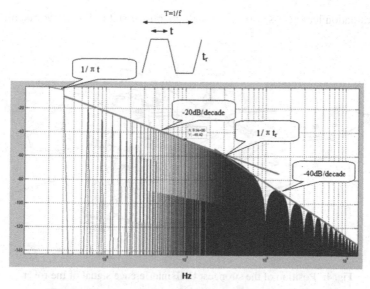

Fig. 3. Spectrum diagram of trapezoidal impulse function

According to the calculation, the main interference sources of the UHF transceiver are: the fundamental frequency signals and related harmonic components generated by the baseband digital clock circuit, the clock signals and harmonic components generated by the FPGA internal DCM core frequency division and frequency multiplication, the IF signals and harmonic components of DA output, and the IF frequency and harmonic components of AD output.In addition, there are many nonlinear devices in the digital circuit of UHF band transceiver, which will lead to useful signal and useful signal, useful signal and useless signal, useless signal and useless signal mixing frequency, and produce more useless frequency components.Multistage frequency components are mixed to form intermodulated frequencies, including frequencies of 43X.XX MHz, which are radiated out by radiation path, and enter the receiver system by receiving antenna through wireless transmission, resulting in false lock of channel 2 and affecting the normal function.

3.2 Interference Path Analysis

The interference path of radiation leakage ultimately affects the receiver system. By comparison, the receiver has no such interference state in the wired case. Meanwhile, based on the detection of radiation intensity, the intensity of radiation interference is mainly concentrated in the front end of the rover, and there is a cable outlet hole nearby, and the UHF antenna is also concentrated in this area, as shown in Fig. 4 and Fig. 5.After verification and comparison, EMC radiation leakage has the following characteristics:

1) The strongest radiation is concentrated in the cable exit hatch;
2) Through the wireless path coupling into the UHF band antenna, and then affect the receiver;

3) EMC radiation leakage is correlated with the on-off state of a single machine.

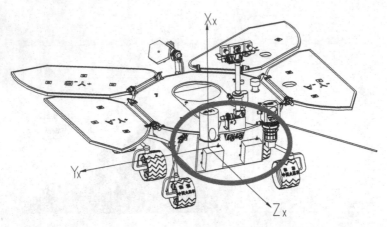

Fig. 4. Position of the strongest UHF interference signal of the rover

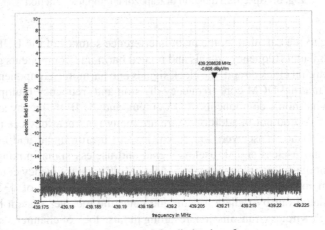

Fig. 5. Spectrum of radiation interference

After investigation, multi-signal crossover is found in the internal cables of the low-frequency electrical connector of the transceiver.Harmonics exist between the data and the clock, and intermodulation occurs in the frequency domain, generating intermodulation signal. The intermodulation radiates through the low-frequency connection cable, forming a strong radiation source, resulting in overerror of RE102.

4   Improvement of Anti-interference Ability

1) Interference path optimization

EMC interference signals are mainly caused by external low-frequency cable radiation. After verification, the interference channels can be reduced by strengthening cable shielding. The EMC radiation can be effectively suppressed by fully shielding the connection lines of single machine and multiple tubes, as shown in Fig. 6. After the test verification, the radiation interference has been significantly reduced. The signal leakage decreases by more than 10 dB, which can meet the requirements of the communication system. The EMC test results are shown in Fig. 7.

Fig. 6. Cable optimization diagram

2) Communication system optimization

Radiation leakage caused the receiver performance degradation problem, exposed a number of weak points of the communication system, including:

a) It is susceptible to interference clutter under high sensitivity conditions;
b) After mis-trapping, it cannot exit effectively and has poor anti-interference.
c) Useful signal and interference signal can not be effectively distinguished.

In UHF band communication, the channel is mislocked due to interference clutter. The interference signal is less than the required threshold and within the receiver margin.Because there is no exit mechanism in UHF band communication, useful signals cannot be captured and tracked normally in the process of mislocking.At this time, the useful signal is larger than the interference signal.

In terms of system optimization, the joint decision mechanism is added, and the communication exit mechanism is introduced to improve the communication reliability of the system. The joint decision of carrier lock tracking and bit synchronization lock tracking can set a good decision timeout time. After the timeout, the acquisition and tracking process is re-initiated.

Based on the CCSDS protocol, the standard protocol of single carrier + idle sequence + information + tail sequence is followed in the normal communication process of UHF (see Fig. 8). In this framework, the timeout recapture protocol is introduced.Through simulation, test and joint trial, it is verified that this mechanism has no impact on normal communication. This measure effectively improves the reliability of communication system and strengthens the anti-interference ability of Mars relay system.

Fig. 7. Radiation diagram of EMC after optimization

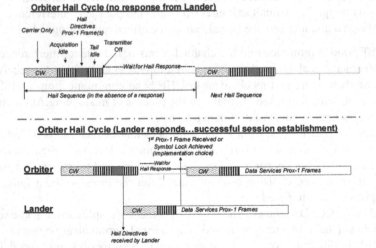

Fig. 8. Diagram of the communication process

5 Conclusion

In this paper, the radiation interference problems encountered in the Mars UHF band communication link are analyzed, and effective measures are proposed.

1. Optimizing the interference source, cutting off the interference signal propagation path: Cable optimization;
2. Improving the anti-interference ability, etc., to minimize the impact of EMC: The timeout recapture protocol is introduced.
3. Through analysis and test, the modification of measures can effectively reduce the impact of radiation interference, and improve the anti-interference ability of UHF band communication system. At the same time, the improved measure can provide data support and application method accumulation for the subsequent design of wireless systems.

References

1. Ju, X., Wang, C., Zhu, Q., Cui, R., Chen, X.: Design and implementation of deep space receiver synchronization algorithm. Spacecraft Eng. **24**(2), 62–67 (2014)
2. Wang, Y., Zhang, G.: Autonomous radio receiver technology based on deep space planetary network exploration. Space Electr. Technol. **2**, 21–24 (2013)
3. Cook, B., Dennis M., Kayalar, S., et al.: Development of the Advanced Deep Space Transponder, IPN 142-156. NASA's JPL, Pasadena, CA (2004)
4. Liang, G., Gengxin, Z., Wei, S., et al.: Development and prospect of deep space communication network. Digit. Commun. World **1**, 54–59 (2012)
5. Smith, J.G.: Ka-band (32 GHz) downlink capability for deep communications. NASA, Washington D.C. (1986)
6. Rebold, T.A., Kwork, A., Wood, G.E.: The Mars Observer Ka-Band Link Experiment. NASA, Washington, D.C. (1994)
7. Yiran, W., Xiaochuan, L., Kaiyuan, L.: Development status and trend of international deep space exploration technology. Space Int. **2**, 12–16 (2003)
8. Jiaxing, L.: Characteristics and main technical problems of deep space TT&C communication. J Aircraft TT&C **24**(6), 1–8 (2005)
9. Li, H., Yang, Z., Jiao, J., Zhang, Q., Wang, R.: A store-and-forward-based relaying CFDP over weather-dependent Ka-band space channel. IEEE Trans. Aerosp. Electr. Syst. (2012)
10. Jiaxing, L.: Challenges of deep space TT&C. Man. Space Flight **2**, 42–47 (2009)
11. Zhu, Z., Li, H.: Atmospheric attenuation analysis of deep space TT&C Link. J. Aircraft Trans Theory Commun. (2009)
12. Jun, S., Jay, G., Shambayati, S., Modiano, E.: Ka-band link optimization with rate adaptation for Mars and lunar communications. Int. J. Satell. Commun. Netw. **25**, 147–165 (2007)
13. Xie, J., Chen, J., Zhu, J., Wang, X.: Analysis of characteristics and key technologies of deep space communication. Commun. Inf. Technol. **4** (2011)
14. Ding, Z., Li, H.: Research status and development trend of deep space transponder. Deep Space Explor. Res. **8**(1), 18–23 (2010)
15. Li, H., Zhang, Z.: Design of relay CCSDS file transfer protocol for deep space KA-band. Shenzhen: Harbin Institute of Technology (2012)

Design and Implementation of Power Supply and Distribution System for Mars Landing Mission

Yan Chen[✉], Dong Yang, Hai Ping Shi, and Cheng Xiong Tang

Beijing Institute of Spacecraft System Engineering, Beijing, China
cheeringyan@126.com

Abstract. Combined with the characteristics of Mars exploration mission, the functions, main indicators and system schemes of the power supply and distribution subsystem of China's first Mars landing and rover mission are briefly introduced, and the design of high-specific energy lithium fluorocarbon batteries, the design of Mars solar spectrum-matched solar cells, the design of dust-proof coating, the design of MPPT, the estimation and management of on-orbit capacity, etc. are briefly introduced, and the design problems of power supply and distribution systems in the extreme environment of Mars landing and rover mission are proposed. The results of the on-orbit flight test show that the power supply and distribution system has normal function, reliable work and excellent performance, and the design scheme of the power supply and distribution system proposed for the landing and rover mission has successfully supported China's first interplanetary exploration mission. Through the design and implementation of this project, a large amount of valuable experience and data have been accumulated, which provides a high scientific and engineering reference value for the design and verification of power supply and distribution systems for subsequent Mars sampling and return missions.

Keywords: Mars · landing and rover · power supply and distribution system · lithium fluorocarbon battery · spectral matching solar cell · dust-proof coating

1 Introduction

"Tianwen-1" is China's first probe to implement an extraterrestrial planet exploration mission, and to achieve the "orbit, landing and rover" mission of Mars through a single launch. Tianwen-1 was launched from the "Long March 5" Yaosi carrier rocket at Wenchang Cosmodrome on July 23, 2020, and the landing rover successfully landed on the Utopian Plain of Mars on May 15, 2021, and successfully completed the 90-day regional rover and exploration mission of the fire surface on August 30, 2021. The rover successfully entered a dormant state after successfully completing the expansion mission for another 9 months. The power supply and distribution subsystem effectively ensures the safe power supply of the system throughout the mission period, and is a key subsystem that restricts the on-orbit work project and life of the rover.

© ICST Institute for Computer Sciences, Social Informatics and Telecommunications Engineering 2023
Published by Springer Nature Switzerland AG 2023. All Rights Reserved
R. Li et al. (Eds.): MOBILWARE 2022, LNICST 507, pp. 256–268, 2023.
https://doi.org/10.1007/978-3-031-34497-8_22

The Mars rover has a long flight time, many key and unique links, faces many extreme environments and uncertainties, and has high requirements for multi-mission coupling design [1]. The landing and rover power supply and distribution system is responsible for the power supply, regulation and transmission of the full-cycle landing rover, and is a key subsystem of the Mars rover, which is crucial to the successful completion of the Mars exploration mission [2].

From the pre-launch to the end of the mission, the probe is divided into six mission stages: active section, ground fire transfer section, Mars capture section, Mars mooring section, de-orbit landing section and scientific exploration section, and the power supply and distribution subsystem has the following characteristics and design difficulties in the whole mission cycle.

2 Power Supply and Distribution System Design

2.1 System Functions

The functions of the power supply and distribution system are: the function of charging the lithium-ion battery of the landing rover by the orbiter in the state of the detector assembly, and the function of independently supplying power to the landing rover when the power of the orbiter is tight; After separating from the orbiter, the power supply of the landing rover is guaranteed by the battery pack of the landing rover, of which the battery pack of the entry module is the main part and the battery pack of the Mars rover is used as the backup; After the entry module and the rover are separated, the two vehicles independently supply power, and the rover forms an independent solar cell array-battery pack joint power supply system to provide electrical energy for the rover.

2.2 System Design

The landing rover power supply and distribution system is designed for dual-cabin combined power supply and adopts an unregulated busbar. The entry module is equipped with a short-term power supply and is equipped with a set of 120Ah lithium fluorocarbon batteries, which is mainly responsible for completing the power supply task of the Mars EDL (entry, descent and landing) section; The rover is equipped with a set of Mars spectral matching solar arrays with dust-proof coatings, a set of 80Ah lithium-ion battery packs, and a power controller using MPPT power conditioning technology, which is mainly responsible for the power supply task of fire and rover detection (Fig. 1).

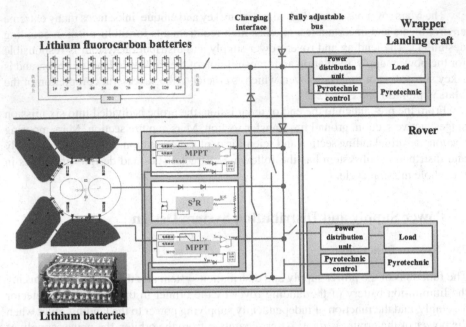

Fig. 1. Topology of the power supply and distribution system of the Mars landing and rover mission

3 Key Technologies of Power Supply and Distribution Systems

3.1 Mars Spectral Modification Technology for Solar Cells

The surface of Mars is affected by the atmosphere and shows a spectral "redshift", and the proportion of long-wave bands is high. The performance of the three-junction gallium arsenide solar cell developed for AM0 spectrum will change abnormally under the light conditions of Mars ground, and the originally matched interjunction current will mismatch, affecting the power output of the solar cell, and the current mismatch under the Mars 30° spectral condition will reach 9.3%, resulting in a decrease in the photoelectric conversion efficiency of the solar cell (Table 1).

Table 1. Current values of the battery under various spectral conditions

Spectral conditions	Top battery Jsc_top (mA/cm^2)	Medium battery Jsc_mid (mA/cm^2)	Bottom battery Jsc_bot (mA/cm^2)	Top middle battery current mismatch (%)
Earth AM0	16.989	17.265	27.703	1.62
Mars 30 degrees	5.476	5.994	9.439	9.46
Mars 60 degrees	2.747	3.133	4.844	14.05

In view of the above problems, the rover adopts the Mars spectral matching three-junction gallium arsenide solar cell technology, adjusts the top-cell and medium-cell structure of the three-junction gallium arsenide solar cell during the design of the solar cell, so that the top cell and the medium cell current match, thereby improving the conversion efficiency of the three-junction gallium arsenide solar cell in the Mars spectrum, so that the solar cell output is reduced by more than 9% to about 2% in the Martian 30° latitude spectral environment, and the photoelectric conversion efficiency is increased from 29% to 31.7%. Enables solar cells to achieve the best performance and power output under special lighting conditions on the surface of Mars.

3.2 Dustproof Coating Technology on the Surface of Solar Cells

There is a large amount of dust in the atmosphere on the surface of Mars, and there will also be violent dust storms, which will make the surface of the solar cell receive a large amount of sunlight due to dust deposition, which will eventually lead to a decrease in the output power of the solar cell, which will seriously affect the safety of the probe's power supply. The power of the Courageous solar cell array is approximately linearly linearly decayed, with a decline of about 9% per month. The accumulation of dust on Mars and the dust storm effect accelerate the decay of solar cell output power.

The rover adopts dust-proof coating technology on the surface of solar cells based on micro-nano structure. The technology has short, medium and long full band high transmittance, high surface hardness, temperature shock resistance, UV/charged particle radiation resistance, low vacuum volatility and many other advantages, in terms of composition, mainly by introducing hydrophobic silicon methyl groups to reduce the force between inorganic dust and coating; In terms of structure, the bionic micro-nano structure design similar to the lotus leaf was carried out to reduce the contact area between the dust and the glass cover and thus reduce the force; The new space dust removal technology based on the new coating has made a useful attempt to develop the dust removal technology on the surface of Mars under the premise of ensuring the safe and reliable power supply of the probe.

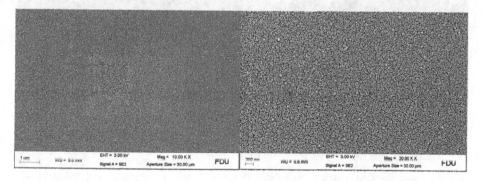

(a) Magnification 10000x, ruler 1mμ   (b) The magnification is 20,000x, the ruler 200nm

Fig. 2. SEM (scanning electron microscope) photo of the dustproof coating

3.3 Design and Management Technology of Wide Temperature and High Specific Energy Battery

(1) Enter the cabin lithium fluorocarbon battery.

Lithium fluorocarbon battery has the advantages of high specific energy, long storage life and good safety, adapting to the long-term storage needs of Benhuo, because it saves the on-orbit charging link, it is more conducive to on-orbit maintenance, so that the weight of the entry cabin system is reduced by more than 5kg. However, there are also limitations in its use, which is suitable for discharge rates below 0.1C, and high discharge rates under the original design will lead to heat accumulation, increased temperature rise, and affect battery safety. The lithium fluorinated carbon battery is selected as the main energy source of the EDL segment, which will face the high rate discharge demand of 0.5C long-term discharge and ultra-1.1C pulse discharge, so the lithium fluorocarbon battery needs to be adaptively improved.

In the Mars mission, a high-specific energy lithium fluorocarbon battery based on a new cathode material was adopted to effectively improve the conductivity of the cathode material, improve the discharge rate of the battery while ensuring the high specific energy of the battery, effectively suppress the heat generation under the high rate of discharge, improve the working safety of the EDL section of the battery, and realize that the specific energy of the battery 0.2C discharge is better than 500Wh/Kg, and the self-discharge rate of 10 months in orbit is 1 5% high specific energy design.

Due to its excellent performance, since Tianwen-1, lithium fluorocarbon batteries have appeared on the historical stage as the main energy source of spacecraft, and have become the first choice for primary batteries for China's spacecraft follow-up missions (Fig. 3).

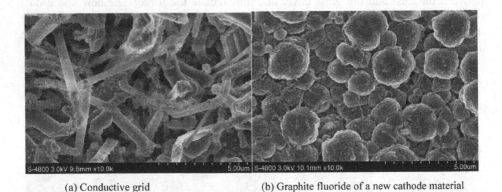

(a) Conductive grid   (b) Graphite fluoride of a new cathode material

Fig. 3. Conductive grid of lithium fluorocarbon battery and SEM photo of cathode material

(2) Mars rover lithium-ion battery.

The rover landed near 30° north latitude of the fire surface, and the lithium-ion battery pack faced a wide temperature environment of −30 °C ~ 55 °C per day, and the rover had no nuclear source support to design the battery pack Challenges. The following figure shows the charge and discharge curve of the lithium-ion battery unit of the rover at −20 °C, and it can be seen that the discharge capacity of the lithium-ion battery pack at a low temperature of −20 °C is less than 80% of the normal temperature capacity, and less than 50% of the −30 °C.

The power supply and distribution system adopts a wide temperature range high specific energy lithium-ion battery, through the positive and negative plate parameters, electrolyte formula, etc. to optimize the adjustment, so that the specific energy of the lithium-ion battery for Mars reaches 193Wh/kg, the −20 °C low-temperature charge-discharge capacity retention rate is better than 90% (compared to normal temperature, the same below), -30 °C low-temperature charge-discharge capacity retention rate is greater than 73%, 10% higher than the conventional long-life lithium cobalt oxide battery, and the normal operating temperature range of the battery is extended from 0 °C ~ 50 °C to -30 °C ~ + 55 °C, on the basis of maintaining high specific energy, improves the wide temperature adaptability of lithium-ion batteries, and improves the robustness of Mars rover to cope with various complex working conditions on the Martian surface;

(3) Lithium-ion battery pack capacity assessment and management.

Based on the calculation of the residual charge of the lithium battery pack based on the fusion estimation of the charge state and calibration method, the results of the fuel gauge and the lookup table method are combined, and the fuel gauge integral data is usually used, and in specific cases, the battery capacity of the battery pack is calibrated by the meter power, so as to ensure that the battery capacity is always known in the case of complex working conditions and reawakening after long-term sleep It provides favorable support for the realization of spacecraft autonomous management under unmanned intervention.

3.4 Hardware-Based Solar Array Maximum Power Point Tracking (MPPT) Technology

According to the overall input, the daytime temperature range of the rover on the surface of Mars is −65 °C ~ + 40 °C, the impact factor of ambient temperature on the output voltage of solar cells is −6.8mV/°C, and the effect factor on the output current is 0.011 mA/^{cm2}. °C。 Since the temperature change has a great impact on the output voltage of the solar cell, in order to make full use of the output power of the solar array, the power supply and distribution system adopts the maximum power point tracking (MPPT) technology of the solar cell array based on hardware circuits for the Martian environment. It solves the problem of efficient utilization of solar cell array power under the complex light and wide temperature conditions of Mars, and the comprehensive utilization efficiency of solar cell array reaches 91%, which effectively reduces the area and weight of the solar cell array and improves the specific energy of the power supply system.

The MPPT main power topology circuit adopts a super-buck circuit with continuous input and output currents, which is tracked by the interleaved perturbation method.

The circuit control mode includes two modes: MPPT ring and constant voltage ring. At heavy loads, the full capacity output of the solar array is required to operate in the MPPT ring. At light loads, not all solar array power is required and works in a constant voltage ring. In order to realize the step-by-step access and exit function of the opposing array power, a three-way solar cell array is designed, the solar array 3 constant voltage point is 29.1V, and the solar array 1 constant voltage point is 29.0V, solar array 2 constant voltage point is 28.9V, so in the process of gradually increasing bus voltage, the three-way solar cell array will exit the MPPT control mode in the order of solar array 2 → solar array 1 → solar array 3.

3.5 Rover Sleep Wake-Up Technology

According to the data, the temperature change range of the Martian surface is −103 °C ~ + 27 °C. During the night of fire, because the solar cell cannot produce electrical energy and the surface temperature is low, the heater must provide a thermal control environment for the basic survival of the rover. The rover's normal operating mode takes into account the power consumption requirements of maintaining a minimum power mode at night; Considering that under the worst conditions of a strong dust storm, the output power of the solar array during the fire day is seriously reduced, and in order to avoid excessive discharge of the battery, the rover will enter sleep mode.

In view of the long-term survival problem of the fire surface caused by bad weather such as random sand and dust that is difficult to predict the time and duration, a fully autonomous wake-up circuit based on dual enabling of light and temperature is designed to ensure safe and reliable wake-up when the battery temperature and solar cell output power meet the standard, which is the first application in the world (foreign nuclear sources, regardless of temperature problems). Compared with the sleep wake-up circuit of the rover, the rover sleep wake-up technology has the following two main improvements:

Circuit Design: Since the rover adopts MPPT technology, in order to achieve bus cut, a secondary power supply and corresponding switches are added.

Sleep Wake-Up Strategy: Add parameter items such as battery discharge depth and Mars time to the sleep condition; The wake-up load voltage threshold in the wake-up condition is designed to correlate with the battery pack temperature.

4 Test Verification

4.1 Solar Cell Mars Spectral Matching Modification Technology Verification

High-efficiency gallium arsenide solar cells for conventional space have a photoelectric conversion efficiency of about 29% in the Martian spectrum. The photoelectric conversion efficiency of high-efficiency gallium arsenide solar cells developed for the Martian spectrum is about 32%. The following figure shows the ground test data (TE: top battery; ME: Medium battery) (Fig. 4).

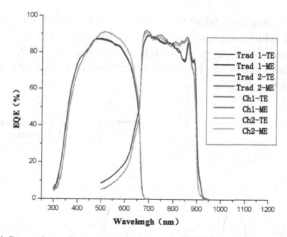

(a) Comparison of quantum efficiency test results before and after improvement

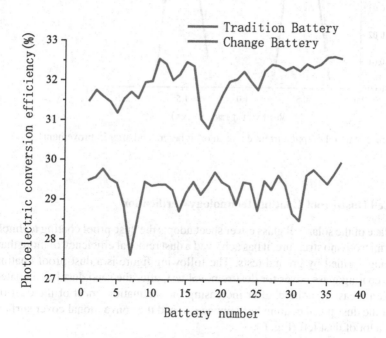

(b) Improve the surface measured photoelectric conversion efficiency curve before and after

Fig. 4. Spectral matching solar cell ground validation data

The rover carried four calibration batteries in orbit, namely the improved front single battery, the improved rear top battery, the improved medium battery and the improved single battery, and the on-orbit output current of the four calibration batteries also intuitively showed the output effect before and after the improvement. Evaluating the power generation capacity of the vehicle, the solar wing power generation capacity is 2900Wh/day, the load power consumption is about 1000Wh per day, and about 1750Wh of energy can support additional tasks, and it can be seen that the Mars rover has sufficient energy in the early stage of the fire (Fig. 5).

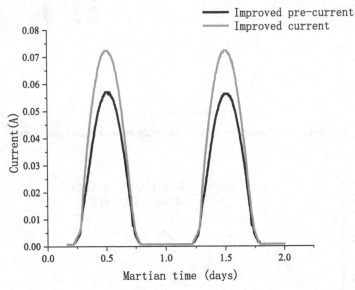

Fig. 5. Solar cell output current curve in orbit before and after improvement

4.2 Solar Cell Dust-Proof Coating Technology Verification

After the surface of the solar cell glass cover sheet adopts the dust-proof coating technology based on micro-nano structure, it has achieved a dust removal efficiency of more than 87% after being verified by ground tests. The following figure is a dust-proof coating and dust-free coating glass cover for dust removal test, after the sand dust has a coated cover sheet is not easy to adhere, after increasing the inclination, most of the dust on the surface of the dust-proof coating has slipped off, and the conventional cover surface There is also a lot of dust left (Fig. 6).

Fig. 6. Ground dust removal test

The solar cell has excellent results in orbit, because the top plate solar cell circuit is the priority output, and the on-orbit is the full power output state, and the decline trend of the output of the solar cell array can be judged by the change trend of the output current of the top plate. The output current range of the rover is 0 to 1.493A at sunset on May 16, and the output current range is 0 to 1 413A, from landing to mission end, power generation decays by about 2% / month. The output current curve of the top plate solar array 3 is shown in the figure below. It can be seen from the curve that the attenuation of solar cell output power is flat, and which is much less than the dust decay data of 9% / month abroad (Fig. 7).

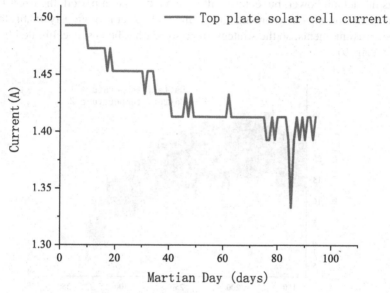

Fig. 7. Top plate solar cell output current

4.3 Wide Temperature and High Specific Energy Battery Design and Management Technology Verification

(1) Enter the cabin lithium fluorocarbon battery.

The heat generation of lithium fluorinated carbon batteries has been reduced by 76.3% after improvement. The landing rover successfully landed on Mars in the early morning of May 15, 2021, and was degraded by telemetry from the EDL segment to the fire on the day of landing, and the EDL process entered the cabin bus bar voltage from the post-fire stage to the post-fire stage, and the voltage was stable and satisfied 25V index requirements, discharge current stability without abnormal transition, the cumulative discharge of the battery is about 37.7Ah, the discharge depth of 30%, in line with the design expectations, successfully completed the landing task of the EDL section (Fig. 8).

(2) Mars rover lithium-ion battery capacity assessment and management.

Lithium-ion battery pack in orbit life (Sol90 within), the difference between the peak of the integral power and the meter of electricity are within 3Ah (temperature at 10 °C ~ 32 °C), during the extended mission period, as the rover enters the winter, the solar altitude angle gradually decreases, and the temperature of the rover gradually decreases. The temperature of the battery pack also gradually decreases, see Fig. 2 0, Sol328 began to calculate the daily calibration of the battery pack can not achieve the integral full charge, the difference between the integral charge and the meter power gradually increased, and the battery capacity error caused by the integral power error gradually appeared, see Fig. 2 for details 1。 Since the temperature of the battery pack is stable above 10 °C during the life period, it is feasible for the rover to use the integral power as the default power, but entering the extended mission period, the rover faces a more stringent working environment, and the integral power is obviously unable to meet the mission requirements, so the strategy since sol331 has been self-calibrated for each Mars day (Fig. 9).

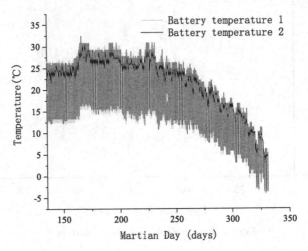

Fig. 8. Sol136 ~ Sol331 battery pack temperature curve

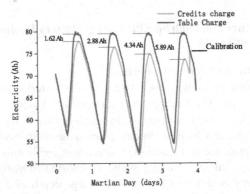

Fig. 9. Sol328 ~ Sol331 battery pack power curve

4.4 Hardware Circuit Based Solar Array Maximum Power Point Tracking (MPPT) Technology Verification

The MPPT circuit works normally in orbit, the solar cell power is fully output at the beginning of the fire day, and as the battery pack voltage gradually increases, the square array gradually exits, realizing the dynamic power regulation function. Figure 10 is the output current curve of the solar cell array on the second Martian day (Sol2), and it can be seen from the figure that when the battery pack is in a low state of charge, the solar array 1 and 2 are both operating MPPT mode, solar array 1 ~ 3 full output, the battery pack is in charge state. As the battery pack voltage gradually increases, solar array 2 begins to exit MPPT mode, solar array 1 still operates in MPPT mode, and solar array 3 still outputs full. Sun Array 2 operates in constant voltage ring mode, gradually moving from the maximum operating point to the open circuit point, and the current of Sun Array 2 is gradually reduced by the maximum power point current. If the battery pack voltage continues to rise, Solar Array 2 operates at the open circuit point and does not output. If the battery pack voltage continues to rise, Solar Array 1 begins to exit MPPT mode and Solar Array 3 is still fully output. Sun Array 1 operates in constant voltage ring mode, gradually moving from the maximum operating point to the open circuit point, and the current of solar array 1 is gradually reduced by the maximum power point current.

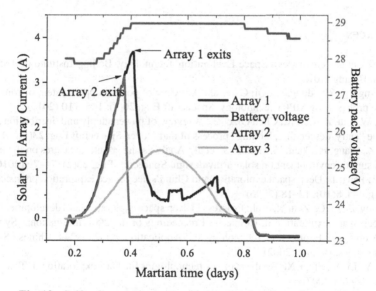

Fig. 10. Sol2 solar array output and battery pack voltage change curve

4.5 Rover Sleep Wake-Up Technology Verification

(1) Sleep process

Mars rover daily into the fire night to judge the battery pack capacity, when the fire during the solar array output power is insufficient, the battery capacity will decrease, when below the design threshold, the rover began to look for the appropriate terrain, set the body orientation, set the whole unit into the minimum working mode, when the battery pack continues to discharge to the discharge depth is greater than 50%, start the sleep setting, sleep setting through the number of tube program control to achieve.

(2) Wake-up process

When the solar wing output power gradually rises during the fire day, the wake-up load voltage also rises, and when the wake-up load voltage reaches about 27.4V, the power controller automatically wakes up the rover through the autonomous wake-up circuit.

5 Conclusions

The power supply and distribution system of the Mars mission proposed in this plan has broken through many key technologies with ultra-high specific energy and innovative design concepts, and successfully completed the Mars landing and rover mission at a very small cost. It provides important reference and reference for the design of power supply and distribution systems for future Mars rovers and other deep space probes.

Acknowledgment. This work is supported by National Natural Science Foundation of China (No. 52007007).

References

1. Sun, Z., et al. (eds.): Deep Space Exploration Technology. Beijing Institute of Technology Press, Beijing (2018)
2. Zhigang, L., Xiaodong, C., Qi, C., et al.: A review of power supply system of foreign deep space probes using MPPT technology. Spacecraft Eng. **20**(5), 105–110 (2011)
3. Guo, W., Liu, Z., Cai, X., Chen Qi, et al.: A review of power supply and distribution schemes for the "entry, descending, landing" process of mars rover. Spacecraft Eng. **23**(5), 111 (2014)
4. Liu, Z., Wang, F., Chen, Y., Huang, S., et al.: Analysis and countermeasures on the impact of mars surface environment on solar array design. Spacecraft Eng. **25**(2), 74–79 (2016). 1/6
5. Ye, P., Peng, J.: Deep space exploration and China's deep space exploration prospects. Chin. J. Eng. Sci. **8**(10), 13–18 (2006)
6. Ouyang, Z., Li, C., Zou, Y., et al.: Progress in deep space exploration and development strategy of deep space exploration in China. In: Proceedings of the 2002 International Symposium on Deep Space Exploration Technology and Application, pp. 237–244. Chinese Society of Astronautics, Beijing (2002)
7. Chu, Y., Li, X., Zhou, X.: Analysis of key technologies for Mars exploration. J. Test. Technol. **21**(6), 63–66 (2007)
8. Barlow, N.G.: Mars: an introduction to its interior, surface, and atmosphere. In: Wu, J., Zhao, H. (eds.) Translated by Beijing, pp. 17–20. Science Press (2010)
9. Shijun, M.A.: China Aerospace Press, Beijing, pp. 254–255 (2001)
10. Chen, Q., Liu, Z., Zhang, X., Fu, L., et al.: Spacecraft power technology. Beijing Institute of Technology Press, Beijing (2018) .3
11. Jensen, H., Laursen, J.: Power conditioning unit for Rosetta/Mars express. In: Proceedings of the 6th European Space Power Conference, pp. 249–257. ESA, Paris (2002)
12. Loche, D.: Mars express and venus express power subsystem in-flight behaviour. In: Proceedings of the 8th European Space Power Conference, pp. 1–7. ESA, Paris (2008)

Research on Integrated Operation Design of Low Orbit Remote Sensing Satellite for Intelligent Application

Du Jie[✉], Li Zhuo, Yixin Liu, Mengjie Shi, and Haihua Li

China Academy of Space Technology, 104 Youyi Road, Haidian, Beijing, China
qi_tianlong@126.com

Abstract. In this paper, from a remote sensing satellites that orbit earth operation characteristics and application conditions, combined with the elliptic orbit agile imaging and application characteristics of huge amounts of data transmission, and both remote sensing satellites that orbit earth in the next 10 to 20 years on the integration of electronic systems and application requirements of the system software, in view of the existing electronic system, the application of gap is given star to integration of heaven and earth satellite data application interface design, This paper provides a direction for the system software design of the future integrated electronic system on board.

Keyword: Low orbit · remote sensing satellite · in-orbit application requirements analysis · integrated operation design

1 Preface

Different from geosynchronous orbit satellites, low-orbit remote sensing satellites frequently enter and exit the country and work intermittently. The resources of reconnaissance, operation and controlcc and measurement and control arc are very valuable. Payload missions are intermittent (orbital characteristics), diverse (target characteristics) and uncertain (burst characteristics). Complex mission plans are made based on daily optimization and calculation of satellite and ground operation parameters.The satellite has a complex operating mode and strong orbital maneuver and attitude maneuver ability, which requires very high mission coordination and real-time performance of imaging payload, data transmission link, measurement and control link and platform.Due to the constraints of orbit, T&C and data transmission arcs are important resources for satellite in-orbit operation.At the same time, the on-orbit work of satellites is also restricted by orbit revisit characteristics, atmosphere, on-board system mission coordination (including attitude maneuver, storage, energy, payload working time), high data rate transmission, etc.

For remote sensing satellites that orbit earth transported accused of complicated, risky, high operation cost, etc., the research and development to use and easy to use

R. Li et al. (Eds.): MOBILWARE 2022, LNICST 507, pp. 269–284, 2023.
https://doi.org/10.1007/978-3-031-34497-8_23

software, the satellite has a strong ability of independent task management, including independent task management ability, independent health management ability, the ability of onboarrefactoring and automated testing capabilities, is the development trend of remote sensing satellites that orbit earth software design.

2 Demand Analysis of Low-orbit Remote Sensing Satellite In-Orbit Applications

2.1 Demand Analysis of Satellite Imaging, Data Transmission and On-Orbit Applications

Satellite Imaging Mode Analysis

At present, low-orbit remote sensing satellites can have strong agile maneuvering ability and realize the following agile imaging modes:

- Multi-target imaging in the same orbit: the satellite can frequently maneuver sideways to ensure the rapid completion of multi-point target imaging tasks.
- Multi-band splicing imaging mode in the same orbit: the attitude maneuver of the satellite in the direction of pitch and roll is used, and the piece-together push sweep along the track direction is carried out several times to obtain a wide multi-band splicing image.
- Multi-angle observation mode in the same orbit: push and sweep images of different facades of the same target were carried out through the pitch and roll of monorail and disorail satellites to obtain different facades information of the target that could not be observed in the traditional side-swing observation mode.
- The same orbit stereo imaging mode: using the high attitude maneuver ability of agile satellite, the satellite can observe the same area with different pitch angles in one orbit to obtain the information of different stereo planes of the same ground object, and finally complete the stereo mapping function through the ground processing.
- Continuous strip imaging mode: the satellite images subsatellite points or ground targets continuously at a certain pitch Angle with high attitude stability and high attitude pointing accuracy. To improve the timeliness of imaging, the satellite imaged long and narrow ground objects in the non-track direction (Fig. 1).

The typical agile imaging mode is shown in the figure below.

Analysis of Satellite Massive Data Transmission Mode

As shown in Fig. 2, compared with the low-orbit remote sensing satellite developed in 2013, the payload data volume of the satellite developed in 2018 has increased by 20 times, while the storage capacity has only increased by 4 times, the earth-to-earth data transmission capacity has increased by 2.3 times, and the relay data transmission capacity has increased by 2.0 times Fig. 2.

As shown in Fig. 3, compared with the low-orbit remote sensing satellite developed in 2013, the imaging power of the satellite developed in 2018 increased by 5.6 times, the earth playback power increased by 13.3 times, and the relay playback power increased

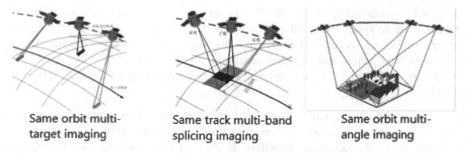

Same orbit multi-
target imaging

Same track multi-band
splicing imaging

Same orbit multi-
angle imaging

Fig. 1. Typical agile imaging mode of satellite

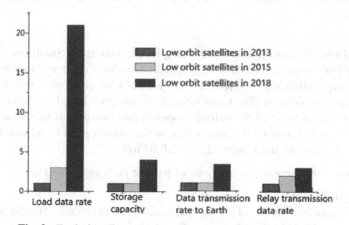

Fig. 2. Evolution diagram of satellite data balance configuration-

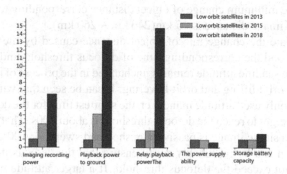

Fig. 3. Evolution diagram of satellite energy configuration-

by 14.8 times. Figure 3 the satellite power supply capacity is reduced by 22.4%, and the battery capacity is increased by 71.4%.

The new generation of low-orbit remote sensing satellites can improve the load data transmission capacity by improving the modulation mode, coding mode, increasing

EIRP, polarization multiplexing and other means. At the same time, the satellite integrated electronic system adopts the dynamic cooperation system of energy, storage and data transmission resources to improve the data storage and transmission efficiency, so as to support the acquisition and transmission of massive data.

The new generation of low-orbit remote sensing satellites has the following capabilities:

- The scheduling strategy of "pre-pointing and cross-using in advance" is adopted to reduce the loss of data transmission arcs caused by antenna cutting stations;
- Intelligent cloud judgment algorithm is used to eliminate the useless massive information and improve the efficiency of effective information transmission.
- The preprocessing technology is used to provide end-to-end in-orbit data service for tactical users.

Analysis of In-Orbit Autonomous Focusing Requirements of Satellites

The imaging of low-orbit remote sensing satellites with different attitudes in orbit will lead to the large difference of object distance between imaging tasks, which will bring a certain degree of defocus. The focus strategy planning is carried out according to the influence of the decrease of the defocus transmission function of the camera in orbit is not more than 5%, that is, the focal plane of the camera must be adjusted when the cumulative defocus amount reaches $\pm\delta/3$ (±0.07 mm).

(1) Analysis of the focusing requirement of passive push and sweep mode

- Elliptical orbit

    The change rate of object distance caused by the change of orbit height does not exceed 0.35 km/s in the range of common attitude maneuver of passive thrust-sweep. Meanwhile, under the current orbit design and camera optical system design, the minimum change of object distance corresponding to 1/3 focal depth change of image distance is 15 km(246 km ~ 260 km).

    A. Calculate the change rate of object distance caused by the change of orbit height and the corresponding time of defocus threshold under the condition that the satellite attitude remains unchanged in the process of passive push and sweep orbit lifting and orbit lowering. It can be seen that within the range of commonly used attitude maneuver, the shortest time for the defocus caused by orbit height to reach the defocus threshold is about 100s. That is, theoretically, when a single image is passively pushed and swept for 100s, the focus plane position can be reasonably set to ensure that the defocus in a single image does not exceed the defocus threshold. If a larger attitude maneuver Angle, such as 45°, is considered, then when the single imaging time is less than 40s, no focusing is required during the imaging period.

    B. At the same time, if only the defocus caused by the attitude maneuver is considered, the minimum point-to-point attitude maneuver Angle corresponding to the defocus threshold is about 20° and the corresponding attitude maneuver time is about 48s(stability $5 \times 10)^{-4}$°/s)/28s (stability 2×10^{-3} / s). At the same time, during 48s/28s, the orbital height of the satellite may also change about 10km/5km, that is, in the worst case, the attitude maneuver between the two targets of the satellite may not exceed 20°, but it may also need to focus. At this time, excluding the stabilization time after focal plane adjustment, the shortest time window for focusing between the two missions is about 40s/ 20s. When the two tasks are very close to each other, the controller should be powered on during the two tasks in order to complete the focal plane adjustment.

C. The actual situation of in-orbit mission arrangement is more complicated than the single factor analyzed in this paper. Factors such as orbit height change, attitude maneuver Angle and direction between two imaging, and orbit rise/fall will exert a combined effect on the change of focal plane position during two imaging. Therefore, for each imaging task, the acceptable focal plane position interval should be calculated separately, and the focus decision should be made. When the user arranges the imaging mode, it can be analyzed according to the specific situation.

• Circular orbit

The satellite adopts passive thrusting mode in orbit, so the change of object distance during a single mission imaging is mainly caused by the change of elevation, and the maximum surface elevation is not more than 9 km, which is far less than the change of object distance corresponding to the acceptable defocus threshold when the object distance is greater than 490 km. Therefore, it can ensure that no focus is needed during a single imaging.

The change of object distance between missions is mainly caused by the attitude Angle and the elevation of the satellite. Since the change of object distance caused by elevation change is small, the change of object distance caused by attitude maneuver Angle change is shown in the following table (Table 1).

Table 1. Object distances corresponding to different attitude angles of circular orbit

Attitude Maneuver Angle (°)	5	10	15	20	25	30
Object distance (km)	492.0	498.1	508.7	524.1	545.3	573.3
Attitude Maneuver Angle (°)	35	40	45	50	55	60
Object distance (km)	609.9	658.0	721.9	809.3	934.8	1131.6

From the above table:

• When $0° \leq$ attitude maneuver Angle (relative subsatellite point) $\leq 25°$, the same focal plane position can be adopted.
• When $25° <$ attitude maneuver Angle (relative subsatellite point) $\leq 35°$, the same focal plane position can be used.
• When $35° <$ attitude maneuver Angle (relative subsatellite point) $\leq 45°$, the same focal plane position can be used.
• When $45° <$ attitude maneuver Angle (relative subsatellite point) $\leq 50°$, the same focal plane position can be used.

- When $50° <$ attitude maneuver Angle (relative subsatellite point) $\leq 60°$, the same focal plane position can be used.

Therefore, in circular orbit imaging, different attitude maneuver angles of the satellite -- the annular map of focal plane position can be calculated. When the attitude maneuver angles of two adjacent imaging missions are different, focal plane adjustment will be needed.

(2) Analysis of the focus requirement of active push and sweep operation mode.

Active sweep mode is mainly used in elliptical orbit near Earth arc.In active sweep mode, the imaging time of a typical imaging task is 20s. According to the design conditions of 96(the most commonly used on-orbit) and 48 (the least commonly used on-orbit) integration series, the integration time corresponding to 54 μs (level 48) and 27μs(level 96), the simulation analysis is carried out. In the process of analysis, a total of 8 characteristic orbital heights were selected for the near-earth arc with the orbital height of 250 ~ 490 km, and one characteristic value was selected for every 10 degrees of the side-swing Angle of the imaging center from 0 to 40 degrees.

Within the orbit range of 250–490 km, the change of object distance is no more than 10 km within 20 s of a single active scan, and the minimum change of object distance corresponding to the defocus threshold is 15 km. That is, after the focal plane position of the imaging task is properly set, the focal plane position does not need to be adjusted during the single active scan.

For the focus requirements between adjacent tasks, active backscanning is more complicated than passive thrusting. Besides the time needed to switch orbit height and attitude Angle, the establishment time of attitude angular velocity should also be taken into account.Via simulation, establish active flyback attitude about 60 s longest, imaging position return to zero after the completion of time of about 80 s, both the sum of the time, caused by orbital altitude change as is close to or more than from the focal distance change threshold, consider adjacent tasks at the same time image center points to differences, a single imaging distance real-time variation during the influence of such factors, It is more difficult to set a general judgment condition to determine whether to focus or not. Therefore, it is necessary to calculate the decision focusing action before each imaging mission according to the orbit, task information, current focal plane position, etc.

2.2 Analysis of Efficient Satellite Measurement and Control, Operation and Control and Application Requirements

The requirements of satellite in T&C and O&C are as follows:

- Efficient mission injection: with the rapid growth of the attitude and maneuver ability of satellites, the number of missions carried by satellites grows rapidly every day, so it is urgent to improve the efficiency of mission injection.
- Autonomous closed-loop operation and control optimization: Satellite business data mass growth, a variety of imaging model, a variety of tasks orbit of different control strategies, to receive, decomposition, scheduling tasks require satellite system,

detection and control to realize comprehensive optimization, consider including orbit, imaging model, agile attitude maneuver, data transmission, energy, store a variety of factors such as stars, fine management, in order to realize the star - integration optimization using, To improve the application efficiency of the system;

- User-oriented control: application satellites in orbit and attitude maneuver ability, energy, ability, tactical service aspects put forward the new requirements, independent task management was adopted to realize the demand of various application environments, a support long-focus camera elliptical orbit environment, support for multiple attitude maneuver strategy, to support the whole closed-loop energy management, etc.;
- Emergency mission response: the satellite has the ability to respond to emergency missions directly without the ground operation and control system.
- Software maintenance: Most of the on-board software has maintenance capability, which can adapt to AIT test and adapt to various orbital imaging applications in orbit.

2.3 Analysis of Requirements for Autonomous Mission Management

Low-orbit remote sensing satellites have the capabilities of attitude maneuvering, imaging control, data transmission and resource optimization, which puts forward higher autonomous management capabilities for on-board integrated electronic systems, and requires them to meet the requirements of multi-mission, high-dynamic, multi-application orbit and high-precision autonomous mission management with higher collaboration and real-time performance. The on-board integrated electronic system needs the capabilities of incremental mission planning, mission optimization, decomposition, scheduling, and collaborative data service.

- Incremental mission planning: JB-16 satellite has the capability of incremental mission planning, realizing autonomous timing conflict detection, autonomous data balance management, mission arbitration, on-board resource balance, etc., and rapidly responding to emergency imaging services.
- Decomposition: the user's various application modes are decomposed into basic working modes, and the number of basic working modes is reduced by combining the modes to reduce the complexity of implementation, testing and autonomous health management.
- Scheduling: reasonably arrange the timing of task-related parameter calculation, instruction generation, focus, refrigerator switching and platform data processing to ensure the rationality of task-related equipment control scheduling;
- Task optimization: improve system efficiency through task parallelization; Based on the "critical path" optimization method, the camera power consumption during continuous imaging is reduced. Satellite-ground integration analysis software is used to autonomously arrange the satellite attitude swing according to the time interval of continuous imaging missions. Based on the task distribution, the focus, memory clearing, data preprocessing and other tasks were arranged by selecting the machine. Affected by the uncertainty of elliptical orbit operation, real-time satellite calculation is used to realize in-motion imaging according to the imaging latitude and longitude information injected from the ground, and the imaging time error and orbit prediction

error caused by the long prediction time of the traditional ground operation and control mode are corrected.

- Collaborative data service: Imaging satellites need load, control, dual mode, data processing, antenna receiver, task management computer, load data processing, such as computers, work together to achieve user tasks in a timely and high quality, especially the control subsystem, camera subsystem, data transmission subsystem, navigation receiver to work together to achieve perigee flyback, The navigation receiver, control subsystem, and integrated electronic subsystem cooperate to provide fast and low-delay integration time data service, and adjust the camera integration time in real time during the backsweep attitude maneuver imaging process.

2.4 On-Board Autonomous Health Management and On-Orbit Maintenance Requirements Analysis

- Autonomous health management: satellite operating mode is complex, data flow relationship is complex, complex application mode, it is urgent to use on-board autonomous health management to improve on-orbit support capacity;
- Mission operation process monitoring: the satellite uses on-board mission management to achieve autonomous operation and control. The ground system lacks prior knowledge to predict the working status of the satellite, and the satellite automatically diagnoses the health status according to the real-time operating status.
- Health evaluation: it provides health evaluation capability to facilitate users to take necessary maintenance measures.

2.5 Automated Test Requirement Analysis

Intelligent testing methods are urgently needed to reduce testing cost and shorten development cycle for satellites.

- Incremental verification: the product status of each subsystem is new, the development difficulty is inconsistent, and the function is highly coupled, so it must have the incremental verification feature to ensure the credibility of the test verification when the equipment is not fully set.
- Automatic mode test and orthogonal test: satellite platform, load working mode highly coupled, more attitude maneuver model, three kinds of application environment, system working mode/validation test sequence mass growth, test verification cycle is long, need to be improve work efficiency and automation model test and orthogonal test, on the premise of ensure testing strength, ensure the reliability of the satellite design;
- Temporal fault immune design: satellite requires highly coordinated platform and payload, and high frequency and low delay data services make system verification more difficult, so it is urgent to adopt time-driven design system.
- Software without assembly maintenance: the high-coupling design makes the whole satellite test the only link of system physical verification. When the ground test encounters a fault, the SMU, CCU and other complex software with multiple interfaces and large scale can be updated online without assembly.

- Interlock protection of dangerous instructions: multiple protection measures jointly designed by software and hardware are adopted to ensure that the satellite equipment will not be damaged by errors in the operation of test sequences of explosive products, propulsion and moving parts.

3 Gap Analysis

3.1 Task Management

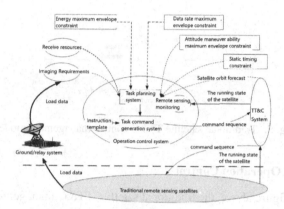

Fig. 4. Traditional satellite mission management mode-1

As shown in the figure above, the traditional satellite mission management mode has the following shortcomings:

- Poor coordination and real-time performance between platform and payload mission: At present, all satellites are static mission management, which cannot meet the requirements of high-dynamic and multi-mission missions. That is, both platform and payload work in serial mode, and the imaging control chain is slow and not real-time, which does not meet the real-time control requirements of dynamic parameters of satellite attitude maneuver imaging (Fig. 4).
- Poor resource management ability and low combat effectiveness: as the "passive executor" of the mission command sequence of the ground operation and control system, the satellite lacks the ability to optimize user tasks according to the real-time operation state, and the utilization of on-board resources, satellite-ground transmission resources and ground resources is low.
- Poor response ability to emergency missions: satellite applications rely on the ground mission planning system, so they cannot directly receive emergency missions, realize mission planning independently, and directly serve tactical users.

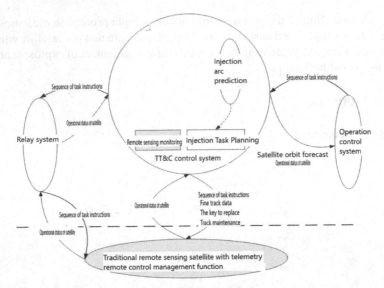

Fig. 5. Traditional satellite TT&C control management mode2

3.2 TT&C and Operation Control

As shown in the figure above, the traditional satellite TT&C management mode has the following shortcomings:

- The mission injection efficiency is low: the ground system directly controls the on-board equipment and sets imaging parameters based on the command template, the command template increases exponentially, the utilization of measurement and control resources is low, and the satellite operation and control cost increases significantly, which cannot meet the rapid growth requirements of reconnaissance and illumination missions caused by the rapid improvement of attitude maneuver capability.
- Lack of user-oriented maneuvering design: lack of user-oriented system-level design, high control threshold, users need to know technical details before using the satellite, complex satellite-earth system operation and control, poor equipment capability; User manipulation errors may affect the success or failure of the mission, or even bring catastrophic effects to the operation safety of the satellite.
- Mission planning with large time delay between earth and earth cannot be optimized in real-time operation and control. There are many satellite imaging modes and different orbit operation and control strategies, and the predicted orbit, agile attitude maneuver, data transmission, energy and on-board storage strategies based on the ground system are rough in resource management, and the overall efficiency is low (Fig. 5).

3.3 Health Management

- On-orbit service is not guaranteed: at present, satellites lack independent health management ability. Ground personnel diagnose satellite status based on original telemetry. The satellite operation mode is complex, and original telemetry interpretation requires professional knowledge and is difficult to interpret.With the rapid increase of the number of satellites in orbit, manual interpretation will be more difficult, and the on-orbit operation of complex satellites lacks reliable guarantee conditions.

- The ground maintenance cost is high: the capacity of T&C channel is limited, the original information is too much, and the ground maintenance cost is high.
- Poor fault location ability: when the satellite is faulty, overseas telemetry can only locate the time period when the fault occurs, and the on-orbit maintenance time is long, which affects the use of users.
- Lack of health evaluation ability: the necessary maintenance measures cannot be taken in advance, and the fault is not handled in time;
- Lack of on-orbit maintenance ability: most on-board software cannot be maintained, and poor adaptability to changes in application conditions/usage constraints;
- Low level of autonomous management: over-reliance on artificial decision-making on the ground, inadequate and timely on-board safety protection measures for emergency failures, and high risk; Except for the control system, all the other systems have no autonomous management ability, which still stays at the low level of the ground switchover, and lacks the system-level safety management strategy and reconstruction strategy, and the satellite operation robustness is poor.

3.4 Test Automation

- The lack of system-level design for fast testing, fault diagnosis and security protection leads to long development cycle and high development cost. The system-level test mode increases exponentially with the user usage mode. The whole process from the whole satellite development to the orbit application relies too much on the ground manual test, interpretation and diagnosis;
- Test no incremental: at present, the remote sensing satellite based on strength test verification system functions, test results closely related to product running environment, single machine testing, subsystem and try and bus, the star test, environment test, test results do not general, lead to more testers, test, strength, testing cycle is long, high test cost;
- Exponential growth of test mode: Currently, remote sensing satellites carry out enumeration test of working mode based on instruction template, and the test verification sequence of complex satellites increases exponentially, resulting in high test and verification cost.
- There are many timing conflicts: At present, remote sensing satellites use event-triggered mechanism to realize work cooperation. More than 90% of the quality problems in satellite system integration are related to timing conflicts, and the timing error location analysis is difficult, the probability of recurrence is low, and the detection cycle is long, which seriously affects the test schedule.
- High software maintenance cost: lack of self-test-oriented design, ground test in the event of failure, disassemble equipment to zero or replace equipment, long troubleshooting cycle.

4   Integrated Operation Design of Heaven and Earth for Intelligent Applications

The new generation of integrated satellite electronic system is advanced in design and can meet the requirements of tactical applications in the field of medium-low orbit remote sensing satellites in the next 10 to 20 years. The satellite is maneuverable, has independent operation, management and survival capabilities, and has the ability to continuously optimize combat performance throughout its life cycle, providing users with high-resolution, multi-imaging mode and high-availability tactical services. Guided by satellite technology innovation, the satellite-ground integration optimal design meets users' application requirements for high performance satellites to be easy to use and easy to use.

The new generation of integrated satellite electronic system has a high level of intelligence, new technical status and complex functions. The operation and control mode, measurement and control mode, relay application mode and on-orbit maintenance mode of traditional satellites have all undergone significant changes. This chapter defines the technology status of satellite-earth data interface, which is used as the input for the design of satellite subsystems.

As shown in the figure below, the new satellite-earth data interface is explained.

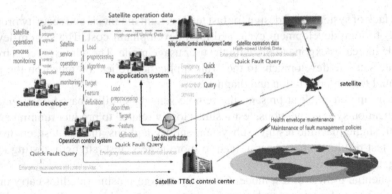

Fig. 6. Architecture of satellite satellite-Earth interface-1

4.1   Transport Control Interface

The satellite operation and control system realizes the transformation from static mission planning to dynamic mission planning, from dedicated operation mode to general operation mode, and from satellite-earth open-loop management to satellite-earth closed-loop management. The new generation of satellite-earth data interface is shown in Fig. 6, and its features include: Fig. 7.

1) Construct a digital satellite model, dynamically modify the usage constraints based on the on-board real state, and change from static mission planning to dynamic mission planning to improve the utilization efficiency of bottleneck resources:

- Energy balance management: change the static constraint of energy "circle balance", realize dynamic energy calculation based on satellite Pro/E model, and arrange user tasks based on "battery discharge safety depth" to improve the efficiency of satellite energy use.
- Storage resource management: the static storage estimation mode and data playback mode of "record interface rate × recording time" were changed to dynamically estimate the amount of imaging data based on attitude, orbit and digital map to improve the on-board memory usage efficiency.
- Transmission arc management: the data arc is estimated according to the real configuration, attitude, and orbit of the satellite, and the playback data is dynamically arranged based on the "actual data volume and task priority" to improve the efficiency of the data arc.

2) Business-oriented control interface is adopted to improve task injection efficiency, avoid irregular operation security risks, and realize the transformation from dedicated control mode to general control mode:

- Satellite control specifications: establish unified, efficient and easy to use satellite and ground control specifications.
- Dynamic timing analysis: Develop a "satellite autonomous command generation and optimization simulation system" to dynamically simulate agile imaging, data playback, recording and playing, camera focusing, antenna presetting, retention cleaning, data preprocessing, platform data processing and other processes, so as to avoid timing conflicts during task scheduling.

3) A closed-loop operation control optimization mechanism of forecasting-execution-Checking-correction (PDCA) was constructed to achieve an efficient and practical business process through integrated satellite-ground design:

- Innovation of satellite-land collaboration mode: Change the traditional satellite on-orbit application according to the state at the end of life, and users can't the lack of "dynamic" adjustment key operation parameters, a day to receive satellite operation data, analysis the actual operation process and the ground "digital satellite model" to predict differences, regular fixed energy model, the attitude maneuver model and so on, implementation strategies and satellite features matching, To realize the fine operation and management of the whole life cycle of the satellite.
- Rapid maintenance design: To change the shortcomings of tight coupling of traditional satellite satellite-based design, rapid reconfiguration of satellite application

strategy can be achieved without upgrading ground software, and multiple imaging modes and multiple orbits can be supported.

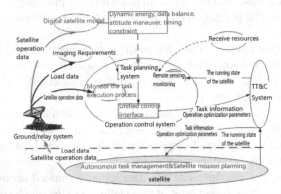

Fig. 7. Architecture of the new generation of satellite operation and control interface-

4.2 TT&C Control Interface

The satellite TT&C system has been transformed from business support and operation monitoring to high and stable operation, high availability of services and long life guarantee in orbit. The satellite-ground data interface is shown in Fig. 8. Its features include:

1) Build a digital satellite model, improve the use efficiency of measurement and control arcs based on the real state of the satellite, and improve the on-orbit monitoring capability of the satellite:

   - TT&c arc simulation: a satellite TT&C antenna occlusion model was constructed to provide accurate TT&C arc prediction for the TT&C system and improve the use efficiency of agile satellite TT&C arc based on user task distribution and TT&C antenna configuration layout characteristics.
   - Operation process simulation: the satellite operation process model is constructed to expand the user task into an on-orbit command sequence, provide the occurrence time of each action on the satellite and the corresponding satellite state, provide accurate operation state prediction for the TT&C system, and improve the ground monitoring and fault diagnosis ability.

2) Construct a closed-loop optimization mechanism of foreseeing-execution-checking-correction (PDCA) for autonomous health management, and achieve efficient and practical autonomous health management through the integrated design of satellite and earth:

   - Health management strategy modification: according to the real on-orbit operation state of the satellite, the autonomous health management model is added and modified to continuously improve the autonomous operation management level of satellite.

- Health envelope modification: according to the real on-orbit operation state of the satellite, the health envelope of key characteristic parameters is regularly modified to achieve the matching between the health diagnosis strategy and the characteristics of the satellite, and to achieve the refined autonomous health management of the satellite throughout its life cycle.

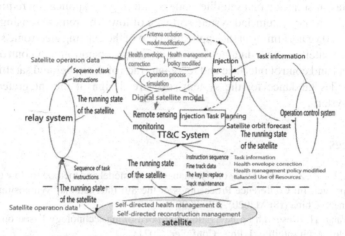

Fig. 8. The interface architecture of the new generation of satellite measurement, control and control-

4.3 Relay Interface

The satellite relay system provides high-speed uplink data injection, satellite operation process data downtransmission, and independent establishment of emergency measurement and control chain to meet the needs of satellite applications. Its features include:

- High-speed uplink injection management: configure the ground equipment required by high-speed uplink (5Mbps) to optimize the satellite operation and control strategy, upgrade the payload preprocessing algorithm, inject the mission-related data form and calculation model, optimize the space attack and defense strategy, and upgrade the onboard software, etc.
- Satellite operation process data transmission: provide detailed original data of satellite operation process for operation control and application systems, measurement and control systems, and satellite developers, and realize closed-loop optimization of satellite operation management.
- Autonomous chain construction for emergency TT&C: The relay system senses the emergency TT&C request of the user star by using the idle time window. When the user star has a serious fault that the autonomous management strategy fails, it

immediately autonomously allocates the T&C channel, notifying the ground system of the emergency TT&C request of the user star, and the ground system starts the emergency rescue procedure.

5 Conclusion

Based on the operational characteristics and application constraints of low orbit remote sensing satellite, combined with the application characteristics of agile imaging and massive data transmission of a satellite, and considering the application requirements of integrated electronic system and system software of low orbit remote sensing satellite in the next 10 ~ 20 years, aiming at the application gap of the existing electronic system, The design of the satellite-earth data application interface, operation and control interface, measurement and control interface and relay interface of the integrated satellite is given, which provides guidance for the system software design of the integrated on-board electronic system.

References

1. Wang, C., Jia, Z., Zhou, H.: Study on risk management model and method for low orbit satellite internet project. In: Conference Proceedings of the 8th International Symposium on Project Management, China (ISPM2020), July 2020
2. Li, S., Wang, H.: Research on navigation and positioning technology based on opportunity signal of low orbit satellite. J. Phy.: Conf. Ser. (2021)
3. Kim, Y.J.: Commercial legal issues in satellite remote sensing. Bus. Law Rev. (2019)
4. Gao, Y.x., Ge, Y.m., Ma, L.x., Hu, Y.q., Chen, Y.x: Optimization design of configuration and layout for Queqiao relay satellite. Adv. Astronaut. Sci. Technol. (2019)

Author Index

Printed in the United States
by Baker & Taylor Publisher Services